THE RATIONALIZATION OF TERRORISM

To Our Children

Nina and Avivah Rapoport

Dean and Daphne Alexander

THE RATIONALIZATION OF TERRORISM

EDITED BY
DAVID C. RAPOPORT
AND
YONAH ALEXANDER

UNIVERSITY PUBLICATIONS OF AMERICA
Frederick, MD

Copyright © 1982 by
University Publications of America, Inc.
Frederick, MD 21701
ISBN 0-89093-413-4
ISBN 0-89093-414-2 (pbk.)
LCCCN 81-70296

Manufactured in the United States of America

Contents

Preface	vii
Acknowledgments	ix
Introduction	1
Terrorism: The Immorality of Belief A.R. Louch	8
Why Does Terrorism Terrorize? Lawrence Z. Freedman	17
Discussion: Panel I	29
Moral and Ethical Considerations in Defining a Counter-Terrorist Policy Ambassador Anthony C.E. Quainton	39
Discussion: Panel II	46
Some Thoughts on State and Rebel Terror A. James Gregor	56
Discussion: Panel III	67
Religion and Terrorism—a Romantic Model of Secular Gnosticism Moshe Amon	80
Measures of the Impact and Appeal of Terrorism Frank Rackley	91
Cults, Liberty, and Mind Control Louis Jolyon West	101

Discussion: Panel IV   108

*International Terrorism and the Moral Structure of
International Society*   115
James A. Nathan

*The Moral Factor in Interstate Politics and
International Terrorism*   136
C.E. Zoppo

*Arab Terrorism and Israeli Retaliation: Some Moral,
Psychological, and Political Reflections*   154
Edward B. Glick

*Morality of the Use of Violence: A Conceptual Dichotomy
in the Indian Perspective*   160
Nemai Sadhan Bose

*A Courtship with Terrorism: The IRA Yesterday, Today,
and Tomorrow*   178
Thomas Hachey

Discussion: Panel V   188

Eliminating the Terrorist Opportunity   205
George H. Quester

Contributors   231

Preface

Although the number of scientific conferences on terrorism have proliferated during the past decade, the question of how terrorists rationalize or explain their activities has been largely ignored. To begin bridging this serious gap in scholarly inquiry and discussion, the Center for International and Strategic Affairs, University of California, Los Angeles (UCLA), and the Institute for Studies in International Terrorism, State University of New York (SUNY), convened a three-day conference at UCLA, March 14-16, 1979.

The papers presented provoked sharp and interesting interactions from the floor, which seemed particularly illuminating as a guide to the problems and to the range of differences among scholars in the field. For these reasons, and in the hope of stimulating further dialogue, we decided to make some of the floor discussions a central feature of this book.

The principal editing problem was how to adapt materials presented originally in an oral context to meet the requirements of a written one without undermining the spirit of the conference and the give-and-take of the discussions. The task was much more formidable than we imagined it could be, especially for those sessions where the original materials consisted of tapes solely. Our objective could not have been achieved without the prompt, enthusiastic help of most participants who resisted strong temptations to polish their remarks.

To many at the conference it became clear that we needed, but did not then have, a clearer picture of the nature and history of the terrorist tradition from its origin in religion to its present secular manifestations which embrace both state and rebel activities. To meet that need, the editors recently completed a second volume. Some contributors appear in both books, but all the essays with two exceptions are different.[1]

---

1. David C. Rapoport and Yonah Alexander, *The Morality of Terrorism: Religious Origins and Ethical Implications* (Elmsford, N.Y.: Pergamon Press, 1982).

Acknowledgments

It is a pleasure to acknowledge the many debts incurred. We want to thank the contributors, University of California, Los Angeles, State University of New York (Oneonta), the UCLA Council on International and Comparative Studies, and the Sidney Stearns Memorial Foundation for their indispensable support. Andrzej Korbonski, chairman of political science at UCLA, and Roman Kolkowicz, director of the Center for International and Strategic Affairs, were especially encouraging and helpful. Donna Beltz exhibited extraordinary skill and poise as she managed the administration of the conference. Professors Hans Baerwald, Robert Gerstein, Andrzej Korbonski, Richard Sisson, and Zeev Sternhell, all from the UCLA political science department, chaired (and sometimes refereed!) the discussions. Professor Marvin Hoffenberg (UCLA political science) provided the original impetus. Ellen Bauerle of University Publications of America gave us much thoughtful work. Barbara Rapoport prepared a magnificent welcoming dinner for forty-five conference participants and helped establish a warm atmosphere which persisted throughout the sessions. She also aided us in different ways during the preparation of the manuscript.

David Rapoport wishes to make some special acknowledgments. A Reason Fellowship in Santa Barbara during the summer of 1980 provided him with some much needed time. He is dedicating his share of the volume to his daughters Nina and Avivah, who accepted his absence on numerous important occasions including, alas, one this very day when at the last moment he withdrew from a family expedition to explore the South Downs in order to complete some final details.

David Rapoport

Yonah Alexander

Introduction

Most people familiar with the large body of literature on terrorism will acknowledge that it does not display serious and sensitive attention to the many moral meanings and ramifications of the phenomenon. The neglect is surprising because the feelings terrorists want to arouse are moral outrage and sympathy and not simply terror. Characteristically, rebel terrorists act to call attention to their moral complaints, and they provide justification for each attack. Those justifications are intended to impress everyone who will listen—the sympathetic, the hostile, the undecided—and those within the organization who may be experiencing doubts.

This perpetual need to repeat justifications, and sometimes to provide fresh ones, gives terrorist campaigns a quality which distinguishes them from military campaigns with which they often are confused. A war obviously needs moral justifications, but its successive military campaigns and actions require arguments based on military prudence or effectiveness, arguments directed primarily to those interested in these concerns. When military operations breach the accepted rules of military conduct, moral explanations are sought and given. But it is precisely because terrorists always violate accepted norms, and their actions are unprecedented sometimes by the practices of the terrorist group itself, that justifications can never cease.

The example illustrates why I think it impossible to discuss *any* aspect of terrorism without invoking moral questions. My view is not the common one, of course, but I think we can agree that many people interested in terrorism are troubled that its moral meanings have been ignored. I would cite as evidence the positive responses so many of our conference invitations received even though we could not pay their way and many assumed their expenses. We who teach courses on terrorism are painfully aware of the problem, because moral questions more than any other engage student emotions and curiosity, and these are precisely the ones we feel least prepared to discuss.

No dimension of terrorism has been muddled more than the one we shall discuss. The existing academic commentary seems dominated by a single tiresome cliché: one person's freedom fighter is another's terrorist. This may be a way of saying that one cannot ask moral questions about terrorism; more likely it seems to be an argument that we judge terrorists only by the end they seek and, furthermore, that it is entirely proper to do so.

Coercion, of course, is always justified as an unpleasant but necessary means to achieve some desirable end. It is right sometimes to punish, just as it is right sometimes to wage war. Should terror not be understood in the same way? Certainly, this is a question the conference will discuss, but I wish to point out that a moment's reflection indicates those in the academic world and those in the United Nations who brandish the cliché that a freedom fighter cannot be a terrorist are making a very different point. When the actions of soldiers and jailers are justified, they remain soldiers and jailers; indeed, that justification *establishes* their identity. But in the case of the freedom fighter the opposite is true, because when the freedom fighter uses terror we are not permitted to acknowledge this as a fact. The implication of the slogan is not that terror as a form of coercion can be justified by the end sought, but rather it leads us to the paradox that terror is *not* a form of coercion at all because it cannot be justified! In this connection, it is pertinent that those who coerce freedom fighters are not described as soldiers or policemen by freedom-fighter sympathizers because that might suggest their actions could be justified. Hence, those who repress freedom fighters are called terrorists.

In various ways terror nowadays signifies a violence which no one can justify. The repulsive connotations of the word are so conspicuous that partisans believe that it is an important political task to make certain that the word is used "properly," which in fact means that they have a decided interest in abusing it! In public no one will acknowledge being a terrorist, any more than one would acknowledge being dishonest, and for precisely the same reason; by the same token, one will make every effort to see that the enemy is perceived as a terrorist.

Those who control the language used to describe a struggle have important, sometimes decisive, advantages in shaping the outcome of that struggle. A government always tries to have all rebels against *its* authority described as terrorists, and this is true regardless of the character of rebel violence. Rebel terrorists, for their part, want to be known as soldiers but, at the very least, they insist on being called guerrillas.

The abuse of language leads necessarily to numerous consequences. A generally unnoticed one is that when governments treat all captured rebels as terrorists, rebels will be "encouraged" to avoid military targets and to strike defenseless or civilian ones. A more observable, demonstrable reaction is embodied in the reporting practices of the American mass media which are always anxious to demonstrate that they are not being used by either side in order to maintain their reputation for impartiality. Examine virtually any account of rebel violence. You will discover a pattern, one so uniform that it is difficult to believe that it could have emerged without collaboration and without design. In one sentence the rebel is called a terrorist, in the next he or she becomes a guerrilla. To break the monotony, perhaps, the journalist (who must be self-conscious in his practice) sometimes will write of *soldiers* but soon afterwards will "balance" or "even the score" by using the word *criminals*. Do the media care if our language is corrupted? Do they worry if our ability to understand the world diminishes as a consequence?

Academics do not manipulate the language as blatantly, at least in this case. Perhaps we do not have such a pressing case of self-interest to serve. Yet we contribute, too, to the debasement of language. In order to strip the term of its abusive connotations, and thus make it "objective" or "scientific," most academics define terrorism as illegal political violence. Though the purpose or intention is different, the definition is remarkably similar to that of governments. But can any good purpose be served by attempting to obscure the meaning of a term and that of the concept to which it refers? Surely, Humpty Dumpty was wrong to tell Alice that a word could mean anything he wanted it to mean. Even if we could make a word change its meaning, we could not eliminate the phenomenon which gave birth to the word. Sooner or later, we would require another word to signify *dishonesty* if we agreed to give the word *dishonesty* a new meaning. The same thing is true with the vocabulary for terrorism; certainly it would be surprising if we continued to find ourselves outraged by a type of violence and were unable to find language to comprehend it.

One way toward an adequate definition of terrorism, one which helps illuminate the moral questions associated with the phenomenon, is to go back and examine the original understanding, that provided by terrorists themselves at a time when they were not yet embarrassed to refer to themselves as terrorists. They were reasonably explicit then about their intentions and activities and did explain why terror had to be distinguished from coercion, or at least from coercion which could be justified by conventional standards and practices, war, and punishment.

Among contemporaries, terror most often is used as a method to achieve insurrection, and we think of it as war. In war, however, we are supposed to assail those who intend to hurt us and are capable of doing so, those who are armed. To attack the defenseless *deliberately* is to commit war crimes, atrocities, and murders. The Russian anarchists who invented the strategy of terror for insurrection knew that they were engaging in a very different kind of struggle, which may be why they never thought of calling themselves guerrillas, an old and perfectly familiar term. For although guerrillas fought in unconventional ways, they waged war nonetheless, because they assailed combatants only. (The meaning of guerrilla in Spanish, "little warrior," underlines this point.) The Russians argued that it would be suicidal to restrain themselves with such rules or principles. Their concern was to find targets which would provide maximum political value by making the revolution known, creating sympathy for its purpose—by establishing evidence that resistance was possible—and by undermining the government's moral case. Characteristically, the early terrorists who called themselves terrorists and the modern ones who want us to call them guerrillas demand their enemies observe the moral rules of war which terrorists themselves reject. Every captured rebel terrorist claims the immunities of a prisoner of war.

When terrorists do not refer to themselves as soldiers, they describe their deeds as acts of punishment, made necessary by a decision of a people's court, as happened when the Italian Red Brigades killed the former Premier Aldo Moro. The reason for such language is that most people believe it to be justifiable to kill a defenseless person only if it can be established that the person has committed serious wrongs. Yet the explanation for the creation of the people's courts in the French Reign of Terror clearly indicates that the purpose of the device was just the opposite; the aim was to free the revolutionary government from the restraints entailed by the notion of punishment as it was, and still is, understood. In the ordinary courts of law—and they persisted during the Reign of Terror—a citizen was punished for *actions* which violated specific laws, actions which could be demonstrated through established rules that provided proven mechanisms to weigh and dispute appropriate evidence. Enemies of the people, not citizens, were brought to the people's courts and they were killed not because of what they did but because of who they were, what they might do, and most of all because their deaths might stimulate desirable behavior from citizens, which would secure the triumph of the revolution.

An enemy of the people was a political not a legal status. It designated persons outside the law in virtually every sense of that phrase. Note, too, that the French category of persons whose "character" deprives them of all legal and moral protection, and the description of the freedom fighter as one whose ultimate purpose entitles him to freedom from restraints derived from rules are opposite sides of the same coin; the head depicts victims and the tail assailants.

This characterization of terrorism raises many questions; some authors discuss them directly, while others provide materials for the discussion sections to develop. Examples of these questions are: How must the world be perceived in order to disregard claims made by the innocent and the defenseless? Can one provide a moral defense for such actions? What sort of moral climate have we produced which enables some to gain moral sympathies from people by committing deeds which those very same people persistently condemn as outrageous? What is the moral cost that those who resist terrorism must be willing to pay?

The word *terrorist* today is normally restricted, or has been corrupted, to signify rebel activities only. But as recently as the decade after World War II, as E. V. Walter's pioneer study *Terror and Resistance* indicates, terror was more likely to refer to particular kinds of state activity. And we all know that the term originates from the explanations which the revolutionary government in France gave for the policies it introduced in 1793 to secure a new principle of legitimacy, that all power ought to come from the will of the people. State terror still persists and, as the examples of Cambodia, Iran, and Lybia among others suggest, is immensely important. The organizers of the conference thought it necessary, therefore, to provide opportunities to discuss state terror not only because the subject has intrinsic merit but also because we wanted to invite comparisons between state and rebel terror.

In the last decade everyone has become more aware of the fact that religion and terror are often associated. Millenarian cults, like the Fruit of Islam, which terrorized San Francisco (1973-1974), and Jim Jones's People's Temple have flourished. Religious terror is present in Islam. A "liberation theology" has been created by priests in Latin America which some have used to justify secular insurrections. Religion plays a role in the political terror of Northern Ireland. After World War II it was indispensable in Cyprus, Algeria, and Kenya. Religious doctrines helped stimulate Indian terrorism at the turn of the century. Although the Russian anarchists who created modern rebel terror were largely atheists, their literature is dominated by powerful religious imagery. To a lesser but significant extent, nonetheless, the same pattern appears during the French Reign of Terror.

These relationships should not be surprising. Much more often terror is linked to religion than it is to secular ends, for only since the French Revolution has it been possible to justify terror publicly for purely secular purposes. Prior to that time, in Judaism, Christianity, and Islam many groups like the Zealots, Anabaptists, and Assassins explicitly endorsed terror as opposed to coercion as the only way to achieve the millenium or the messianic era. All these facts invite questions. What relationships are there between the moral appeals of contemporary secular and religious terror groups? How do their doctrines compare with those of religious groups before the French Revolution? Why does the belief that legitimacy derives from God or from the people seem to produce outbursts of terror periodically? Five of the papers discuss these and other pertinent matters pertaining to religion, subjects virtually untouched by the existing literature. We will not settle these questions here, and we will not settle the ones posed earlier either, but we will be richer for having discussed them.

David C. Rapoport

Terrorism:
The Immorality of Belief

ALFRED LOUCH

Are there actions so abominable that no reasons could justify or contexts excuse them? Answers, I suppose, may differ. My list would include torture, killing for the fun of it, and blowing up the innocent in order to demoralize those one supposes guilty. Others will say the first two surely, the Shah of Iran and Charles Manson; but the third, in spite of the apparent atrocity of it, is after all the response to atrocity. The innocent suffer and that is unfortunate, but their death and dismemberment are stages in a radical social surgery. At the end of that process is the millenium, when repression and exploitation will cease.

If we believe that only terror can bring about the millenium, we will be well on the way toward admitting its necessity. Even so, we may find it hard to shake off a rather different impression of the terrorist—the person who carries out the ghastly assignment. This may be so for two related reasons. First, terrorists, like kidnappers, put us in the unenviable position of acceding to their illegitimate demands or becoming accessories to their atrocities. If we comply we only make further demands more likely; if we refuse we feel a joint responsibility for the fate of their victims. Rage is the natural response to this dilemma, and rage does not exactly diminish feelings of moral, as well as personal, outrage.

Second, it is cowardly to attack the defenseless. It speaks of an indifference to violence that is not suitable psychological material for the millenium. Most of all, terrorists are arrogant, acting on beliefs about social causality that the available evidence does not license. Their moral perceptions are equally dulled, since they seem quite unable to distinguish between the repressiveness of totalitarian regimes—Hitler's, Amin's, or Stalin's—and those, like the Western democracies, that—even if they limit human freedom—do so within recognized constraints on political or economic power and in an atmosphere that allows for some freedom of opinion. They are, in short, fanatics, and fanatics are not part of the good society. They are the effluvia of social unrest, ambition, frustration, and hatred. Even if we allowed that only through fanaticism are great social objectives ever attained, we would still be repelled by the fanatic.

Are we hypocrites if we tacitly approve the consequences while condemning the doer and the deed? It has been suggested to me by my friend and former student, Professor Keith Quincy, that morality has to do with what is done, not with the agent who does it. So we might consistently approve a deed and condemn the doer—approve terror and condemn the terrorist. On the face of it, this distinction amounts to a utilitarian account of action. Of the act we ask: does it result in a balance of good over evil? Of the person: is he or she someone we could like, trust, or regard as a friend? But if we reject a utilitarian calculus—as unworkable or as false to our moral intuitions—we might believe that the judgments about persons are a better index of the morality of actions than the consequences that issue from those actions. If, along these lines, we saw that only a repulsive character could perform certain acts, we should find this a reason to condemn them.

And this applies to jailers, secret agents, soldiers, informers, and all sorts of people whose business and talent it is to do violent, sordid, and unpleasant things, as well as to terrorists. But most of us acknowledge the necessity of nasty functions and try not to think about the agency of them, even while condemning noninstitutionalized terror. Are we in the position of Bolingbroke?

> They love not poison that do poison need,
> Nor do I thee. Though I did wish him dead,
> I hate the murtherer, love him murthered.
> —Richard II, V. vi. 38-40

So the first question is: do we have a leg to stand on in condemning terror?

Another question arises also from our equivocal attitude toward violence. We don't condemn all instances of random or sudden violence. We applaud the act and at a distance admire the actor, when terror is directed against regimes as hideous and oppressive as Nazi Germany. Many, though obviously not all, will feel similarly equivocal about the methods of internal warfare employed to bring down Chiang Kai-shek, Batista, or Somoza, or to establish the state of Israel. We say that the evil against which we fight is both serious and powerful; only by fighting fire with fire can we hope for a remedy. If at the same time we condemn the PLO, the Red Brigades, the IRA, or the SLA, it must be because we think the targets of these groups are neither evil enough nor powerful enough to warrant such extreme measures. Or we may feel rather more fastidious than they about targets—it is one thing, we say, to blow up dictators, banks, or bridges, quite another to plant bombs in supermarkets, where the victims are innocent. We must then ask, is our condemnation of terror selective? And if so, does our distinction between allowed and disallowed forms of terror rest on an assumption that Western societies are really not so bad? We shall doubtless feel at least somewhat tepid about this assumption—embarrassed, perhaps, at finding it in our ideological baggage. This is a second challenge to the moral condemnation of terrorism.

Finally, we shall need to face up to the moral strains under which terror places us. What are we to think of terrorists and how are we to respond to them? Terrorists commit us to a response which is itself violent, for they are intractable to peaceful methods of persuasion and compromise. Terrorists are outside the reach of law, because they do not acknowledge its authority. They are thus outlaws. But we have few, if any, instructive precedents for dealing with outlaws. This is perhaps the most important dimension of terrorism, but I have, alas, the least to say about it.

Are we hypocrites in condemning terror? Or without sin in casting stones? Suppose we draw the following distinction: there is all the (moral) difference in the world between public institutional sanctions and random individual reprisals. The difference is that the first expresses community consent and gives advance warning of the consequences of acting in certain ways. The second raises an idiosyncratic conception of the good, or the just, above the consensus, and applies sanctions without warning. In a community dominated by terror there is no way that citizens could know their guilt or how to avoid it. In contrast, settled communities have at least institutionalized their barbarities (allowing for the sake of argument that all forms of force applied by the state on individuals are barbaric). An individual has grounds for predicting the state's use of force and knows how to act in order to avoid it.

Now, terrorists say the distinction is meaningless. Law and authority are illusions that tempt the imperceptive to cooperate in their own exploitation. It is odd that this argument has so often paralyzed moral judgment, for it is the most transparent instance of a *tu quoque*. We don't appeal to examples of admitted wickedness as models and justifications of our own conduct. Corporations, banks, and the democratic process, in their various ways may be instruments of exploitation and coercion; for that very reason they hardly serve as an excuse for greater violence. That would be like using the existence of capital punishment in one jurisdiction as a motive for another to resort to torture.

But to construe the argument this way is to miss its effect. Political societies are described in the language of exploitation not to license violence but to paralyze the will of those who give at least tepid allegiance to such societies. We bourgeois feel, hearing the charges, the twinge of guilt at our own practices or those in which we have acquiesced. We are people in glass houses, and that is a frame of mind in which we lose our grip on the important distinction between practices admittedly needing improvement or rectification and those that are incorrigibly evil.

Nonetheless, here is a sketch of an attempt to maintain that distinction. Unless we are fanatics, we don't believe that a perfect society is possible. Bourgeois regimes, which are so often vilified by revolutionaries as the paradigms of exploitation and repression, are marked by severe disparities of advantage and opportunity and by obstacles to legitimate pursuits and the airing of righteous grievances. Nonetheless, some mitigation of these evils is better than none. A state in which, for example, it is possible to appeal through the courts to win relief from police misconduct has to be preferred to one in which the police are wholly immune from citizen complaints, and brutality and torture are the rule. We shall not, having made that judgment, justify the brutality of our own police, or fail to take note of gross injustices to which venality or race or class-consciousness of public officials exposes us. But we will argue that a system like ours, with its partially working constraints on police power, is immensely to be preferred to one in which torture or imprisonment without trial are accepted practices. We don't want to be complacent about our faults, but neither do we want to obliterate the distinction between capricious and lawlike exercises of the police function, simply because both rest on coercion. A policeman's reluctant reading of the *Miranda* warning to the quaking suspect is not to be compared to the interrogations of a secret police or the stage executions of terrorist justice. If we cannot find it in our hearts to condemn the terrorist because the police carry guns and sometimes use them too rashly, we evidently believe that violence is evil. Otherwise, the example of police brutality would not embarrass us. If we do believe this, we should be able to distinguish greater and lesser degrees of violence, or greater and lesser control over it. I therefore see no reason to suffer paralysis of judgment on account of *tu quoque* arguments. Let us agree: the act of terror is evil.

If anything more is to be said, it must be by way of extenuation. The terrorist's reasons, or the context of his or her action, must make a difference. And here, I think, the friends of terror say one of two things. First, they say you must sometimes fight fire with fire, a slogan designed to show that violence is the only means to a worthy or a necessary end. Second, they complain that systematic (and cunningly disguised) repression prevents legitimate points of view from being heard; violence is the only remaining way to express a certain range of beliefs about politics and society. Let us look at these apologies in turn.

(1) If the fighting-fire-with-fire principle applies, terrorists must have good reason to believe either that worse things will happen unless they throw their bombs, or that a more than offsetting good will be brought about, and can only be brought about, in this way. Terrorists seldom trouble themselves about the eventual good; their future extends only to the destruction of present institutions. So we

and they don't know what positive qualities of life the destruction of society aims at. To kill in the name of unspecified and unspecifiable benefits is to kill for no reason at all. This is gratuitous violence, for which no extenuation is produced or sought. It is an immorality of thought, as well as act.

Terror as preventive action may seem more promising. Most of us allow that violence might be necessary in self-defense, or to subdue a madman or assassinate a tyrant. These cases sometimes—even in the critical light of hindsight—warrant violence. Hitler and Amin are not open to persuasion or vulnerable to other lawful pressures. We know, moreover, that they will certainly commit further atrocities if we fail to kill them. If we are lucky, a single bullet may put an end to the imminent evil. But usually the method is more like war. There will be regretted casualties, as war always brings in its wake—but still more will die and still more rot in prisons, if the chance isn't taken.

The argument is not unpersuasive. But before it can be assumed to help the terrorist, distinctions must be made. The assassin and guerrilla soldier kill so that atrocities may cease. They may be mistaken, but it is at least plausible to believe that on occasion they are not. It is possible that the evidence supports their actions and excuses the suffering they cause.

But are guerrillas soldiers or terrorists? I have no zeal for definitional disputes, but a matter of importance hangs on the answer to this question. Terrorism, guerrilla warfare, and assassination share a form of extenuation. Bloody work is done to prevent bloodier consequences. But in attempting wicked things for virtuous ends, stronger than usual evidence is required to show that the work will indeed bring about the desired future, that it will not have unforeseen effects that cancel out the accomplished good, and that other options for action are unavailable. The Vietnam War protester who sits on the White House lawn may or may not have adequate grounds for his views about the evil of the war or the consequences of withdrawing from it, but because his action is not itself morally momentous—causing at most minor inconvenience to public officials and passersby—we do not oblige him to prove his case beyond the shadow of a doubt. He is, we say, entitled to his opinion. But the assassin who supposes a President must die to end the conflict, or the terrorist who—seeing the war as a symptom of social malaise—attempts to destroy society by random violence, cannot claim immunity, because these are privately held opinions. Can an assassin ever be sure that with the death of his or her target evil will cease, or that it will not bring other unforeseen evils in its wake? Rarely, we say. And those cases for which we may find the grounds sufficient are tyrannies in which present evils are so frightful that our inability to rule out untoward consequences of tyrannicide simply cannot matter. Can the terrorist's theories of social repression ever offer grounds for capricious violence? Here, I think, the answer is that the antibourgeois terrorist cannot profit by sharing a common label with the guerrilla or the assassin of lunatic despots. Those who rail against bourgeois society and attempt to bring it to its knees by leaving bombs in supermarkets cannot claim to be frustrating demonstrable and about-to-be-committed evils. They do not know what specific evils they are preventing; the rhetorical flourishes of repression and exploitation do not serve to identify the alleged evils. They have no evidence to show that the social structure will crack under the pressure of their sporadic violence. And nothing, surely, is more horrifying than the use of tendentious slogans of social theories as bills of indictment against individuals. Yet this is the proposed extenuation offered on behalf of terrorists in the Western world, in Ireland, or in Palestine. No greater atrocity will be prevented by their exploding bombs. Such reasons do not mitigate violence, but simply make light of it.

(2) Sometimes terrorists are described as seeking an audience for their views in the only way open to them. We cannot therefore accuse them of doing terrible deeds on the merest pretext of evidence as to their efficacy, because efficacy is not part of the terrorists' immediate intention. Rather, their bombs dramatize their condemnation of the social order. I find this idea bewildering. The message of dismembered housewives is at the very least unclear. By what twisted reasoning can it be supposed that the exploitation of persons will succeed in stating a message about exploitation? Should I be awakened to my status as a wage slave or a manipulated consumer by contemplating this ultimate use of people as a means?

Why should I not learn instead the lesson that my current exploited state is much to be preferred to the exploitation I may expect at terrorist hands? Those who can say that terrorists are only expressing opinions they have a right to hold and express have failed to appreciate what the exploitation of persons means. They can demonstrate it in their social theories and fail to notice it in dreadful fact. These are threadbare defenses indeed.

One last effort at extenuation. Sometimes it is argued that no man is innocent, therefore the terrorist is not guilty—or at least not of slaughtering the innocent. This argument shifts the grounds of mitigation from the reasons for acting to the context in which it takes place. But what can that mean? Not, surely, some Kafka-like eschatology, which, when applied to practical affairs, converts killers into agents of divine retribution, even though an element of just such madness can be detected in the minds of many terrorists. In a more mundane spirit, one might suppose that the loss of the status of being innocent means only that a state of total war exists. Many who could not be connected positively to the war effort died at Dresden and Hiroshima, but their presence there made them accidental victims of a strategy with a rightful cause, the defeat of the Axis powers. So terrorists are at war with society, fighting for its demise through tactics imposed on them by the logic of the situation. To argue in this way, whether about bombing Hiroshima or the Bank of America, sidesteps the issue as to whether the probabilities of good results can justify such atrocities. We might answer—as many friends of terrorism would—that we lacked such warrant in Dresden or Hiroshima. What, then, would lend us to suppose that the terrorist declaration of total war is any different? Indeed, it is ludicrous to suppose that a half-dozen self-appointed rescuers of humanity are in any position to declare war, total or otherwise, or to appoint themselves just executioners of the wicked against a nation of 50 or 250 million people. Such a defense is just another instance of banal reasons thought adequate for the commission of violent crimes.

It is, of course, part of the terrorist's eschatology to believe that citizens of modern states are hopelessly corrupted by their affiliation and by their exploitation. To say no one is innocent may mean just this—some are exploiters and die for that, others are exploited and are thus past saving. So in pulling down prisons as centers of repression, guards should die as agents of repression, and the prisoners as victims of it. Such a bloody salvation can only be self-immolating; terrorists must be victims of the social order also. At least they do not, as far as I know, come down from the sky, though some of them, or their defenders on university campuses, may appear to have come up out of the earth.

So much for extenuation. But what of us? Terror is a fact of life to which we must respond somehow or other. Terror tempts us to violent reprisal because it strikes us as irrationally violent. By the same token, we want to say that terrorists are mad. And so our minds are diverted to thoughts of therapy and commiseration. This response is self-deceiving, unless we remember Conrad's remark in *Lord Jim*: "How much certain forms of evil are akin to madness, derived from intense egotism, inflamed by resistance." On the other hand, a violent response to violence caters to the propaganda of terror. *Our* violence supports the terrorists' otherwise shabby case, or seems to do so for many. And so we seek accommodation, which appears as a sign of the success of terrorist methods. In the end, we must reluctantly recognize that the terrorist's uncompromising position makes it impossible to treat him or her as other than the enemy—as an outlaw. Except in war, we lack the conventions of violent reprisal. And even in war we maintain conventions of civility; we recognize that our enemies hold other, but still plausible, allegiances. Men and women who blow up supermarkets and glory in their deed have moved beyond the reach of that courtesy. But what it means to treat someone as an outlaw is a matter on which I fear I have no more to say, except to say that it is what we ought to think about.

Why Does Terrorism Terrorize?*

LAWRENCE ZELIC FREEDMAN

Why does terrorism terrorize; why does the terroristic event have such a powerful impact; why does the media focus upon it and why do vast audiences seem transfixed by it? The answers are not self-evident.

The personalities of terrorists often differ greatly. Their personal motives are usually unknown. Their publicly stated goals may be political, or religious, or obscure. These issues and their apparent importance vary enormously. Yet the widespread fascination, the fear charged with awe, the sense of the uncanny they engender compel attention like a powerful magnet.

Terrorists seem to be driven by an irresistible moral imperative to carry out their terrifying acts. This morality appears to be absolute, unimpaired by the bewildering and paralyzing ambiguity of values which are experienced by the audience. Political terrorists aim to rectify wrongs inflicted on the community, religious terrorists want to assuage an offended and demanding god. The psychopathic terrorist like Charles Manson justifies himself as attacking political and religious wrongs which mimic those of the true believers.

The religious terrorist sometimes assaults the community like an ancient prophet or messiah. He seems charismatic in the divine origin of his vision of a terrifying blessing from some god. His style is both empathic and dominating. The public acceptance of his visions and his awful commands are effectively transmitted through the projection of the aura of a powerful personality.

---

*The author gratefully acknowledges the valuable assistance of Sandra E. Schmidt, M.A.

The messianic and prophetic message reached its ironic and paradoxical climax in the most secular terrorists of the nineteenth century, Nechaev and Bakunin, who wrote:

> The revolutionary is a dedicated man. He has no personal inclination, no business affairs, no emotions, no attachments, no property and no name. Everything in him is subordinated towards a single exclusive attachment, a single thought, and a single question—the revolution....
> To knit the people into a single force which is wholly destructive and wholly invincible—such is our organization, our conspiracy, and our task....[1]

Marx, originally a Jew, carried on the prophetic tradition of the desert prophets in the name of secular and psychological humanism. His thesis, like theirs, was that man's inhumanity to man carried the seeds of its own destruction. He reasoned that the deprivation inflicted upon workers by the merchant-industrialist dispossessed the workers and their children. He perceived the psychological alienation of workers through the inhuman fragmentation of their atomized, industrialized role, subordinated to efficiency and profit.

Yet Marx and Engels, prophets of the proletariat, ambivalently rejected terrorism themselves, as they did social meliorism. Terrorism for them was ineffectual romantic adventurism, while social reforms postponed the collectivist triumph of the proletariat and the withering away of the state.

Bakunin and Kropotkin, the prophets of anarchism, preached terror in the service of an inherent goodness of man. Man for them had been forced into demonic distortion by the viciousness of government and autocracy. Therefore Nechaev, Kropotkin, Bakunin, and even Marx prophesied the end of the human hells, but did not specify the alternative political and social arrangements that would replace the hells, because it seemed self-evident to them that destroying the devils of human oppression would free the spirit of the innate goodness of man.

In his evolution, Homo sapiens developed self-awareness and with it a Janus-like consciousness: he looks in, self-consciously, and he looks out, apprehensively.

Why Does Terrorism Terrorize? 19

Emergent Homo sapiens saw threats to his existence and frustrations of his desires through the impositions of his natural, dangerous physical environment, the predatory animals which surrounded him, and the human animals who might punish, ignore, or worst of all, abandon him. The primal fantasy shared by all these people was transfused with anxiety, dread, and loneliness; with terror of the unknown and of the murderous elements. This anxiety arose early in the evolutionary birth of our species. It remains today the initial experience of the fetus, born with strain and pain from a warmly protective amniotic fluid to a dry, cold, separate existence.

Man's incapacity to survive without the care, in both senses of the word, of adults accounts for a quarter of his lifetime. This prolonged dependency is unique to the human animal. The significance of crucial others around him for survival is essential to our understanding of his vulnerability to anxiety, to previsions of disaster, and to terrorism.

Activity, feeling, thought, and will become enmeshed in this existential angst. Fear of illness, pain, poverty, and loss of love are condensations of that original terror, which is projected upon the background of the ancient cosmic anxiety of helpless loneliness felt by a creature grown self-conscious and afraid.

The human species's survival is based on the growth of its central nervous system, its open-ended mechanism for adaptation, and its prolonged period of dependency and need for adults to attend its newborn. For these means of species survival humans pay in horror, disquietude, and a sense that the narrow boundary of the circle of survival is surrounded by evil, darkness, and terrible demons. The inward primordial dread is projected to the vast, insensate, and threatening outer world.

In the early stages of human development, action and feeling were directed toward survival and escape from fear. Over millenia arose gods, propitiatory rituals, and prohibitions; religious systems provided taboos and ceremonies for atonement when their laws were infringed.

Arising from this primal terror, the gods and goddesses were ambivalent ones, incorporating the fear which begot them into their images. For example, with the idea of the mother's womb as a delightful place of shelter and rest there is inextricably associated a profound sense of anxiety. Referring to the Primal Mother, a Babylonian hymn says, "Whoever catches sight of her shall perish from dread."[2]

The All-Mother or Earth Mother of Greek mythology was Gaia, who conceived her daughter Echidna with Tartarus, the personification of the underworld. The top half of her body in the form of a beautiful maiden, the lower half a hideous serpent, Echidna herself was "the mother of all terrors, of the Chimera, Scylla, the Gorgon, of frightful Cerberus...and of the eagle that devoured the liver of Prometheus." With her own son Orthrus, the dog of the monster Geryon, Echidna begat the misshapen female strangler, the Sphinx.[3]

Hecate was also identified with the Mother Goddess. A "spook-goddess of night and phantoms, a nightmare," she sent "the horrible and fearful nighttime apparition, the Empusa, which Aristophanes says comes wrapped in a bladder swollen with blood." She is "the deadly mother," an incubus or vampire who appears in the form of a "man-eating lamia," and is the Terrible Mother of witches and witchcraft. Hecate is "the wild huntress prowling at night," and was called the "far-hitting" or "she who hits at will."[4]

The Greek Father-God, Zeus, was capricious, revengeful, and malignant. Euripides wrote, "The gods' one concern is to make us suffer. The wrath of the Heavenly Father has neither meaning nor purpose." "It would be far better never to have been born," chants the chorus of the elders of Colonus, "but if thou livest, the next best thing is, as speedily as possible, to return to the place whence thou camest."[5]

Among the lesser Greek deities were a host of frightening figures, the dread-inspiring demigods such as Medusa and the Harpies. Pan was the god that dwelt on earth, whose sudden appearance caused unreasoning terror, giving rise to the term *panic*.

Other cultures show similar patterns. In the East, Ishtar, the goddess of love, "never embraced without slaying." Kali was a Hindu goddess of terror, the bloody and destructive consort of Shiva. Her devotees, the Thugs, practiced ritual murder in her name well into the nineteenth century. In Mexico an important earth goddess was Cihuacoatl, "the goddess of adversity," "through whom sin came into the world."[6]

Mankind found it intolerable to go on believing itself a subject of the unceasing spite of an all-powerful evil spirit. The terrible tyrant gods were transformed into benevolent and just deities, but even after the creation of a just god, the dread persisted. A just god must be perceived as one who treated people according to their just deserts. But if there is divine justice, then man must be to blame for the world's imperfections.

Thus, out of man's own conviction that he was guilty developed the idea that he had to atone for the Fall which had brought a curse upon the whole human race. Pangs of conscience and guilt made mankind tremble in the face of this idea of a just god. The same dread that had produced the taboos of primitives overcame the civilized peoples who had struggled to construct the idea of a just god. His very justice became itself an intimidating and frightening prospect.

The Catholic church incorporated many of the models of the earlier terrible gods and cults. The danger of falling into the eternal damnation of Hell was emphasized, but believers were provided with rituals that protected against the ancient demoniacal gods. Catholic architecture preserved the demons but demonstrated that they could be exorcised through faith. The fear-inspired conviction grew that men could avoid the fires of Hell only by completely transforming themselves, by atoning for their offenses through the sacrifice of their egos. The sense of original sin grew keener, and with it came an increasing need for self-chastisement, for a sense of guilt.

In the Middle Ages the great autarchic states emerged. Families of king-gods who owned the lands controlled the people. Nationhood became the predominant value, both mystical and rational, the protective device against the terror of the now-humanized king. The prophet who had formerly spoken for the god in the name of the god's values, visiting terror for sins against that god, became the prophet not only of the humanism that protected against terror, but also for nationalism. The prophecy that the terror of existence could be overcome by millenarianism became a worldwide movement.

The existence of the nation and of religious systems both required the sacrifice of impulsivity and subordination to the values and symbols of the nation and of the gods.

The Renaissance, the Enlightenment, and the triumph of reason precipitated a breaking away from the rituals of the Catholic church and, likewise in the name of reason, a breaking away from the mystique of the nation. But reason itself gave birth to the term *terrorist* during the reign of Marat and Robespierre in France. In the name of reason they had revolted against their god-king, but they themselves began to terrorize all who would undermine the work of the revolution, including each other.

In the late nineteenth and early twentieth centuries arose the messiahs and prophets of industrialism and nationalism. Karl Marx, descended from a long line of rabbinical leaders, took up the messianic message that would protect the most oppressed or terrorized of mankind, not only from the physical deprivation inflicted by people and nations, but from the terrors of industrialism: the alienation of the worker and the subordination of the human spirit. In Russia, a group called the People's Will, having failed to reach the peasants, turned to terrorism and assassinated the Great Father, the divinely inspired Alexander II, in 1881. In the same year, Charles Guiteau, who had spent six years in a Christian communist community, only to be discharged as miserable as he had arrived, killed President Garfield. However, the killers of Alexander II protested that in a free nation it was immoral to kill the head of state.

The American experiment, which sought and had a unique opportunity to reject the terrorist traditions of more ancient states, has had its own experiences with terrorizing the indigenous population and with terror carried out in the name of competing religious institutions. The great Civil War, fought in the name of national unity and over the moral issue of slavery, was followed by the assassination of the President and the emergence of terrorist and guerrilla practices for the subordination of the formerly enslaved. This terrorization was successful for a century, and its effects remain in the consciousness and in the reality of American life—in this, the most powerful and affluent of nations.

And yet today, within American borders, terror—except as expressed by minor, if spectacular, predominantly religious episodes—does not manifest itself as it does, for example, in comparable Western European nations such as Italy and West Germany. There are a number of hypotheses that might explain this difference. Certainly we cannot ignore the striking emergence of leftist antigovernmental terrorism precisely in those nations that experienced terrorism by governments in previous generations. This is a necessary but insufficient explanation. In the 1960s, a number of major American institutions—not excluding the government—found themselves under active challenge by college-aged people, particularly those attending large universities. Changes in lifestyles and the practice of dropping out gradually became politicized. This particular change in lifestyle meant a dropping away from many of the values of bourgeois society, from which, not incidentally, the leaders of these groups had come. The sexual mores of postmarital monogamy yielded to sexual experimentation and a marked increase in acceptance of other forms of sexuality. Dress became radically altered to assume the characteristics once associated with the American hobo of the nineteenth century. There was a celebration of sensuality, of love, and a seeking after different levels of consciousness. The drug culture exploded, with particular emphasis on LSD and other ego-shattering and sense-accentuating substances. Society was labeled plastic; there was a strong reaction against the corporate society and similarly against the values of the young activists' middle and upper class families. Vague political substitutes were offered, but these were not coherent.

The activists tended to believe in ideologies of an exotic or distant nature, in direct proportion to a lack of familiarity. For example, Soviet communism was adopted by very few; Maoism, in the days before Richard Nixon traveled to China, was a preferable ideology, although acquaintance with that doctrine might have consisted of little more than the possession of the Red Book of Mao Tse-tung. These foreign ideologies were mixed with a combination of sexuality and aggressivity and, peculiarly enough, mysticism. Sexuality was explored through the writings of Herbert Marcuse and

Norman O. Brown; aggressivity through Fanon, Eldridge Cleaver, and for some, even Sorel and Pareto; mysticism in the Vedanta and the Hare Krishna movements and in the affiliations with a number of gurus.

Early in 1962 a serious, politically aware student, Thomas Hayden, and a group of like-minded others became concerned for the survival of the social democratic values which they had been taught represented the American ideal. They issued the *Port Huron Statement,* which read today sounds like a remarkably thoughtful and temperate affirmation of traditional American values. The Establishment, however, responded with something akin to hysteria. Confrontations on campuses rapidly accelerated in the intensity of provocation and counterprovocation until finally all the leading universities in the country were involved. The decade which had started for these young people with the assassination of the young President Kennedy in 1963 accelerated in its frightening hideousness to the confrontation between the youths and the police of Chicago during the Democratic convention, to the assassinations of Robert Kennedy and of Martin Luther King, Jr., and to the black riots in the major cities of this country.

Within the youth movement, the SDS—Students for a Democratic Society—fragmented into an ineffectual, liberal, social democratic group; an organized, ideologically coherent, humanly remote Maoist group; and a third group, the Weathermen. The Weather Underground borrowed its name from the lyric of a poet of the counterculture, and moved from student activism to the beginnings of underground violence.

However, shocked by the deaths of two of their leaders in an accidental explosion and moved by a concern for human life (such had at first characterized their nineteenth-century Russian precursors, the People's Will), the Weather Underground avoided the taking of human life. But they moved to destabilize the Establishment by blowing up buildings and structures symptomatic of the corporate state.

This twentieth-century American terrorist movement may be said to have been characterized by humanism, mysticism, anarchism, and feminism. The feminist movement, for many of the previously leftist politically radical women, surpassed in significance their earlier ideological allegiances. The emergence of female leaders was striking in the 1960s and 1970s as it had been in earlier American history—in the abolitionist, the temperance, the suffrage, and the birth control movements, and in the creation of such powerful religious movements as Christian Science—but was not substantially different from the European terrorist movements. Very important also to American terrorism are the continuing dilemmas of the black community, whose equality—economic, social, and political— has yet to be attained.

But most important in the long historical perspective is the recurrent, eternally optimistic experimentation with utopias, which has been an integral part of the American experience. Throughout this country today, there are communes experimenting with alternative lifestyles—as did Brook Farm, New Harmony, and Oneida in the nineteenth century.

A new phenomemon emerged in September 1975 which suggested a convergence of many of these trends. Within seventeen days, two women—Sara Moore and Lynette "Squeaky" Fromme— shot at then President Ford. Squeaky Fromme and Sara Moore represent the coalescence of most of the important elements of the activist movements. Fromme was a veteran of the Manson Family, a terrorist group that was only marginally political but was deeply involved in mysticism, sexuality, aggressivity, and lifestyle changes. Its charismatic leader drew the Family's political element from its fear of a black-white war, which only the Family would survive. Fromme said that she had shot at the President in the name of ecology. Sara Moore, a middle-aged divorcee with an upper middle-class background similar to Fromme's, had become involved in social activism when she volunteered for PIN, the distribution program of some $2 million worth of food donated by the Hearst family on the demand of the Symbionese Liberation Army when it abducted Patty Hearst. To an extraordinary degree, both female assailants have brought together through their affiliations and the locales of their respective crimes some of the more bizarre manifestations of the American counterculture of the late sixties and early seventies. Included are elements of the Manson Family, the Symbionese Liberation Army with its murder of Marcus Foster and its kidnapping of Patty Hearst, the entire Berkeley commune culture and its involvement in the Black Liberation Union, the introduction to now-politicized black prisoners of the psychiatric model for social change, and finally the psychiatric model that characterized the counterculture movements of the sixties and seventies.

In the sixties, American adolescents and young adults were not unlike their peers in Western Europe and Japan. But in the seventies, Italy, West Germany, and Japan exploded into a frightening orgy of terrorism, both national and international. This had little echo, however, in the United States. We can only speculate why this has been so. There is, it seems, a significant difference between the breakdown of social controls and economic stability in Italy as compared to the United States. However, these differences in circumstances do not carry over to comparisons of the United States with West Germany or with Japan. In either case we must look with interest on the phenomenon of terrorism on behalf of the left arising from the children in precisely those countries where the preceding generation had been involved in the terrorism of totalitarian states.

The intent of this essay has been to explore not the genesis of the terrorist himself, but the even more puzzling phenomenon of the extraordinary excitement, fear, and indeed terror that he or she creates. This excitement resonates through millions of people, via the media, while the mutilations and deaths of tens of thousands through accidents, conventional warfare, and natural disasters go virtually unremarked.

It may aid us to work within a framework, which we may label "a model of terroristic resonance," in exploring this significant but puzzling phenomenon. First, the terrorist as perceived through the media is single-minded in his or her purpose, uncaring in his or her aggressivity and unafraid of the vengeance of powerful figures. Thus, the perception of the audience is extremely important. Secondly is the sense of randomness. Although in the past, high-ranking officials or heads of state have clearly been selected for propagandistic purposes (as in the case of the assassination of Alexander II and President Garfield), the target of small terrorist groups in recent decades more commonly appeared to be randomly selected and generally unpredictable. Indeed, many of the victims have been "symbolic" only in their insignificance. For example, the passengers in a hijacked airplane are as victims interchangeable with any number of equally anonymous figures in the audience.

Terror may be defined as extreme anxiety infused with an awesome sense of the uncanny. This emotional response is evoked by the tactics of the terrorist who appears to play out his aggressive impulses untroubled by feelings of guilt or remorse. He appears suddenly on the scene, an anonymous figure who attacks the very structure of society either by selecting a powerful figure or by challenging authority and social mores by violating the security of accepted social procedures. This sudden assault and apparent fearlessness communicates a sense that the terrorist can in fact work miracles in upsetting the state. The terrorist's belligerent denial of the normal affective reactions, other than anger and resolution, assaults the sensibility of the spectator. The sudden transformation of the human target from free agent to vulnerable victim assaults the sense of autonomy of the spectator. The sudden, unexpected fall of someone in power assaults the sense of security of the spectator.

In psychoanalytic terms, it is as though an irresistible impulse from the id assaults the personification of the social representative of the superego. These manifestations of unconscious psychic institutions arouse not only fear but also the sense of the uncanny: the terrorist is seemingly omnipotent. His force of will is impenetrable. He has produced something inevitable. The suddenness of appearance, the lack of psychic preparation, and the indefinite time span of the terroristic act all unsettle the sense of time and orderliness. This element of unreality tends to depersonalize all the actors in the drama, including the audience. Thus, the powerful resonating impact of limited interactions amidst a few people reflects the awe, fear, and terror in which the apparent enactment of the unconscious, infantile apprehensions of every man is evoked.

In sum, then, the role of the messiah and the prophet has always been to sustain personal and social equilibrium, to overcome primordial dread. The messianic message has been that the terror of existence will one day be replaced by harmony and serenity. The prophet predicted and threatened; he predicted social justice and the god's grace with conformity to the god's rules, but he threatened terrors unless sin ended and propitiation of the gods was successful. From prehistoric man with his primitive and jealous gods through the early Judaic, Hindu, Buddhist, Christian, and Islamic periods, the twin themes have been constant. The terrors of an individual's life are omnipresent. Only behavior and feelings suitable to the injunctions of the god or the god's designated messiahs and prophets could bring respite.

The divine tyrant, the national leader, the political philosopher—all have carried the same message. Live according to ordained rules or suffer the terror of those who violate the gods and goddesses of both supernatural and rational origin.

The terrorists of the twentieth century carry on this messianic and prophetic tradition. Their horrors are visited upon man because man has violated the absolutist value that for the nationalist, spiritualist, or nihilist transcends all other values.

When the humanist, egalitarian commune of planetary man has become the absolutist value, man will not have eliminated terrorism. But he will come as close as his species can—given its range of evolutionary adaptive capacities.

NOTES

1. *The Revolutionary Catechism* (1869), quoted in Robert Payne, *The Terrorists: The Story of the Forerunners of Stalin* (New York: Funk & Wagnalls Co., 1957), pp. 21-27.
2. Rene Fulop-Miller, *Leaders, Dreamers, and Rebels: An Account of the Great Mass Movements of History and of the Wish-Dreams That Inspired Them,* trans. Eden and Cedar Paul (New York: The Viking Press, 1935), p. 9.
3. C. G. Jung, *Symbols of Transformation,* trans. R. F. C. Hull (Princeton: Princeton University Press, 1956, 1967), p. 182.
4. Ibid., pp. 369-70
5. Fulop-Miller, *Leaders, Dreamers, and Rebels,* p. 12.
6. Ibid., p. 6.

Discussion
Panel I

LEITES: Professor Louch presented the moral dilemma of terrorists as deriving from the incommensurability of what they impose with the benefit they aspire to confer. The typical terrorist, it would seem to me, does not perceive any incommensurability in this regard: the cost appears to him tiny in comparison with the benefits of damaging the status quo. The status quo seems to him highly resistant to all other means than his own, but vulnerable precisely to them. There are a number of precise rationales which predict the sharp impairment of the status quo by terrorist acts. For example, there is a belief that the society contains a high incidence of highly repressed revolutionary attitudes; the terrorist will be their derepressor by at least two mechanisms. First, he will show that a moral man such as he finds the status quo horrible enough to resort to extreme deeds against it. Second, he will show that it is possible to exercise violence against the status quo even if only in a limited or temporary fashion. It is possible to monopolize the attention of the rulers as well as of the population to the extent that a state of siege may be produced in the regime for a period sometimes of considerable length. This, the terrorist foresees, will change forecasts as to how the battle between the regime and its enemies will turn out, and such changes of forecast work in favor of the derepression. Besides these that I have just sketched there are others.

LOUCH: I don't suppose, in fact, that most terrorists engage in what we would think of as utilitarian calculations. But the point is that if you believe actions will have large-scale social effect, and act *because* you believe it, you are bound to consider what the consequences are going to be of derepression. What's going to happen? And, of course, one characteristic of terrorist rhetoric is the absence of any planning for the future. It's not enough just to say, "Get rid of the repressive regime"; you need to have a view about the mechanics by which some other kind of regime is going to emerge. It's the lack of such a view that leads me to say that the rationale for terrorism is essentially irresponsible.

POSSONY: From the perspective of practical strategy we should recognize that terrorism is rarely an effective means of waging conflict. It is propaganda of the deed, specifically a sort of psychological crescendo. You pay blood for blood, and blood activates people. Hence morale is expected to rise. But it is an unpredictable enterprise.

Even if the terrorist movement is very, very large, as it has been in some places, it doesn't crush the state, and it rarely destroys important targets. In Italy the state still is functioning, and the terrorists are viewed as little more than reckless drivers who add to the number of traffic fatalities. God knows it's a bad state; God knows nothing functions well in Italy. But everything is functioning in a way, and the economy still is making progress.

Let me give you another example which Professor Louch mentioned himself: the attempt on Hitler's life in 1944. There was no question about the logic of killing him, about the morality of doing so: he was one of the greatest criminals and murderers of all time, and he had usurped state authority. What is there left to do in a case like this? Yet the operation did not work, a typical outcome of terrorist operations. It did not work even though it was reasonably well organized. Rather than alleviating repression, it intensified Hitler's irrationality. Many people were killed in the repression which followed, a result that should be counted in the balance sheet. It was a crime of the Allies that we did not attempt to use imaginative means to conclude the war earlier, and to get rid of Hitler by means which were not exclusively terroristic and not exclusively military. We ignored the anti-Nazis within Germany and we drove responsible Germans into the desperation of terrorism. Basically, just as the

Nazis believed there could not be one good Jew, so the democracies believed there could not be one good German. We are loath to admit the reality of mirror-imaging in this case.

KNUTSON: I think one of the aims at a meeting on terrorism is to follow our own first premises; one of the first premises of Dr. Freedman was that terrorists are not uniform in their ideologies and actions—different terrorists have different perspectives. I want to discuss a few very specific things concerning that premise. It's possible to kill human beings only by making them into objects—an understanding which we probably all share. Such dehumanization of victims comes either because of certain psychiatric disabilities through which people really are experienced as objects (the psychopath or sociopath, depending on your choice of terminology) or, in terms of what we call more "normal" psychology, it occurs when we make people into objects—as in wartime.

Now, I think it's very difficult, at least for American and Canadian terrorists-executioners, to dispose of their victims by employing the second psychological strategy. There *is* a thin veneer of ideology, but when they talk about a "class victimizer," when it comes down to specifics, it's very hard for American terrorists to hold on to the reality of the abstract enemy. I think that distinction is important, and I would suggest that at least the North American terrorist who executes his victim is more likely to employ the first psychological strategy.

However, most of the American and Canadian terrorists with whom I am familiar are *not* executioners and, for them, the employment of terror involves a real moral crisis. Beforehand, denial is practiced to an amazing extent. Frequently, they perceive that terror is an unwanted, though unavoidable, aspect of what they feel is necessary to do politically. I have explored in detail with a number of them how it is possible that one can take over a plane or plant a bomb without an ordinary degree of anxiety that somebody might die of a heart attack, the bomb might go off, etc. That lack of anxiety is such an unusual phenomenon, if you consider normal psychology. However, most of the people to whom I talk do not accept responsibility for the final consequences of their terror, and thus are *very* different from the Irish, from Okamoto (the remaining Japanese terrorist from the Lod massacre), from the Palestinians. I hope that this distinction will remind us of the differences which we are going to be discussing.

The terrorists to whom I have talked who did not intend to be executioners display three phenomena that made their terroristic acts possible, within the general category of denial. The first one is a lack of a pragmatic orientation, problem solving, and goal orientation—an ideational pulling away from reality that really distorts reality and that prevents a plan which deals with ultimate consequences. The second is a definite lack of a future orientation so that the question of what happens after the event is never seriously considered. The plan ends at the point that the act begins. The third phenomenon, which several of the terrorists I've interviewed felt very strongly, was a sense of omnipotence. Somehow, *simply by their willing it*, they would be able to avoid the possible consequences of terror—by the magnetism and righteousness of their cause, by becoming personally involved with the hostages to disallow their being victimized by feelings of terror, etc.

NATHAN: It seems to me that terrorists, at least as we have come to know them in the United States, do make a utilitarian calculus. If I understand what people in the Weather Underground were saying, it was that 1) we live in a hierarchical society, 2) that society is repressive, 3) change is not possible by ordinary means, and 4) those who believe in equality are left with violence as a remedy. They argued that "innocents" should be avoided, and they blew up remote power plants or planted explosives in corporate headquarters—the symbols of society's repressive hierarchy—when nobody was around. But if "innocents" were injured, it was for a greater service—a better, more just society. Now, that simple formulation is "pragmatic" and "utilitarian" if one uses the words normally, that is, as a rational, prudential calculation of ends and means. I say this, of course, not in defense of terrorists, but as an indictment of "pragmatic" thought when it comes to the use of violence for collective aims and societal change.

HACKER: There is, or at least there should be, general agreement to the opening remarks that one should not be satisfied with the trite but true statement that one side's freedom fighters are the other side's terrorists. However, this reminder is quite important in order not to fall into the error of naive ethnocentricity. Without discussing the question of effectiveness of terrorism in detail, it could be argued that many of the Third World nations owe their recently won independence to at least a phase in their liberation struggle that could be called terroristic. Professor Louch talked about moral indifference and moral insensitivity as characteristic of the terrorists, a view supported by the remark of the French intellectual Henri who, throwing into a Paris café a bomb that killed many people, exclaimed, "There are no more innocents." The innocence of the victims is indeed irrelevant for the terrorist, but then he feels that society by its injustice also punishes innocents without even recognizing that society's victims are indeed victimized. The terrorists protest against the conception that it is blind fate and not biased society which is mainly responsible for victimization. The dramatic terrorist act is supposed to show, by its seeming insensitivity, how insensitive and immoral society is. Thus the terrorist means to point to the repressive, unjust immorality of society which, however, poses as the only possible morality. The essential aloneness of the terrorist is at least counter-matched in his fantasy by his conviction of speaking and acting for a group and for a higher, more sensitive form of universal justice.

I believe that one should pay a great deal of attention to what Dr. Freedman said, namely, that for the unconscious, the great omnipotent protector is at the same time the great destroyer who is to be feared. The destroyer therefore commands considerable attraction because people are not only afraid of him but also identify with him. For this and many other reasons, I believe that the question of terrorism from below cannot be isolated and has to be seen in connection with terror from above, that is, the terror of the established rulers and institutions. In coming to a valid moral evaluation (and rejection) of terror and in order to find effective means of combating it, one cannot afford to make any value distinction between terror from above and terrorism from below. One has to see their interconnection and interaction because they are indeed existentially related to each other, causing each other and justifying each other.

RAPOPORT: As usual Dr. Hacker is eloquent, and I am pleased that he wants to pursue my opening remarks. I did say that state and rebel terror have certain common distinguishing characteristics and that we ought to talk both about those characteristics and about the relationship between them. I regret that Dr. Hacker does not address himself to the first question, because a response might help illuminate how we should treat the second question—the relationship of the two forms. He argues that the terrorist has a "fantasy," that his actions are a response to the Establishment's terror. He then suggests that in fact "terror from above and ... from below ... are indeed existentially related to each other, causing each other and justifying each other." One cannot, therefore, make any value distinctions between them.

Dr. Hacker's logic is, however, faulty. I think that we would all agree that *every* terrorist says that he is defending us against a fascist state. The terrorist does this because this is the strongest possible justification for terror. He wants to convince himself and everyone else that he has an obligation to do what he is doing. I suspect that those who justify state terror might be making similar claims, as Stalin did. But why should we believe either, without at least looking at the evidence and asking for some definition of the terms? In fact rebels rarely mount a terror campaign against a vigorous state terror. They are much more likely to be active in democratic and/or weak states. Terrorism thrives on hope. State terror deprives the individual of hope.

If we accepted Dr. Hacker's characterization of the relationship and believed that state and rebel terror are the cause of each other, we would *have* to sympathize with the rebel because we know that the state is too strong not to have options. Dr. Hacker wants us to be more detached; but in fact he has so defined the situation that we must take sides.

ZAWODNY: I would like to plead for several refinements. We should recognize that there may be differences in the scenarios to which we want to apply moral judgments: two kinds of terrorist movements requiring different kinds of scenarios would require different kinds of judgments. One kind of terrorist movement is directed against its *own* government. That is when the "terrorists" and "oppressors of terrorists" are of the same culture, as was the case with the SLA. In the second scenario, the terrorists represent the people who fight against an enemy from a different culture, as was the case in most colonial uprisings. In that instance an "oppressor" is dressed in a hostile uniform. These two basic situations require different criteria for moral judgments about terrorist activities.

Another refinement is even more complex. In the discussions here it seems to me that many people assume that a terrorist represents some sort of chronologically consistent entity. That is, that the motivational factors are the same from the inception of the desire to join the terrorist group to actually pulling the trigger. This, in my judgment, is a great oversimplification. This is not the case. And if you assume that it is not the case, then refinements ought to be made about different stages of the development of a terrorist. For example: different variables are operational when the man (or woman) is joining the terrorist movement, and when he (or she) acts violently as a member of a terrorist group.

I can testify from experience as an urban guerrilla that there are several psychological thresholds which people like myself had to cross before the trigger was pulled. And each of these thresholds had a different motivational ambiance. Therefore, it occurs to me that the moral implications, to be correctly assessed, ought to be related to each of these thresholds and anchor on them. In other words, a very simple distinction ought to be made between the moral implications of why people join the terrorist group and why they pull the trigger. There are several psychiatrists here and I am sure they will agree. Incidentally, you seem to be presenting your view about terrorists from other countries with incisiveness, elegance, and sensitivity; however, it appears to me that your generalizations are very much culture-bound. On the other hand, I don't believe this can be helped.

WEINBERG: I wanted to follow up on the observation about the cultural biases of these judgments. We have been evaluating the terrorists as if they were graduate students. As would-be philosophers, they are deficient because they don't seem to understand the utilitarian calculus. As potential social scientists, they clearly lack an adequate understanding of the statistical probabilities of achieving the goals they seek by the means they employ. Perhaps the terrorists should be required to take another course in research methods. The implicit question about terrorist behavior we have been seeking to answer is this: do the terrorists really deserve Ph.D.s?

LOUCH: Let me respond very briefly to that. It seems to me that once judgments of political action, particularly violent political action, are made, there is a responsibility on the terrorist's part to meet just those kinds of standards. It's the failure to meet them that has to do with the moral indictment of the act.

RAPOPORT: I want to supplement Professor Louch's response because I think that Professor Weinberg's irritation has less to do with the question of philosophic standards and more with whether we ought to pay any attention whatsoever to justifications. Professor Weinberg has forgotten that it is not the violence, but the relationship between the violence and the moral claims, which gives terror its peculiar quality. The terrorist *is* always attempting to speak a moral language. If we are ever to understand him, let alone deal with him, we *have* to pay attention to what he is saying. Those of you who have been hostage negotiators (like Dr. Hacker and Dr. Hatcher) I'm sure will agree that a negotiator who didn't listen would fail. And then there is something else. I teach a course on terrorism. Sometimes I get students who sympathize with this or that act, with this or that group. They provide moral arguments for their positions. Am I supposed to ignore them, tell them to shut up? Would it not be better to try and see if they really understand all the implications of their position?

FREEDMAN: I, too, want to respond to the intriguing challenge of Professor Weinberg. Professor Steven Marcus of the Department of English at Columbia University and others who teach the literature of the late nineteenth and early twentieth centuries have found that students respond to those works of authors such as Conrad and Dostoevski which are concerned with terrorists and terrorist activities in two remarkable ways: they personally identify with and often admire the terrorists, and they put the terrorists and their conflicts in a dramatic or theatrical context. So, the absurdity which Professor Weinberg has described has, in this absurd world, a real existence in the minds of graduate students in this country.

LIEBSTONE: What I have been able to pick up regarding a psychology for terrorists is that in order to perpetrate crimes and violence, terrorists must undergo a kind of psychological conversion. They must begin to believe that an idea or an abstraction is more significant, more important than human life. When they accomplish this they have their justification for violence. Whether they are reactionary or radical doesn't matter much once that psychological conversion takes place. If we're talking about younger terrorists, I suppose for them the conversion is easier because they're at that age when a new identity is being sought.

FREEDMAN: That's precisely the point. In studying personal murders, which occur in the thousands each year, I have found a sequence of subjective reactions which is quite common amongst convicted murderers. There is a profoundly intimate love-hate relationship which explodes into a homicidal attack. Subsequently there is usually a profound depression and sometimes amnesia. Amongst a large proportion, there is a religious conversion, usually taking the evangelical form of being born again in Christ. I have studied a man who killed his six beloved children. He became amnesiac, and while in this state he experienced a profound Christian conversion. He came to believe that his children were in heaven and that if he lived a godly life, he would join them there. It was only after he had accomplished this internal adjustment of psychic defenses that we were able to break through his amnesia. He then described in great detail and with a profound reenactment of his emotions the killing of his children. He had in fact been in a dissociative state in which he believed that he was himself committing suicide and that his father, who had in fact committed suicide many years earlier, had returned to kill his children.

In our studies of the politically violent assassins and terrorists, we have found that this conversion experience, not necessarily Christian, but deep involvement in a cosmic belief system, precedes the murderous attack. The conversion takes place before the act and suffuses the self, so that while it is true that there is a great deal of moral justification, the act itself results from a sense of a moral imperative. Characteristically, it is not followed by depression, amnesia, or conversion. On the contrary, there is relief of tension, and often exhilaration. Some have reported that they had their first restful night's sleep on the night following the political murder.

POSSONY: I think you must distinguish two types of terrorists. One is what you might call a "soldier-terrorist." This sort of person doesn't have many of the problems psychologists talk about, least of all does he or she suffer from moral suppression. The second type is the "psycho-terrorist" who does have all the problems analysts are interested in. Most terrorists in the first group are military types; recruited and moved into action like soldiers, they come from the barracks. The psycho-terrorists are self-recruited. They come from the home, the bed, or the classroom.

Moral and Ethical Considerations in Defining a Counter-Terrorist Policy

AMBASSADOR ANTHONY C.E. QUAINTON

Albert Einstein once observed, "Any power must be the enemy of mankind which enslaves the individual by terror and force." There was evidently no question in Einstein's mind that the use of terror deserved condemnation. The word *terror* itself is invariably used in a pejorative sense in our world. We think in terms of combating it, of taking measures to eradicate it, and of eliminating its root causes. But before we can succeed in these endeavors, we must have a clear understanding of what kinds of violence should be designated as terroristic.

The standard definition of terrorism is in itself normatively neutral: the threat or use of violence for political purposes when such action is intended to influence the attitudes and behavior of a group wider than its immediate victims; its ramifications transcend national boundaries. The definition of Thomas Thornton, a former member of the State Department's policy planning staff, is equally neutral. Thornton has called terrorism "a symbolic act designed to influence political behavior by extranormal means entailing the use of threats or violence." These definitions do not solve the dilemmas of the policymaker, operating in a world where some uses of violence are acceptable and others are not, where some political purposes enjoy our support and others do not. We, like the terrorists, seek through a variety of political means to influence a wide spectrum of target groups.

Obviously, when we talk of terrorism, we talk of those violent political acts, whether symbolic or not, of which we disapprove. Those of which we approve are categorized as legitimate liberation struggles or valid defense of vital national interests, or justified responses to state or institutional violence against which we might be struggling. One person's terrorist is another's freedom fighter only because moral judgments about ends and means differ.

This problem of definition has bedeviled the development of an effective counter-terrorist strategy at both the national and international level. Even within our own government, the desire of the Congress and the administration to put the United States on the side of a negotiated settlement in the Middle East, majority rule in South Africa, and a democratic evolution in Nicaragua or El Salvador poses problems for us as long as El Fatah continues its bombings and assassinations, Zanu and Zapu shoot down civilian aircraft, and the Sandinistas take innocent civilians as hostages. How do we separate means from ends? This is the basic dilemma of any antiterrorist policy.

I certainly do not have any magic answers. Beauty continues to be in the eye of the beholder, the legitimacy of violence in the mind of the perpetrator and his or her supporters. To deal with this problem, we increasingly have been working to separate means from ends. We are seeking to build an international consensus that certain heinous acts are inadmissible in civilized societies, irrespective of the causes in which they are used.

This effort is not new. The international community has been actively struggling with this problem since the mid-1930s. The 1937 League of Nations Convention set forth a series of acts that were considered inadmissible in the context of the post-World War I political environment. That convention condemned international acts against the life, physical integrity, health, or freedom of heads of state and others vested with public duties and responsibilities, or acts which imperiled human lives in creating a common danger. Since 1937 a series of conventions have enlarged the consensus. The Geneva Conventions of 1949 and their additional protocols cover acts committed both in conventional wars and in national liberation struggles. The Hague and Montreal Conventions of 1970 and 1971 deal with hijackings and aircraft sabotage. The 1977 New York Convention outlaws certain acts against internationally protected persons. Most recently a convention has been drafted on hostage taking. As yet, however, there is no convention or any consensus on other acts, such as assassinations, letter bombings, or attacks on nondiplomats, and the American effort in 1972 to put forward a comprehensive antiterrorism convention failed to obtain the requisite international support.

The drafting of all of these conventions has been time-consuming and has had to overcome a series of deeply felt commitments among Third World delegations. These delegations have been concerned that the conventions not in any way derogate from the legitimate rights of national liberation movements nor weaken the struggle against racism, imperialism, and colonialism. Other states have tried to limit the principles of state self-help that were involved in the Israeli rescue operation at Entebbe. Formulae have ultimately been found to deal with these issues but only after prolonged and sometimes bitter debate.

In almost all the conventions the basic principle is that of traditional international law: *aut dedere aut punire*—either hand over or punish. However, a particular problem arises when the perpetrators of any of these acts seek political asylum, arguing, for example, that they have committed a hijacking to obtain "freedom" or that if they are extradited to another country for prosecution they will be unjustly treated. Many countries in Latin America consider the granting of asylum to be a more important principle than criminal punishment. Our consistent effort in the last decade has been to insist that the obligation to prosecute is not inconsistent with the right to seek asylum. Hijackers seeking freedom have been prosecuted and, once having served their sentences, have been granted asylum. These precedents should be extended to the prosecution of other terrorist acts, so that terrorists cannot assert that their political views exempt them from prosecution for their actions.

Most international conventions suffer from a fundamental weakness: they contain no effective enforcement machinery. In 1972 at Rome we tried to put teeth in the Hague Convention and failed; the economic and political self-interest of a majority of states precluded their agreeing to any sanctions mechanism. However, in July 1978, seven states (Canada, France, Great Britain, Italy, Japan, the United States, and West Germany) agreed to cut off air services to and from any state that failed to extradite hijackers or prosecute them. The agreement, the Bonn Declaration on Hijacking, is the first major step towards enforcement of the Hague Convention obligation to prosecute or extradite. It is a credible step, considering that these seven states conduct some 70 percent of the non-Communist world's civil aviation. We have actively been seeking to extend international acceptance of the objectives of the declaration, and over thirty countries have publicly indicated their support for it.

In addition to the issues posed by international conventions in the domain of global policy, there are other more specific issues that arise in the course of managing specific terrorist incidents in which lives are at stake. The fundamental issues are whether to negotiate with terrorists, and if one decides to negotiate, whether to meet the terrorists' substantive demands. Meeting demands may save lives. It may also encourage terrorists to make other attacks or to escalate their future demands. The private sector's policy almost universally is to pay a ransom when it is demanded. Many governments, including the United States, have a firm policy not to pay ransom and not to release prisoners. Other countries, such as Japan, have been willing to make substantial concessions.

Neither approach requires that negotiations be strictly avoided. Virtually all governments are convinced that it is desirable to keep a dialogue going with the terrorists in an effort to talk them into freeing their hostages. More often than not, such a strategy is successful. The alternatives—the precipitate use of force or making concessions—are less satisfactory. When in the past terrorists have been released after hijackings, they have often come back to plague the government and the international community. A flexible approach is needed that combines a sure sense of priorities with firmness of purpose, and in which a dialogue is maintained but fundamental values are not sacrificed. Such firmness is not easy in hostage situations in which lives are at stake.

For the negotiator, irrespective of the policy framework in which he or she must act, there are many perils. The extent to which he or she should be aware of rescue or assault plans is a case in point. A negotiator's task is to keep the discussion going; it may be necessary to try to convince the terrorists that their demands will be met, even though an assault is in fact being planned. The time that the negotiator buys may only ensure the death of the terrorists. Most experts with whom I have talked are convinced that negotiators must act in good faith and should not necessarily be aware of other measures under way to rescue hostages. Nonetheless, an element of duplicity may be involved with which the unfortunate decision maker will have to grapple.

In the private sector, where there are frequent kidnappings, a different issue arises. Many American executives working abroad are insured by their employers against kidnapping. Should they be kidnapped, professional negotiators are often hired. Such negotiators are interested not only in the release of the prisoner but also in a reduction of the ransom demand. Success with the latter may prolong the detention of the hostage at some cost to his or her health and psychological well-being. Is this delay justified? Some of these issues are currently under review in the courts because a former hostage is suing his employer, in part, at least, on the grounds of the "unnecessary" hardship that he was forced to endure while the negotiations were going on.

Another area of potential moral ambiguity lies in the interstices of our human rights and counter-terrorist policies. Looked at realistically, terrorism can be eliminated only when full political rights are enjoyed by all, economic and social grievances are removed, and the inviolability of the human person is respected. Certainly these are and will remain our basic, long-term goals. But in the short run we and many other goverments face the hard reality of violent terrorist acts. These acts must be dealt with by law enforcement agencies under our respective constitutions. Some of our closest friends—Canada, Great Britain, and West Germany, for example— when faced with FLQ, IRA, or Red Army Faction terrorism have taken preventive legal measures. They have lengthened periods of detention without trial and increased prison sentences. In so doing, however, these countries have been concerned to avoid counterproductive, repressive measures. Should the United States be faced with greatly increased violence or terrorism, we also might have to determine where the balance should lie between political freedom and measures necessary to protect society from the terrorist threat.

Society can also be put in jeopardy through the misuse of intelligence. In recent years, we have seen a dramatic decline in the collection of information about the political activities of American citizens. This development obviously reflects past abuses and the unjustified intrusion into the private lives of Americans. One of the results of a decline in the fortunes of the intelligence community has been a notable reduction in the amount of information available about domestic terrorists and the violent acts they may be planning. Obviously, without good intelligence we cannot be successful in halting the terrorists' efforts. Yet we must continually ask ourselves what price, in terms of civil liberties, we are prepared to pay to have the insurance against attack that accurate intelligence might provide.

Even when we have intelligence its use may involve difficulties. Our government's basic assumption is that whenever it has information indicating that a hijacking, kidnapping, or assassination is being planned, it must act on that information in order to save lives. Yet the use of intelligence necessitates its dessemination, and the sources of that information may be exposed. Their lives may be jeopardized, thereby creating yet another dilemma for the policymaker. In such circumstances, we invariably choose dissemination and the taking of necessary protective measures.

One final word about protection. Those of you who have traveled recently will have seen the physical security measures that have been added to our embassies and consulates: access controls, magnetometers, bulletproof glass booths for the Marines. Ambassadors ride in armored or partially armored vehicles. Some have armed bodyguards; others, follow-cars. These steps provide a degree of security, but the killing of five American ambassadors in the last twelve years makes it clear that this security is insufficient. But how much security *is* enough? Here again there is a dilemma. The price for perfect security, like the price for perfect intelligence, is high. If our diplomats must live like prisoners in their offices and are unable to move about without extraordinary security measures, they are no longer able to represent America adequately. We are a free and open society—our representatives abroad must reflect that freedom and openness if they are to do their jobs. Again, a balance between freedom and security must be struck or the terrorists will have won.

This issue of openness versus security is also posed in a government's relations with the press. Terrorism is high visibility theater. Lives are at stake. The public has a legitimate interest in knowing how a particular incident is being handled by its government, yet clearly there cannot be unlimited access to information. The press has a responsibility to ensure that its actions do not endanger the lives of the hostages. It also has an obligation not to glamorize terrorism, not to make the use of terrorist violence an even more attractive means of promoting political causes. Our objectives are governmental commitments to openness and to responsible and restrained reporting in life-threatening situations. They do not always go together.

In our efforts both to deter terrorism and to deal with it when it strikes, the search for an appropriate balance is at the center of U.S. policy. But the definition of the balance, the determination of tolerable limits, is as much an issue for the public and the Congress as for the administration. The public must support a search for an international consensus; the public must decide whether it wants corporations and governments to make concessions or to stand firm; the public must decide how much intelligence collecting it will tolerate and what, if any, restrictions on its freedom it will allow. These dilemmas are at the very heart of government policy. Their resolutions, however, are not matters for civil servants only but for all of us: in government, in business, in academia.

The other day I came across a quotation from a now unfashionable source, Benito Mussolini. In a speech fifty years ago he commented, "There is a violence that liberates and there is a violence that enslaves; there is moral violence and stupid, immoral violence." Our task is to differentiate among these and thereby to ensure that we focus on the stupid, immoral violence that enslaves and that, as terrorism, threatens free institutions and societies.

Discussion
Panel II

ZAWODNY: I want to express my uneasiness concerning the sophistication, pathological sophistication if I may say, of weaponry today. With these kinds of weapons available, I don't see any way to prevent political assassination, that is to say, selective terrorism.

In 1977 on the German black market, nerve gas was available. Soon lasers will be. Let me give you another illustration: the SAM-7 missile called Strela. This is a ground-to-air missile. It costs about $900, weighs about twenty-five pounds, and a child can operate it from a Volkswagen bus with an open roof parked two miles from an airport when a 747 takes off. The plane and its 300 passengers can be dropped like an insect. It is my professional judgment that if factions want to carry out acts of selective terrorism, they will. The State Department should recognize this reality; countermeasures may alleviate the problem, but they won't prevent it.

QUAINTON: Surely there are some kinds of acts against which it is almost impossible to guard without extraordinary measures, measures that we are far from willing to accept. An assassination, as our own society has seen, is a relatively easy thing to carry out, but no President will avoid every contact with the public in order to prevent it.

We are all very much worried about the issue which is implicit in the second part of your question. We are familiar with hijackings, kidnappings, and hostage barricade situations; we have devised quite a number of reasonable strategies for dealing with them. But if you begin thinking about new kinds of weapons which might be of interest to terrorists and which are readily available even without going to the cataclysmic terrorist possibilities of biological, chemical, or nuclear weapons there is a whole range of intermediate technology which is now widely diffused in the world. The SAM-7, which has been used in Rhodesia and which has been found in a number of other places in the world, is the sort of intermediate technology which in the very near future could pose a serious threat and against which we have nothing like the same defenses.

RAPOPORT: Professor Zawodny, I'm sure, has not forgotten that *today* is the ides of March, the day when Julius Caesar got his! Advances in technology might not be so important after all.

I do have a question, however. It refers to the direction that the State Department is *not* going in, the direction of "institutionalizing terrorism." If the problem really is distinguishing between those forms of violence which are permissible and those which are not, when will we make this distinction? There is an enormous difference between attacks on armed soldiers and those on unarmed children. I have talked to terrorists in a number of countries, and many have made one striking point. They maintain that they want to be soldiers, but aren't *allowed* to be; they will be treated as murderers no matter whom they kill so why not go after the most defenseless target? It reduces their casualties and often produces a more useful political impact.

In the seventeenth century when the wars between Protestants and Catholics produced many massacres, Europe faced a similar problem, and decided that it was wrong to allow soldiers to attack innocent or defenseless peoples. Europeans knew that they could not abolish or prevent war, but they did believe that they could reduce its barbarism or "civilize" it. Governments constantly talk about preventing terrorism but never about civilizing it. These are very different problems. I suspect that preventing terrorism is quite an impossible task; civilizing it may very well be feasible. At least, I know a lot of terrorists who have said they would be interested in cooperating.

QUAINTON: Civilizing violence is not that easy.

RAPOPORT: Perhaps not, but we do it all the time. The police and the military both have weapons; each is expected to use its arms in different ways and for different purposes.

QUAINTON: I agree.... The Geneva Conventions are an effort to define what kinds of acts are legitimate in wartime and against military targets. The additional protocols of 1977 extend these principles to national liberation movements which commit acts against military targets. However, when push comes to shove, when you have the tools of violence in your hand, people are going to be more indiscriminate about the choice of targets than a conference such as this would like. But, it's clearly an issue which we have thought about and where some progress has been made, although not as much as we would want.

RAPOPORT: Must we wait for an international agreement? If we were really interested in pursuing this task, we could rewrite our law so that it more truly reflects popular sentiments concerning the difference between murder and combat—a step which could have serious political ramifications. I remember a letter by George Bernard Shaw explaining why the Easter Rebellion was bound to have an enormous impact on Irish and British consciousness. The rebels were hung as criminals, but Shaw pointed out that they were fighting for a purpose and employing methods that any decent person would find honorable. The rebels, you'll remember, fought British soldiers; I wonder what Shaw would have said if they deliberately assaulted children? Or to take another example: Lawrence Durrell's *Bitter Lemons* notes that the execution of Karolis, an EOKA member who assassinated a police officer, destroyed the last bridge between the Cypriots and British. The police, of course, are not legitimate targets during war. Perhaps the Cypriots cannot be expected to appreciate the difference between police and military officials, but they would, I think, know why it is wrong to kill children and would respect a law which protects them. In every state the law which governs terrorist activity is the same as that which determines criminals, but terrorist activity is not simply criminal activity, and if our law does not reflect our sentiments we are asking for trouble.

QUESTER: I am curious as to whether an international agreement will work as well as you imply. For example, someone hijacks an Aeroflot from Moscow to Stockholm and draws a five-year sentence in a Swedish prison. My impression of a Swedish prison is that you much would prefer that to five years back in Moscow as an ordinary citizen. If the word gets out, this isn't going to stop people at all.

QUAINTON: That point is frequently made to me by representatives of the Soviet Embassy! But the point is that some punishment has been meted out. We have indicated that hijacking is not something that is automatically admissible and for which there is no penalty at all. However, this is not necessarily going to deter future cases. They continue to happen. It is important to maintain the principle of prosecution: punishments meted out under most Western court systems tend to take into account the circumstances of the crime—there may well be mitigating circumstances.

POSSONY: It is a mistake to assume that in this area the government has a preventive function. Prevention is an attractive but unworkable idea; neither parliaments nor courts nor security forces have the capability of *preventing* crime. At best it is feasible to minimize danger and damage and to exact punishment. Antiterrorist strategy should aim at deterrence. This means that a security capability of such an effectiveness is created that it persuades many terrorists that their actions will not be successful, that they will be caught or killed if they attack. Effectiveness is dependent on intelligence in the double sense of operational knowledge—know thine enemy—and of political IQ—be a successful problem solver.

QUAINTON: That's our policy; you couldn't have stated it more succinctly.

WEST: We have been talking a great deal about technology and not very much about morality, which is the issue of the conference. It isn't easy for governments to be moral, yet there are moral issues that governments can address. If we try to differentiate among the several types of violence and then try to consider whether one type of violence could be morally acceptable while another type is not, we must look to definitions or criteria of morality.

One such definition was put forward by Martin Buber at the time of the Eichmann trial. It went something like this:

> To take a life in time of war is morally justifiable if it is in defense of one's own country, and thus the lives of one's own people. To take a life on an individual basis can be justified if it is to protect oneself, or to save a life. Throughout, it is life that has the moral value. Thus, violence *for* life can be morally justified. But if a soldier takes a prisoner, binds him, and *then* kills him, under the conventions of war the soldier, having killed a helpless captive, becomes a criminal. If you as a householder capture an intruder rather than shoot him, tie him up, call the police, and then the police come and find that you have subsequently killed him, you are indictable for homicide. Now, what is immoral for the individual cannot be made moral for the group. If it is wrong for an individual to kill a helpless captive, then for a government to kill one is equally wrong, even if that captive is Adolf Eichmann.

This is the essence of the purely moral argument against the use of the death penalty.

Today we are living at a time when the death penalty is coming back, with a vengeance, so to speak. The people want it. The states want it. And the federal government is not exactly hanging back. The number of different crimes considered to be capital crimes is going up again, and the temper of the people is that it is right, proper, and good to solve problems by killing helpless captives under certain conditions.

It strikes me that the federal government could play a role in examining this question, and that we scientists could play a role. For example, there are data to show that the attempt to solve problems of domestic violence by executing the occasional prisoner is self-defeating. Just as the death penalty stimulates more murders than it prevents, executions probably promote and foster more terrorism than they prevent.

Of course, this is a double dilemma. Of all the arguments in favor of the death penalty today, one of the most powerful is that even if you didn't execute anyone else, you should execute terrorists because if you *don't* execute them (and swiftly), then there will be more terrorism by their comrades trying to liberate them from prison. I don't believe that argument is valid. I don't believe that imprisoning terrorists will encourage further terrorism, and I don't think executing them will forestall it either. But here is a moral question, an issue that bears directly on the terrorism question. I wonder if the government intends to study this matter, to pursue it, to analyze it, to inspect the available data concerning it.

QUAINTON: You have obviously hit the fundamental issue: the value that you attach to life. This subject is being debated in a lot of different contexts in our society these days. I have heard the argument that you have put forward about the need for capital punishment for terrorist crimes. The fact is that the vast majority of terrorist acts have nothing to do with the release of captives, although there have been a number of very sensational cases in the past that did. So you are not going to eliminate terrorism by capital punishment, although you might eliminate that kind of act, I suppose—whether that would be sufficient justification for that penalty seems highly dubious. I am not quite sure where in the U.S. government you would have this inquiry take place.

You are posing issues which go far beyond combating terrorism; I certainly am not going to plunge into the vast array of moral and ethical issues that are related to capital punishment or the right to life. I'm not sure that this is something which the executive branch of the government ought to be doing. It *does* need to be developed and articulated in academia and out in the public: you have to tell your representatives what you believe the value of life is and what the circumstances are in which you accept the right to take it. That will change over time, I suspect; it *has* changed over time.

NATHAN: I'd like to get back to Professor Rapoport's question of institutionalizing violence. It seems to me that to some degree terrorism is already institutionalized, in that there are governments that aid terrorist groups. If the United States continues to pursue a policy of not aiding terrorist groups, how can we expect to be left with any option other than prevention? We are, thus, depriving ourselves of the ability to influence the outcome of the inevitable action.

QUAINTON: Are you arguing that we ought to be in the business of helping terrorist groups in order to have influence over them? To arm them?

NATHAN: That's a plausible argument and I have heard it before, but I don't subscribe to it.

QUAINTON: The way we are dealing with the problem is to try and get at the patrons of terrorism. This is also the thrust of legislation that has been sponsored by one of the L.A. congressmen, Glenn Anderson, and by Senators Ribicoff and Javits. It would have imposed a certain number of penalties on those states which provide a "pattern of support" to terrorism. It is a useful approach.

NATHAN: This might make for some difficulty in our relations with China and the Soviet Union.

QUAINTON: It is going to create difficulties with the countries the President determines to be on the list of patron states. If you want to combat terrorism you have to pay the price for it. In the last analysis we may not want to pay that cost, but if so, we have to be prepared for the other costs.

BOSE: Unfortunately, many countries are very quick and strong in criticizing terrorism. But they are reluctant to put equal pressure into eradicating the factors that prompted such acts of terror. The emphasis should not only be on condemning the terrorists but also on the acts and policies that provoke terrorist reprisals. Don't you think that one should attempt to remove the cause itself instead of only seeking to remove the effects arising out of it? It is imperative to take a broader view of the problem and adopt a program accordingly. Otherwise, it will be like trying to store water in a leaking bucket.

QUAINTON: Yes, our human rights policy is doing exactly that: it is trying to go to the root causes and to make us conscious of state violence and coercive measures by states against their own people. The basic grievances which exist in various parts of the world and which may arise through the use of state violence deserve a response by the U.S. I'm not sure, however, that it should be dealt with as terrorism.

BOSE: My main point is neither for nor against the U.S. government. I'm only trying to look at the problem from a general and wider perspective.

QUAINTON: That's what the charter of the United Nations is about. If you took the charter seriously, you would come to grips with all of these issues.

ERMLICH: Ambassador: At one point, Deputy Assistant Secretary of State Morris Draper told the Senate Foreign Relations Committee that the State Department had approved the sale of Boeing 707s and 727s to Libya. I wonder about the morality issue here, when Senator Javits had earlier documented a list of supporters, including Libya, for terrorist acts. How would your particular department react to this?

QUAINTON: We were very much involved in the decision. Our philisophy is that the punishment ought to fit the crime, to borrow a phrase from Gilbert and Sullivan. We don't sell Libya anything that directly contributes to their military capability or to their ability to support terrorism. We have embargoed military cargo aircraft and the comparable civilian version of that aircraft. We don't at present sell anything that would go to the Libyan military, and we have a similar policy with Iraq and South Yemen. We don't have a full trade embargo with any of those countries, nor with any country at the moment—we believe that normal commerce can continue. Perhaps that is the wrong approach, but we try to tailor our response to the policy which you want to change, and by concentrating on those things that might not enhance Libya's military or terrorist capabilities. With regard to civil aviation I might just say in passing that the Libyan policy concerning hijacking has markedly evolved for the better: in 1978 Libya acceded to the Hague Convention, and it has not allowed a number of terrorist hijackings to land in its territory. It seems to me that this is a positive step, and I'm not sure that cutting off all sales of civil aviation equipment to Libya would necessarily be very positive. You also have to weigh up our commercial interests: combating terrorism is not the only interest of the U.S. government. Whether it should be is something else again. If you were to speak to the senators from Washington, you would find that the $850 million in aircraft sales to Libya envisioned for the next three years is very important to the people of Seattle. The making of foreign policy is the balancing of a variety of national interests and objectives. We try to achieve as many of them as possible, and we try not to put all the eggs in one basket. But no decision is ever going to satisfy everybody.

FIELDS: Just a moment ago a colleague eloquently stated the question I intended to ask concerning the policy implications of providing support to countries that either aid terrorist groups or—and for me this is an even more cogent issue—those who employ state terrorism. I think the issue of morality is involved in our aid to specific countries identified as "allies" who request our military aid to fight "terrorism" when they are also recognized by international bodies as human rights violators. Given the propensity of our government to provide aid to such regimes, I'm amazed that there hasn't been even more action taken against representatives of our government by terrorist organizations: the citizens of such countries must view our accommodations and contributions to their government as collusion in their repression. I should think that in the State Department the offices of Terrorism and those of Human Rights ought to be adjacent to each other and have interchange continuously. No populace will support terrorism on a long-term and large-scale program without motivation, such as large-scale violations of human rights. But U.S. support is erratic. While contributing military aid to the British government to put down "terrorism" in Northern Ireland—a process which has included adjudicated violations of human rights according to the European Court on Human Rights—the U.S. also contributed heavily to the terrorist activities of the FNLA in Angola against our NATO ally Portugal, which has been accused—but not judged guilty—of human rights violations.

QUAINTON: I don't quite know what to say in answer to that. Obviously, what you are asserting has elements of truth to it, but the range of governments to which we have provided support over the years and which we support today represents a variety of standards of human rights. Determining what is an appropriate relationship is a basic issue in our foreign policy; those issues have to be addressed by the secretary of state. I have no doubt that we will continue to see violence directed against the U.S. government in countries where the popular perception is that we are too closely associated with a repressive regime. That is a price which we will pay. We have been very cautious in a number of countries in Latin America where we traditionally provided a great deal of assistance, including assistance to their police forces; now we do not provide assistance to police forces which engage in torture. This has been totally stopped. The International Police Academy, which was a thriving instrument of U.S. government policy until the early seventies, no longer exists. We do almost nothing with police forces, and certainly not in any countries where there is a bad human rights record.

Some Thoughts on State and Rebel Terror*

A. JAMES GREGOR

In order to present some responses to a few of the major issues brought forward by Professor Louch and Ambassador Quainton, I think we might distinguish two kinds of questions. First of all, there is the issue of the psychodynamics, or sociodynamics, of terrorism: that is to say, questions about what it might be that makes a person a terrorist or how one might effectively combat terrorism. These seem to me to be essentially social science questions that require empirical data and empirical assessments of the kind that I am not prepared, equipped, or disposed to undertake. What I would like to do is venture on a discussion of the normative aspects of our concerns.

On that level we are all prepared to acknowledge the differences between human beings and animals. Insofar as human beings attempt to justify their actions and animals do not, we recognize a moral distinction between them. Consequently, I think it an important enterprise to consider the normative dimensions of terrorism; that is to say, to have some reflective consideration of the moral rationale offered for the use of force and calculated violence against human beings. Our consideration of those dimensions and that rationale is urged upon us by our very humanity; we are compelled to attempt such reflections because, as human beings, we choose to distinguish ourselves from animals.

Even if men and women who employ violence against others are never required to justify its use, we, as academics, have an obliga-

---

* I would like to acknowledge the assistance of the Institute of International Studies, University of California, Berkeley, in the preparation of this essay.

tion and responsibility to address the issue. And because there seems to be considerable conceptual disorder surrounding the entire problem of human violence, in general, and the problem of terrorism, in particular. If we choose to reduce the incidence of violence and interdict terrorism, it seems essential that we be in a position to identify the occurrence of such acts. If we want to deplore deeds of violence or terrorism, it would be convenient if we could characterize them.

In addressing the kinds of issues evoked in these essays, and the ensuing discussion this morning, I would like to articulate some ideas which are not my own. In general, I feel more confident providing some account of the ideas of others—acting as an intermediary—rather than taking the responsibility of formulating notions of my own. In this case I would like to pursue some of the issues alluded to in the two earlier discussions by outraging your sensitivities—I would like to touch on the entire issue of an analysis of terrorism by providing an account of a "fascist philosophy of violence."

Most of us, of course, are prepared to invoke "fascism" whenever we talk about violence, because fascism and violence seem to be inextricably linked in our minds. Such an association constitutes a kind of pervasive prejudice that afflicts Anglo-American intellectuals. The term *fascism* is used universally as a term of abuse; it is almost invariably associated with violence and terror—and I would argue that there is a quaint sort of justification for such a constant association.

Fascists were among the only modern revolutionaries who actually put together a rationale for violence and sought to articulate a moral rationale for its use. If this claim appears odd, I suggest a survey of some of the available material on violence and terrorism. I recommend Marx's works, because Marx, for all his intellectual gifts, moves artlessly among talking about violence, terrorism, and force without ever clearly distinguishing among them. We can undertake a similar search for such distinctions in the works of Lenin. None are there. Occasionally, Lenin will speak of terrorism as individual acts of violence "unassociated with a mass movement"—a characterization that is not terribly helpful. If we rummage among books with "terrorism" in their titles—Karl Kautsky's *Terrorismus und Kommunismus*, for example—we will find literally no distinction between violence and terror. And when no distinction is made, no distinction can be pursued.

Kautsky sought to deplore the horrors of the Bolshevik revolution, but in doing so he failed to make even the most elementary distinction between violence and terror. In response, Leon Trotsky had little difficulty arguing that revolutions almost invariably involve—in fact, necessitate—violence, and anyone who would abjure violence must abjure revolution. Consequently, Trotsky argued that Kautsky, in rejecting violence, must reject revolution. Trotsky, like Kautsky, made no distinction between violence and terror. Whatever justified the one justified the other.

In any academic discussion of terror, the necessity for a distinction is transparent. Among revolutionaries, on the other hand, such a distinction might well be a pragmatic disability. Revolutionaries generally choose to avoid intellectual niceties, the better to have freedom of action. For that reason one finds very little that might pass as a "philosophy of violence" or an argued "philosophy of terror" among practicing revolutionaries.

This would have to be qualified with one exception: Sergio Panunzio, one such revolutionary and one of the intellectual founders of Italian fascism, produced just such a philosophy. At about the time that fascism was radiating out of Ferrara, in 1920 and 1921, Panunzio published his *Diritto, fòrza e violènza*, a rationale for political violence. In that publication and in his earlier *La persistènza del diritto*, Panunzio articulated a similar rationale and suggested some distinctions that I would urge here. In those works, Panunzio attempted to make distinctions between force, violence, and terror—distinctions that he saw reflected in Fascist tactics and strategy in the struggle for power in Italy prior to, and immediately after, the March on Rome.

In attempting to provide an account of Panunzio's views, I do not intend to investigate the history of the Black Shirt revolution. Whether the Fascists discharged their responsibilities in terms of their own moral philosophy is not a matter that I intend to address. That is a matter of marginal interest in terms of the issues I would like to pursue. What I would note instead is that of all the authors who have written about violence and with whom I have become familiar, it was—curiously enough—Panunzio alone who had something illuminating to say in making critical distinctions. Whether such distinction can be consistently and coherently pursued I have not, as yet, been able to determine. Nonetheless, Panunzio did make an effort that can well serve as a point of departure for further analysis.

To begin with, Panunzio provides several analytic categories, which suffer all the disabilities of analytically generated categories. Whenever such categories are mapped over the real world grey areas invariably appear: areas that seem to occupy uncharted space between two categories, or areas in which categories overlap. But, unlike the writings of Marx, Lenin, Kautsky, or Trotsky, Panunzio's work does advance some distinctions between force, violence, and terror. And it is to those distinctions that some time may be profitably devoted.

Fascism, as we all remember, grew out of the Sorelian tradition that initially made a distinction between "force" and "violence." The distinction made by Georges Sorel was a relatively primitive one; Panunzio elaborated upon it. When we talk about "power," for example, we touch upon some of the features to which Panunzio alluded when he spoke of "force." Panunzio spoke about the various aspects of force: normative force, material force, and coercive force.

The institutions of organized society employ force in all these aspects. We influence the young, for example, through moral suasion in order to have them adjust and adapt themselves to what we take to be suitable patterns of behavior. We socialize them, and we ourselves are continually socialized and resocialized through instruction, peer-group pressure, the media, and a variety of other agencies too numerous to catalog. We easily recognize all this as the exercise of moral or normative force. By training, by providing role models, and by subtle influence we convince and persuade others to behave as we would like.

Beyond that, society employs material force, or material power, to further influence behavior. We as individuals, for example, withhold a variety of welfare benefits from our children, our students, and our inferiors in the effort to shape their responses more in accord with what we consider proper conduct. We generally accept and recognize the effectiveness of this exercise of power or force. *All* societies employ both normative and material force, in varying degrees and measures, in shaping patterns of behavior.

Beyond that, all societies employ coercive force in varying degrees. Every society, in appropriate circumstances, provides for the employment of deadly force against its own citizens: the police carry a variety of weapons for just such purpose. We all recognize all this as a constituent of social life. To Panunzio, all this represents the employment of institutionalized force. All such employments are governed by rules, and when institutions violate those rules they employ *criminal* force.

Panunzio proceeded with his analysis by conceiving of violence as the perfect analog of force. For Panunzio, violence was the revolutionary counterpart of force—a distinction, as we have suggested, he borrowed from Sorel. When a group of individuals decides that they wish an alternative future precluded by extant social arrangements, they undertake revolution. A massive change in social alternatives can be effected by the exercise of normative, material, or coercive violence. Panunzio spoke of normative "violence" just as he was prepared to speak of normative "force"; the distinction he sought to make was between the exercise of power by the Establishment and the employment of power by a contending anti-Establishment. The former he identified as force and the latter as violence. Both use moral suasion, systematic instruction, the exploitation of political "myths," symbolic speech, allusions to the will of history, the evidence of time, etc. We employ them either to lend support to the established social and political arrangements or we use them for contrary purposes. Similarly, both the representatives of the Establishment and their opponents employ material power—material force or material violence, to use Panunzio's terminology—to accomplish their ends. Finally, both employ coercive power—coercive force or coercive violence—when normative or material power is insufficient.

Established polities employ coercive force against revolutionaries in what Panunzio identified as "internal war." Revolutionaries

Some Thoughts on State and Rebel Terror

in turn employ coercive violence against the state. Panunzio considered this to be the perfect analog of society's use of deadly force against criminals or foreign enemies in wartime. Revolutionary violence, according to Panunzio, is governed by the same rules that govern the employment of coercive force. There are legitimate objects of coercive violence, just as there are legitimate objects of coercive force. Just as governments might use *criminal* force when the objects of that force are inappropriate, so revolutionaries might similarly lapse into *criminal* violence.

Panunzio argued that the proper objects of revolutionary violence, that is to say coercive violence, were the sworn representatives and security services of the Establishment, the selected opponents in an internal, rule-governed war. Like enemy soldiers in international war, such "enemy" individuals are the *proper* objects of deadly violence. When they are armed and/or sworn to resist the advent of the revolutionary's alternative future, they are the proper objects of coercive violence. When they are disarmed, compliant, and helpless, they are like captured enemy soldiers and are no longer the proper objects of deadly violence.

In such circumstances, the representatives of the Establishment and their security forces have an option. They know precisely what compliance behaviors are required of them if they should choose to avoid becoming the objects of revolutionary violence. They vacate their respective incumbencies, or surrender their arms. When they no longer have social or political responsibilities and/or are no longer armed, they are no longer the proper objects of violence. The alternatives open to such individuals are fairly specific, and the compliance behaviors that would render them no longer the objects of attack are reasonably clear.

When Panunzio discussed Fascist violence it was always in the above terms. Fascist attacks were violent acts undertaken in the course of revolutionary, internal war. The proper objects of Fascist violence were members of the Communist party, the Socialist party, the Socialist Leagues, and their armed squads. Fascist attacks were directed against such individuals and their support institutions: to avoid being the objects of Fascist violence, such individuals could abandon "enemy" organizations and lay down their weapons. There

62   Rationalization of Terrorism

were reasonably specific compliance behaviors that would have significantly reduced, if not entirely eliminated, the probability of their remaining targets of Fascist violence. All of this Panunzio identified with the rules governing revolutionary coercive violence.

Beyond that, Panunzio sought to isolate acts of deadly coercion that were not simply acts of criminal violence (acts of violence undertaken for personal gain or out of simple vengeance, for example, in the course of revolution). Those acts he identified with *terrorism*. He sought to establish a difference between coercive violence and terrorism based upon this distinction: those who are the proper objects of revolutionary, coercive violence are those who function within the "enemy" camp in some determinable and determinate manner and who have the option of choosing compliance behaviors that would remove them from that category. Terrorism, however, involves the indiscriminate use of deadly power against those who either do not function within the enemy camp or have no realistic alternative to so serving. That is to say, the proper subject of coercive violence has alternatives that will allow his or her escape. Conversely, the victim of terror knows neither that he or she is considered to be in the enemy camp nor what compliance behaviors might significantly reduce the risk of being the object of revolutionary attack. The housewife who is the victim of a terrorist bomb can hardly be said to have recognized her responsibilities or anticipated what compliance behavior might have insulated her against the terrorist. Even if terrorists were to insist that the housewife was a member of a society that enjoyed the profits of "exploiting" the Third World, for example, in the effort to justify the attack, there is no conceivable behavior the housewife might undertake that would have reduced the risk of being the object of terrorist attack. In effect, there is no means of defining the nature of her complicity in the exploitation of the Third World, and so there is no compliance behavior that would reduce that "complicity." The pretended justification for killing or injuring her with a bomb is, as a consequence, simply that: the *pretense* of justification. This indiscriminate nature of terrorism distinguished it, in Panunzio's mind, from revolutionary, coercive violence. A measure of the distance between revolutionary violence and criminal terror is the measure of vagueness, ambiguity, and indeterminance that characterizes any suggestion of compliance behavior that might reduce the individual's exposure to terrorist attack.

On one hand, a revolutionary who prints a manifesto and specifies what compliance behaviors are required to reduce the probability of attack on individuals is laying down, in principle, definition of "guilt" and "responsibility." To be told, on the other hand, that we are "guilty" simply because we are members of a society, is to be told little if anything of consequence. Unless such a charge is accompanied by a realistic catalog of compliance behaviors, it is simply a terroristic pretext for criminal coercion.

On the basis of this kind of analysis, Panunzio was prepared to argue that governments that employ indiscriminate bombing techniques, asphyxiant gases whose distribution cannot be effectively controlled, and blockades that reduce entire populations to starvation are all guilty of terrorism even in the course of a "just" war. Similarly, revolutionaries who bomb public buildings, public transportation, and injure infants and the infirm are guilty of terrorism. Because of its intrinsically indiscriminate character, terrorism, for Panunzio, was always morally objectionable.

Panunzio was prepared to license coercive violence, even intimidation, in the service of revolution. But he was not prepared to countenance terrorism. Intimidation, like coercive violence, is used to bend individuals to revolutionary purpose. A newspaper editor, for instance, could be intimidated into conforming to revolutionary "law"; opposition could be suppressed and dissent punished. As is the case with revolutionary violence, the proper objects of revolutionary intimidation are individuals responsible for *specific*, and *specifiable*, acts that they can realistically abjure. Thus Panunzio could justify fascism's violence and repression and still distinguish it from terrorism: coercive violence and intimidation are applied discriminately, with very specific goals in mind. The point of terror, for Panunzio, was not its victim, for terrorism has no *proper* victim. The point of terror is its *proximate end,* not its *immediate object*; the point of terror is to influence others, not to bend terror's vicitim to our purpose. The *object* of terror is used as a means to an end: the bending of others to our will. The bombing of a supermarket or a civilian aircraft is undertaken to spread panic and demoralize not the objects of attack, but *others*.

The point of *violence* is to alter the behavior of its object and only tangentially to demoralize others. The point of intimidation is similar. Only *terror* is completely indifferent to the human object that suffers its attack—it is this indifference that renders it irretrievably immoral.

Terrorists have come to recognize precisely this distinction argued by Panunzio over half a century ago. Carlos Marighella explicitly stated that the purpose of terror was not to punish offenders or alter the behavior of its object but to make a demonstration. Thus, he urged guerrillas to kidnap "notable personalities *whether or not they have been active or interested in politics* for the purpose of making a demonstration." It did not make the slightest difference whether such a "notable" person was "guilty" of any determinable action, because the purpose of terror was not to alter specific individual behaviors, but to influence others. Terror is to be used *demonstratively* or *prophylactically*—to demonstrate the power of insurgents, or to terrify a subject population and prevent resistance. In no case is there any announcement of compliance behaviors that will reduce an individual's risk of involvement in terror: Individuals are not chosen because of any determinate personal qualities, and in fact anyone would do as well. The objects of terrorism may be totally innocent of any conceivable wrongdoing, but this would not impair their usefulness as objects of terrorism.

What Fascists undertook, in Panunzio's judgment, was a system of force, violence, and repression. By contrast, the Stalinists undertook a program of terror. The individuals who suffered at the hands of the Fascist Special Tribunals were victims of institutionalized violence, repressive force, and intimidation, not terror. This is not to say that, within that political context, there were not any number of cases of *criminal* force and *criminal* intimidation—acts undertaken to satisfy the personal and selfish interests of their perpetrators. But such acts could be accommodated within Panunzio's analysis. They were simple criminal acts, not terror. Only with the advent of fascism's anti-Semitic laws did Fascist Italy approximate a regime of terror.

In the case of Italy's anti-Jewish laws, an entire class of persons was declared "guilty" of some series of ill-specified acts. But even in that instance there were means of significantly reducing the probability of any one individual becoming the object of coercive sanction. Individuals could opt to become "Aryanized," for example, as some did. But such circumstances hardly reduced the terroristic character of the legislation.

Conversely, the regime in Stalin's Soviet Union was unreservedly terroristic. Entire categories of individuals were swept up in the maelstrom of Stalin's purges, with victims often having not even the least awareness of why they were the objects of attack. The most frequent question asked by Stalin's victims was "why?" Many were party officials, many were compliant and committed members of the party. There was nothing that they could do to insulate themselves from the terror: the terror was totally indiscriminate in most cases, simply because its purpose was proximate rather than immediate. In effect, there was no simple or complex compliance behavior that would have saved any individual from injury or death in the Soviet Union under Stalin.

However morally reprehensible Fascist violence may have been, it approached terrorism only with the indiscriminate treatment of the Jews. Other than that, the Fascist regime may have been violent and oppressive, but it was never characteristically terroristic, unlike the regimes of Stalin and probably of Mao Tse-tung. The distinction is fairly clear. Fascism justified violence, repression, and intimidation, but not terrorism. When the regime took on some of the aspects of terrorism, even some of its own spokesmen—Giovanni Gentile among them—raised objections. As long as a distinction is entertained, there is the possibility of principled resistance to terrorism. Under Stalin, on the other hand, no distinction had been, or was, made, and ultimately terror infected every aspect of society. In our own society, the system of terror that was used to maintain the system of slavery and even the comparatively benign terror of the anti-Japanese "relocation" in World War II were recognized at the time by some, and now by all, as violating some fundamental principles of humanity.

The strategic bombing of entire cities for no conceivable military purpose, the murder of hostages, the sabotage of civilian aircraft, and the mining of schools are all instances of terror—the use of injurious and deadly coercion directed against innocent human beings for proximate, rather than immediate, purposes. Almost every established government in the modern world has been guilty of episodic terrorism, but only a few modern movements have consciously adopted terrorism as a "legitimate" weapon of revolution. We see perhaps the most harrowing evidence of moral decay in the contemporary world in the observation that fifty years ago Fascists could make a distinction between political violence and terrorism, but that our learned societies and international forums are no longer prepared to countenance that distinction today. We still talk loosely of conceding that "one person's violence is another's terrorism" and "one person's terrorist is another's freedom fighter," but terrorism's indiscriminate and indifferent nature renders it irretrievably immoral. Fifty years ago, Fascists recognized that to be the case. We could hardly do less today.

Discussion
Panel III

QUESTER: I want to respond to Professor Gregor's dichotomy, which I find quite interesting, but at the same time I see a few problems with it. Let me cite two. People do not use the word *terrorism* in the manner suggested by Professor Gregor. If you ask the average person whether leaving a bomb around to discourage tourists from coming to Paraguay is terrorism, he or she would probably say yes. But by the new definition, I would guess that the answer would have to be no. This is, of course, a minor problem because we can argue about whether ordinary language helps to obscure or illuminate.

Getting down to the nitty-gritty of the definition, I wonder whether in the end the categories do not overlap more than Professor Gregor acknowledges. The proposed definition of terrorism strikes me as being absolutely pointless mainly because it turns upon the circumstances in which punishment is inflicted without any notion of how such punishment might deter others from behaving in a certain way. The policeman who waves his nightstick at anyone near by when there is a possibility of trouble is in a way doing precisely what the terrorist does. He makes everyone less likely to get in his way. When I make someone nervous by making threatening gestures, I am increasing the likelihood that he will alter his behavior to better conform with my notions of what proper behavior might be. Leaving aside the empty case in which terrorism is actually pointless, I see terrorism as a technique for deterrence.

GREGOR: I must apologize for being so obscure and failing to communicate my meaning. What I said was that the distinction between violence and terror turns on the fact that terrorism uses others in the service of proximate ends. Those others are, in fact, innocents. The objects of terror are indiscriminately chosen. That is to say, the individual who uses you as a victim in order to demonstrate or to evoke fear on the part of others is a terrorist. That is the case whether the individual is a policeman or a government official or a revolutionary. If I place a bomb in LaGuardia Airport to deter the passage of tourists, and it explodes and kills five people who were there simply by chance, that is a terroristic act. Innocent persons were used for proximate ends—to deter tourism or to bend the government to my will. A policeman who orders a crowd to disperse is acting quite differently. The crowd's members have a choice: they could choose to disperse. They could reduce the probability of their being the object of violence by dispersing. They understand that if they choose not to disperse, they may well be involved in violence. The fact that the officer is brutal in employing that violence does not change its intrinsic character—it is still intimidation or repression, but it is not terrorism.

The situation is fundamentally different when a terrorist uses a ground-to-air missile to destroy a civilian aircraft. The passengers on that aircraft have not been warned that that flight would be the object of violence. There was no compliance behavior that might have reduced their exposure to violence, and there was no rational course of action they might have chosen to avoid catastrophe.

This does not mean that terrorist acts are pointless or irrational. When Stalin killed millions of Russians, his purpose was to preclude the possibility of resistance or rebellion. And he was probably successful. That does not mean that his actions were not terroristic. The distinction is that the Stalinistic system was, in principle, terroristic according to Panunzio's definition. The Fascist system was intimidating, repressive, and probably brutal, but it was not a system of terror.

RAPOPORT: How would you respond to the argument that the law "prevents" terrorists from making a distinction between the combatant and the noncombatant? Anyone, for example, who knows that I am a terrorist has a legal obligation to turn me in. Those we call innocents or noncombatants are in some sense agents of the state.

GREGOR: That argument turns on the distinction between *potential* and *real* behavior. We all have the potential for criminal acts, and we all have the potential for being "government agents," and conversely, "antisocial elements," but in any civilized society, we are not punished because we have the *potential* for behaving in objectionable ways. The terrorists who claim that we are all somehow involved in criminal "complicity" are simply saying that we are all legitimate targets of their attack. How could I demonstrate that I am not a "government agent" or an "antisocial element"? How might I clear myself of such a charge? How might I show myself to be an "innocent" under such circumstances? Actually, the terrorist argument attempts to make everyone guilty, and by doing this terrorists demonstrate their barbarism. By making everyone guilty, the terrorist has denied that there is any type of behavior that could characterize anyone as innocent. He or she can then indiscriminately attack all of us or any of us. If the terrorist provides a list of behaviors that would evidence the innocence of individuals, he or she would no longer be a terrorist. He or she might be intimidating or repressive but would no longer qualify as a terrorist. The terrorist argument of universal complicity is, on its face, specious.

QUESTER: What you describe as being so unreasonable seems to be what the Chinese were doing to individuals during the Cultural Revolution, or what Stalin was doing to individuals during the purges, or what the Inquisition was doing to suspected heretics. Now in what sense is that so different from straightforward blackmail?

GREGOR: Blackmail is blackmail—it is not terrorism. Joan of Arc on the pyre might have avoided destruction simply by rejecting her heavenly voices. She would then have been "rehabilitated." Joan of Arc knew precisely what was required of her. As long as that is the case, we are dealing with intimidation and blackmail, not terrorism.

QUESTER: What if the demand is that the person make a "sincere change in character"?

GREGOR: While that phrase is admittedly vague, it still involves choice on the part of the victim of violence. Consider the victims of Stalin's purges: they were all prepared to make whatever changes were necessary, and they all debased themselves in every conceivable manner. But that did not save them. They were not, in fact, being "blackmailed."

Consider the terrorists who bomb schools or destroy civilian aircraft in transit. Do they really believe that the children or the passengers involved have the option of "sincerely changing their character"? Of course the terrorist has no such purpose in mind. What he wants to do is influence the behavior of others, not the behavior of his victims. His victims are used instrumentally, for proximate ends. As long as a person is seen as a means and not as an end, the action is potentially terroristic.

HACKER: In my own recent book I have devoted a chapter to the indiscriminate nature of terroristic violence and therefore I am much in sympathy with making a certain indiscriminateness a criterion of terroristic violence. But I cannot accept a distinction that exempts Fascist regimes, including the National Socialist, from the terroristic charge just because they went about their work with considerable forethought, discrimination, and legalistic rationalization. Also, alleged "innocence" of the victims is in and by itself not a good criterion for the definition of terrorism. Mr. Moro and Mr. Schleyer were quite involved due to the positions they occupied in their respective regimes, and hence quite "guilty"—certainly more so than the woman in the supermarket that you are fond of citing—but that does not make the acts directed against them less terroristic.

The question remains: what does lack of discrimination really mean? At some stages of development, for instance, in the initial stages of fascism and of national socialism, the lack of discrimination may be greater than later on. In other words, as terrorism becomes more refined, it also becomes more discriminate in the choice of victims. It remains indiscriminate only in the sense that as a matter of principle it can hit everybody. If prohibited acts are really well defined and if it is in the choice of individuals to avoid these acts, then I would agree with you that the punishment for engaging in these acts is not terroristic. But saying that everything is forbidden which is against the interests of the state provides no such clarity of definition. If, by definition, everything that is evil or destructive in the eyes of the regime is thus forbidden, then this definition is so vague that any action based on it practically amounts to indiscriminate terrorism, regardless of the justification of the terrorists from above or below. The type of indiscriminateness of which you speak is very clear to you and even to me, but it is not clear to the terrorists themselves. Even the members of the Russian Revolution and the French Revolution who killed their own did so for certain reasons that seemed imperative and good to the perpetrators. To us these reasons do not seem valid or sound, but to them they did. In fact, what we call lack of discrimination in others is often merely condescension on our part, and an erroneous arrogation to ourselves of discriminatory powers: we assert that only we are able to make distinctions. Therefore, while lack of discrimination is indeed an important factor in many terroristic acts, it cannot be used as the sole criterion to distinguish terroristic from other violence.

GREGOR: Once again I must apologize—I have unintentionally confused you. It is quite true that the National Socialists used fairly precise characterizations to identify the Jews who were the victims of their terror, but what they did *not* do is identify the compliance behavior that would have reduced the risks suffered by Jews. There was no voluntary behavior any Jew might have undertaken that would have insured him or her against the threat of deadly force. However precisely the victims of terror may be identified, there remains nothing that they can realistically do that would reduce the probability of their being victimized. If there had been something that they might have done to comply with the wishes of the National Socialists, then the violence used against them would have qualified as just that—violence, repression, or intimidation—but it would not have been terror. A similar argument can be used in analyzing the Fascist treatment of the Jews, or the American treatment of the Japanese on the West Coast. The example of the French Revolution is appropriate. Imputed characteristics—the fact that an individual was a member of the nobility—were sufficient to identify him or her as an enemy. There was little, if anything, a French nobleman could do to reduce the risks he suffered as a consequence: he was part of a subsystem of terror. In Stalin's Soviet Union, everyone was a potential victim; the system of terror involved everyone. It seems to me that the Helots in ancient Sparta lived in a subsystem of terror. Helots could be identified with some precision, although that did not mean that they were not involved in a subsystem of terror. There was nothing any one of them might do to reduce his or her chances of being involved. A terroristic system *can* be very precise in identifying its victims, but as long as any potential victim does not know how to effectively reduce his or her chances of being involved in violence, that system remains terroristic.

POSSONY: A friend of mine, a Serb, was three months of age when he was tried and condemned to death by a "legal" procedure run by the Nazi-type Pavelic government of Croatia. He was saved by the Italians and so is in California today. The Italian Fascist must not be confused with the Nazi. After 1938 and once again in 1943, Mussolini adopted Nazi ideas, yet he did not practice genocide; Mussolini does not belong to the Hitler-Stalin class. The indiscriminate application of the term *Fascist* or *fascism* is a semantic trick invented by Stalin, who did not want an association to be made between "socialism" and Hitler's "national socialism." Stalin copied genocide from Hitler, and he practiced "class liquidation" before Hitler appeared. It still is easier for the Soviet Communists to talk about fascism than about national socialism. So far Moscow has refused to publish the documents of Stalin's deal with Hitler: they are fully aware of what their mortal sin was.

RAPOPORT: There is a critical difference between moral responses to violence on the one hand and to terror on the other. There *are* times when it may be appropriate to imagine violence as ennobling or elevating. Ordinary language leads us in that direction—we speak of "fighting like a man," "standing up for our rights," etc. But can most people ever talk about terrorist activity that way? Often we denounce terrorist acts, for example, as cowardly. We do not flinch when someone speaks of battlefield courage, but is it possible to talk about the admirable qualities of those engaged in a massacre?

GREGOR: The distinction I would want to make is the distinction that you have just made. For example, you will never find a Fascist, even the most lackluster figure among them, celebrating *la bellézza del terrorismo* (the "beauty of terrorism"). They would never say that because terrorism is, in principle, objectionable. The use of violence might well be applauded, but you will notice that Mussolini applauded only violence and war, not terrorism. Similarly, Panunzio was very careful to say, "The conditions of violence must be soldierly and cavalier." That is to say, violence must be used against armed opponents, never against women, never against the infirm, and so forth. Violence, for Fascists, was in the romantic tradition. Violence can ennoble. That was Georges Sorel's argument.

We ourselves give people medals for being violent in war; we do not give medals to those who kill children. Even the Nazis did not celebrate the use of terror, for when they employed terrorism, they were very careful to keep knowledge of its use secret from the German population.

RAPOPORT: We deeply value institutionalized combat. Take the Anglo-American legal system, for instance: while the continental systems are organized to get at the truth, ours is organized for *self-defense*. Everyone here could provide other, perhaps more telling, examples to illustrate that we think "fair fights" are a good, perhaps indispensable, part our culture. By the same token, we condemn terrorism because it precludes *reciprocity*. The terrorist does not permit self-defense. He or she wants victory above all else, and when only victory is thought of, I believe that the kinds of problems you have been describing inevitably arise. Am I carrying your argument too far?

GREGOR: No, I think it captures the distinction, which seems to be intuitively clear. We know the difference between violence and terror; what distresses me is that we insist on ignoring the distinction—for some obscure reason we want to resist it. We insist that we are opposed to violence of whatever sort, and yet we have institutionalized violence—as you have indicated. Football games and professional boxing—not to speak of war—are cases in point. They are violent forms of activity in which men can earn public acclaim.

In our ordinary life we do make distinctions. We deplore acts of terror. An act of terror is morally repugnant. The My Lai massacre is a case in point. We punish perpetrators of acts of terror, even when those acts are undertaken in war. Even the Germans punished their soldiers for individual acts of terror. The Germans, in fact, were very systematic in that regard: they recognized that terror simply cannot recommend itself, and that recognition led them to conceal the state terrorism they underook. Terrorism is intrinsically immoral, and I think that the distinction between violence and terror should be preserved for a variety of reasons—if not in public law, then at least in public conscience.

AUDIENCE: The overlap between violence and terrorism in war is the taking of hostages.

GREGOR: Yes. The Germans, for example, used hostages in a program of officially sponsored terrorism. Similarly, when we used hostages in securing villages in Vietnam, we recognized the intrinsic moral disabilities entailed. The Geneva Convention, for example, fully recognizes all the distinctions I have attempted to make.

LOUCH: Professor Gregor, I think we need to make some other crucial distinctions that have not been made very well. There is a distinction between guilt and innocence, for instance; there is another about the possibility of changing one's conduct. These are really different.

GREGOR: Yes. That is true, but I want to escape the dilemma those distinctions would involve. To make a distinction between guilt and innocence in moral terms does not concern me here. Rather, I am trying to suggest some criteria by virtue of which we can remain amoral and still empirically distinguish between an act of violence and an act of terror. What I am suggesting is that even if I cannot identify guilt or innocence in some transcendental sense, I can still make a distinction between them on empirical, or operational, grounds. What I am suggesting is that guilt or innocence can be identified operationally by providing an outline of proscribed or prescribed conduct. When someone suggests that everyone in society is equally guilty, then the term *guilty* has no serious application; only if some set of specific acts can be identified as proscribed would the application of the term *guilty* make empirical sense.

In a perfectly meaningful sense, you are right. I cannot attack the moral quesiton of guilt or innocence directly. All I can do is try to establish some criteria, some indicators, that would signal that the terms are used in some subjectively determinate manner. As to the moral question of guilt or innocence I cannot begin to grapple with that here.

LOUCH: Terrorists can hardly be expected to stop and announce, "This is what we consider sufficient grounds for assigning guilt." They cannot issue a manifesto containing such information; hence, I can never have the information necessary to reduce the probability of my involvement in any terrorist attack.

FIELDS: I have a question. Every man, woman, and child in the state of Israel knows what to do to avoid becoming the object of terrorist attack. All they have to do is move out of Israel. Does that establish that the PLO is not terroristic?

GREGOR: That is a very interesting question. First of all, you must consider that the threat of violence involves an entire category: all the members of a nation. They are all equally guilty—some for no other reason than having been born in a particular place. They may not have chosen to be born in the state of Israel, yet they are as guilty as those who immigrated there. Second, the threat involves children, who are not free to choose their place of domicile. In effect, the threat is indiscriminate: all Israelis are equally guilty in the eyes of the terrorists. Third, there are no time or circumstance qualifiers on the schedule of compliance—if an Israeli citizen does not leave this instant, he or she becomes the object of attack despite having plans to leave tomorrow. Such a schedule of compliance behaviors is indiscriminate and unreasonable. One cannot comply with such demands. If I am instructed to leap over a building in order to avoid attack, I cannot consider such a threat intimidation—it is terroristic, because I cannot possibly comply.

FIELDS: Where do you draw a line?

GREGER: Well, it seems that there are certain kinds of realistic stipulations that can be laid down.

FIELDS: Take, as a case in point, the terrorist demand that the president of Fiat change the entire organizational structure of his establishment.

GREGOR: In such a case it would seem that the recipient of the demand might make "good will" efforts—as was the case in the Hearst kidnapping. In an act of intimidation, the SLA kidnapped an innocent, Patty Hearst, and then laid down conditions for her safe return: $2 million in foodstuffs to be distributed to the "needy." But after Hearst made the requisite "good will" gesture, the kidnappers refused to return his daughter. Their demands became increasingly vague and indeterminate—and, hence, increasingly terroristic. I believe that you are pointing to an important conceptual problem, but I also believe that distinctions can be made. The very unreasonableness, vagueness, and arbitrary character of the compliance behaviors demanded would be one measure of distinction.

FIELDS: It seems to me that state terrorism is predicated on a distinctive political rationalization which in turn rests upon a philosophy of law. I think that the indentification of such an ideology is more readily made if we avoid the ideological labels of fascism, communism, or democracy, and instead inspect the philosophy of law under which the system is operating.

GREGOR: I would agree, but I do not see that it in any way impairs the distinction for which I am arguing. I can provide a rationalization for any kind of idiotic conduct I wish to undertake, since "rationalization" means offering an excuse for doing what you intend to do in any case. What I am suggesting is that once you recognize rationalization for what it is—that is to say, an excuse for doing what you intend to do in any case—it becomes quite clear that Nazi rule, for example, was a system of terror. A Jew under Nazi rule was deemed guilty simply for being a Jew. The Nazis had to contrive "reasons" for making Jews somewhat culpable. They attempted historical rationalizations—that the Jews, for instance, were pornographers. But if some Jews were in fact pornographers, it was those Jews, as individuals, who were guilty, not Jews in general.

What I am suggesting is that a rationalization for terror immediately reveals its shortcomings. Only individuals can be guilty of any intelligible sense; an individual is guilty because he or she has chosen to undertake proscribed acts. A group, as such, can never be guilty by virtue of attributed traits. If a group is guilty it is because, as individuals, its members have chosen to behave in proscribed fashion.

When Stalin used the category "dangerous social element" to identify the victims of his terror, it became obvious almost immediately that there were no determinate criteria that would have made the application of the terms *guilty* or *innocent* at all defensible. Individuals were indiscriminately rounded up and punished. There was not the least semblance of a trial, because the charges were vague and ambiguous and the category indeterminate. The "criminals" were arbitrarily characterized as "guilty," and the category included potentially everyone. The law embodied, as you suggest, a rationalization. It was not a rationale.

NATHAN: If I am forced to choose between two very undesirable alternatives, I think, then, that I am truly terrorized.

GREGOR: That is probably true.

NATHAN: If I am the innocent victim of an explosion in a supermarket, then I am not terrorized; I am a victim of a violent act. And yet those who must go shopping the next day in the supermarket are terrorized.

GREGOR: I think that you are addressing yourself to the psychological dimensions of terrorism—something I have tried to avoid doing. It is quite conceivable that the victims of terror and the victims of violence suffer the same magnitudes of personal, psychological fear, but that is not my concern here. What I am trying to argue is that terrorism, no matter what its victim's state of fear is, is employed for a proximate purpose: the terrorization of others. This is not true of the violent act. In principle, fear begins and ends with the object of violence.

NATHAN: What I am trying to argue against is the "Fascist" distinction between violence and terror: I feel that having alternatives does not relieve terror in any way whatsoever.

GREGOR: Again, I think you are referring to a psychological fact. A soldier on a battlefield, sitting in a foxhole with shells raining about him, can be terror-stricken. Of that I am sure. But for all that, he is not a victim of terror. He is the victim of violence—and war—regulated by law. And that does not qualify as terrorism. On the other hand, an individual who is in an open city under bombardment runs relatively little risk of violence—the probability of his or her being injured by bombs is relatively slight. The person may not feel discomfited by the bombing, but he or she is the victim of terroristic attack nonetheless.

I do not wish to address myself to the psychological aspects of violence or terrorism: some people are terrorized by almost anything, so the issue of psychology is quite complex. But if we accept psychological states as the grounds for identifying terrorism, we have a broad and indeterminate collection of acts that might generate terrorism, depending on how timid our subjects happen to be. I am trying to deal with violence and terrorism empirically, in terms of their victims and their purposes, without entering into the private mental states of those subject to either.

The objects of terrorism are innocent, and the purposes of terrorism proximate. Those who are victims of terror can do nothing to offset its advent, nor have they done anything to provoke it. Terrorists wish to make a demonstration. That is their purpose, and any victim will do. This is not the case with violence. These are the distinctions I am concerned with, not with the psychological impact as such, because that depends on the intestinal fortitude of the victims—and that is too variable to allow any consistent distinctions to be made.

Religion and Terrorism— A Romantic Model of Secular Gnosticism

MOSHE AMON

I call the model employed in this paper gnostic, since I believe that the terrorist rationale closely follows a Gnostic mode of thought.[1] The term *secular gnosticism* is an indicator that we are dealing with the post-"murder-of-God" era, and that in our times the gnostic denial of the present order of things is linked with an aspiration to erect anew the perfect form of man, and is no longer linked with the wish to return to the realm of the good and perfect God. The "murder" is philosophical, of course, based upon the supposedly correct understanding of our origin, our true nature, the reasons for our current corrupted state of affairs, and the escape to redemption. The model is romantic in its notion of re-creation out of chaos, of purging the world by reducing it to nothing, of subjugating it to the primordial fire and redeeming it as a new and final order of things based upon the ultimate or gnostic knowledge—from the Greek word *gnosis*, or knowledge. Gnosticism assumes that salvation can be obtained by the "right" kind of knowledge, and that the present world is evil because it is based upon the "wrong" kind of knowledge, distributed by the wrong kind of governments. Armed with the right kind of knowledge, the gnostic believes that he or she should first destroy the present order of things before constructing the "right" and "final" order according to laws acquired from the right source. The gnostic believes that he or she has the right to destroy the world because it has no right to exist.

Righteousness breeds violence simply by reasoning that all those who are not right are wrong, not mistaken, and therefore deserve to be annihilated, not reeducated. This of course is a devilish mode of reasoning, in the same way that the devil believes himself to be acting justly by rectifying that which is evil and by removing from our midst the corrupt and corrupting elements. The devil sees himself as fulfilling a divine role by purging the world of wicked people who follow the wrong laws. The devil himself is well acquainted with the "right law"—he often assumes the role of a learned lawyer—and therefore he can recognize and obliterate the wrongdoers. The devil is triggered into action by wrongdoing, by evil, but he acts in a manner that we consider to be just, and his actions carry a divine sanction. As such he is accepted by us and is linked in our minds to guilt feelings, which are part of a scheme in which suffering is understood as punishment, even when we are unable to pinpoint the causes for it. Guilt is so much a part of our consciousness that quite often mere suffering gives rise to it. We accept the devil as part of our lives because we believe that we live in a sinful world. Only in paradise, where there are no sinners, is there no place reserved for the devil.

Gnostics "know" that they are righteous and enlightened because they are able to recognize that the world is corrupted, that its rulers are evil and impose upon us evil laws in order to imprison us and reduce us to a state of serfdom. This knowledge puts the gnostics on the side of the angels and induces them to break the law in order to bring down the evil system. The antinomian revolt is thus understood as a process of liberation.

It seems to me that both gnostic and terrorist movements follow a similar rationale, use similar motives, and apply them to similar symbols. In short, both movements act within the framework of a world view based upon a similar mythological model.[2] Both movements are compatible with a world rife with terms like alienation, liberation, and salvation, which point to the illegitimacy of current governments. I submit that religious models and mythological symbols do not die and disappear but are transformed and reappear in different historical periods under a different guise.[3] I therefore suggest that through identifying the model we can diagnose and understand many social phenomena, including the toleration of terrorism in our society under the guise of liberation movements. The legitimacy of terrorist movements may stem from a mythological model adopted by the terrorists and endorsed by large segments of society.

In our relations with the world we usually react to symbols, not to things as they are in themselves. It seems that in specific historical situations we answer to specific symbols and, as each group of symbols forms a certain pattern, it triggers a corresponding mode of reaction. During the Reformation, the German mob disfigured paintings and smashed sculptures of saints, as they represented a world in which the pope ruled as the anti-Christ. During the French Revolution the mob destroyed churches and palaces, not because they were bad in themselves, but because they symbolized the *Ancien Régime*. Today, ideological opponents are approached as Communists, capitalists, Zionists, imperialists, etc.; their actions are unjust, evil, exploitation, and so on. As such, opponents can be treated as objects or part of a scheme: the workers are supposed to be always right, capitalists or imperialists or Jews are assumed to be wrong—to be enemies and consequently should be annihilated. In this way, we do not deal with people but with concepts. Therefore, assuming that the concept is right, we also are always in the right, even when we admit that the same actions toward "people" would be wrong. It takes a philosopher, a scientist, or a lover to approach people individually and as individuals, not as abstractions. The philosopher and the scientist try to find and expose the nature of each thing as it is in itself; in doing so, they destroy the world of those who follow a myth—therefore Socrates and Galileo had to be punished. The scientific approach is step by step, part by part. Mythological thought explains and approaches the world as a totality; the part is understood through the conception of the whole. Thus a person "knows" how to deal with a Zionist, a capitalist, or a Communist as he or she already is acquainted with the nature and the significance of the whole group.

I believe that mythologies serve as proto-models to social structures, and that rather than composing a social form we are "induced" into it. Mythological structures therefore hold a kind of a spell over us; we are drawn into them when they fit a structure which most likely has already preexisted in our subconscious.[4] When two such structures—a universal one and the one ingrained within us—lock into each other, all our sensory and emotional reactions are amplified many times and answer only to signals coming from this kind of structure. In such a situation we seem to feel at home, while all signals coming from different systems are treated as alien, senseless, and meaningless. It may well be that the real meaning of freedom is the ability not to fall prey to such patterns, but this kind of freedom is rare indeed. Mythological adepts live in a dreamlike world in which they feel secure, but precisely because of this dreamlike, elusive quality this world cannot be changed. It may set the adept minds at rest, but it would not allow them to reach the moon or get to Saturn. As long as the laws governing their environments are in accord with their myths, the adepts are at peace with the world; conflicts arise when adepts are forced to live according to laws stemming from a different system. The laws believed to be true are then ineffective and not suited to deal with any situation. The adepts find themselves completely helpless, "knowing" then that they are prisoners, thrown into a hostile world which is ruled by evil and malignant spirits. They strive to get back to their "real" home, to where they "really" belong, and this is achieved only by breaking the surrounding walls. When scientific developments, philosophical schools, or political situations shatter social structures, when traditional institutions and concepts lose their meaning, there are many who feel that they are in just this kind of a situation and have no other choice but to rebel and to destroy the system. While the classical gnostic will look for means to overcome matter, that is to say, his or her body, in order to release the captive soul, the secular gnostic attempts to fight matter in the form of the motherland in order to liberate the "true" self and restore his or her "real" home and land.

Both gnosticism and terrorism belong to the pattern of messianic, redemptive mythologies that stem from such social incongruities. The process of redemption is coupled with rebellion, with a denial of the laws and values that hold sway over the world around us; redemption leads therefore to nihilism and to anarchism. All laws, social as well as ethical, seem to be wrong. Therefore, they should not be obeyed and the order of things that produced them should be destroyed. The nihilistic trends of our era started, as Nietzsche had already noted, with the "death of God," with the declaration that the god who constructed this order of things is not our god and the values of this order are not our values. The death of this god leads naturally to freedom from the laws dictated by him, to a rebellion against the society that still follows these laws, and to the killing of those who supervise the execution of these laws, be they kings, popes, shahs, or presidents. The gnostic rebel posits himself "above good and evil" as practiced in society at large.

The following lines may read like a classical Gnostic text, but they were written by the father of modern anarchism, Michael Bakunin:

> Jehova, who of all the good gods adored by men was certainly the most jealous, the most vain, the most ferocious, the most unjust, the most bloodthirsty, the most despotic and the most hostile to human dignity and libery—Jehova had just created Adam and Eve, to satisfy we know not what caprice; no doubt to while away his time, which must weigh heavy on his hands in his eternal egoistic solitude, or that he might have some new slaves. He generously placed at their disposal the whole earth, with all its fruits and animals, and set but a single limit to this complete enjoyment. He expressly forbade them from touching the fruit of the tree of knowledge. He wished, therefore, that man, destitute of all understanding of himself, should remain an eternal beast, ever on all fours before the eternal God, his creator and his master. But here steps in Satan, the eternal rebel, the first freethinker and the emancipator of worlds. He makes man ashamed of his bestial ignorance and obedience; he emancipates him, stamps upon his brow the seal of liberty and humanity in urging him to disobey and eat of the fruit of knowledge....
>
> God admitted that Satan was right; he recognized that the devil did not deceive Adam and Eve in promising them knowledge and liberty as a reward for the act of disobe-

dience which he had induced them to commit, for, immediately they had eaten of the forbidden fruit, God himself said (see the Bible), "Behold the man is become as one of the gods, to know good and evil; prevent him, therefore, from eating of the fruit of eternal life, lest he become immortal like Ourselves."[5]

Let us disregard now the fabulous portion of this myth and consider its true meaning, which is very clear. Humankind has emancipated itself; it has separated itself from animality and constituted itself human; humankind has begun its distinctively human history and development by an act of disobedience and science—that is, by *rebellion* and by *thought*.

The gnostic rebellion stems from the conviction that the mythological adepts know the reason why our world is as it is and what should be done about it. Their "knowledge" is in the form of a mythology, therefore they are unable to recognize the validity of an argument which follows a different line of thought, believing themselves to be the sole representatives of the universal truth. As such, this truth gives the gnostics a measure for justice and righteousness that may never be questioned. Once questions are raised demanding verification of mythological concepts, they and the social structure based upon them may shatter and break down. Teachings that follow gnostic models will necessarily forbid questioning. An ideal breeding ground for terrorism is an environment that permits questioning and believes at the same time in the availability of answers, because only mythologies can furnish answers that claim to solve all problems, and such mythologies are the breeding ground of terrorists. A search for answers and solutions will too often glide into gnostic models like communism, fascism and nazism, to name but a few, which will forbid the continuation of such a search. The nineteenth century is permeated with such systems of thought claiming to be absolute, like the Absolute Spirit of Hegel, the Ultimate Social Order of Marx, and so on. The failure of gnostic solutions to solve any problems leads to the perpetual search for "traitors" and to a perpetual "purging" within gnostic groups. Within the framework of free society, some will wander to other gnostic models and groups, and the mythological nature of their nostrums will always gain them the support of many segments of society that likewise believe that solutions are indeed possible. We face here an interesting situation—terrorism is tolerated in a society riddled with guilt feelings because it fits into a mythical model in which the devil inflicts deserved punishment. But we should note that the devil is punishing individuals—people who are personally responsible for their wrongdoings—according to an ethical code that is practiced by society at large, in direct contradiction to the terrorist's way. The devil, after all, is interested in good government, while terrorists are interested in no government.

As the thought precedes the act, it is the gnostic, mythological ideology that precedes the acts of violence performed by terrorists. The elimination of terrorism can be achieved only through the realization that the ultimate answers are beyond our comprehension: by recognizing that our answers are derived from the necessity to act without having the certainty of complete answers; by recognizing that democracy allows for free speech and questioning because it knows that it does not have the perfect answers and is looking for better ones; by recognizing that democracy is a good form of government precisely because it is not perfect and admits to its ignorance of the ultimate truths. A society that believes in instant and complete solutions breeds final solutions and terrorism. The way to heaven is through the eternal question, "What does God expect of me?" The way to hell, on the other hand, is paved with "isms" claiming to have the right answers to this question.

If an individual chooses the way leading to hell, he or she will be asked to pay the price of admission. If the person is lucky, he or she may encounter on the way a protective figure garbed in a costume to some degree resembling the outfit traditionally associated with the devil; but in effect this one is a jester, a clown, or a prankster. As foolishness is the boundary of wisdom, it will be the "fool" who will in jest portray to the individual the world as it exists beyond the border line on which they stand: the world into which the person will slide by unwisely breaking the laws and the customs of the traditional order of things. If, finding ourselves in a similar situation, we laugh at the performance and become aware of the limit of our actions, we may be able to retain our human image. But if we choose to emulate the clown, we will go over the verge and become citizens of the netherworld. As such, we will follow the image of the devil, not of the clown, because he is a citizen of no world. If he emulates us, he will cease to be a clown; if we lose our sense of humor and model ourselves after him, we will cease to be human, and the devil will enjoy the last laugh, watching us play the fool.

The point is that we can laugh at the clown because we know that he is a fool. On "fools' days" we all play the fool because we accept foolishness as part of human nature, and we are wise in admitting the presence of the fool within ourselves. Similarly, if we forget that as imperfect creatures we are unable to produce perfect answers, we are assuming a nonhuman role. We play the real fool and we become real demons. God guides us by forcing us to question ourselves: "Who are we?" The devil rules us by supplying answers. Johan Huizinga, in his book *Homo Ludens*,[6] points out that in our modern world we have removed the playful element from our social life. No more do we play "as if" we are fools, or "as if" we are wise and knowledgeable, or "as if" we are gods. Nowadays, we take ourselves as seriously as if we really represented all those things, as if we were indeed creating a new world while destroying the old one. In reality we are only destroying. No longer do we have clowns, "fools," or court jesters to show us when we are going overboard, when we are reaching the point of no return on a course that leads to the negation of humanness and to hell. In dumping the clown and the "fool" as part of our social structure, we lost the safeguard of humor as a constant reminder of the necessary chasm between human aspirations and human nature.[7] When we forget our human frailties and lose the ability to laugh at our pretensions, we come forward with nostrums leading to "final solutions" that give rise only to sorrow and to tears.

The behavior of the clown permits uncontrolled expression of passions and desires and therefore leads the world into the condition in which it existed before the time of Creation, that is, into chaos. In the same way that the child is father of the man, so also chaos, the lack of order, is the father of order; it precedes it in time. In order to create an order there must exist an extraordinary desire. Hence, a period of transition toward a new creation must be characterized by outbursts of desires, passions, and incontinence.

Here we come to the Romantic motif, in which the night is father of the day. The new creation comes about through a release of passions plunged into the kingdom of the demons—into chaos and irrationality. The demons ascend from the subconscious as a redeeming power, the source of a new creation.

The Romantic movement was the renaissance of the Dark Ages. The principles of truth in this movement are derived from the all-powerful primordial and not from the ultimate perfection of God. God is interpreted as spurious and ersatz; the devil becomes the legitimate ruler, dictating laws and principles.

As we shape ourselves and the world in the likeness of the images from our subconscious, we construct not a dream world but a demonic one, in which the unconscious holds full sway and destroys the world of reason. The legitimacy of the images from the world of darkness and from the world of dreams releases the brutal powers that attempt to destroy social order through violence and terror.

Man strives to be in the image of God and therefore he looks for the ultimate knowledge, for the *epistēmē*. The complete knowledge that is ascribed to the Tree of Knowledge is to know good *and* evil, *not* good *or* evil. To be Godlike is to know good and evil as one unit. If we concentrate on only one of the dimensions, we will necessarily get a distorted picture and a confused sense of direction. It is apparent that this existing confusion of values is symptomatic of a major change in our religious concepts in a world where everything including the religious model is in a state of flux. We are used to a static religious model, one which describes God as dwelling above, in heaven, the devil below, in hell, and us in the middle, enjoying the freedom to choose one or the other. Today the model is more dynamic, more in the image of the dancing Shiva: the advancing front, the part that creates new images while in motion, represents God the Creator, while the posterior part, which leaves behind it the shattered and destroyed forms of the past, represents the devil. God is one, creator and destroyer, the giver of life and the angel of death.

In the electromagnetic model, the plus and minus poles belong to the same field, attracting one another. Movement and tension exist only when there is distance between these poles. In the cosmic model, we create this distance by our own existence. When matter and antimatter or when proton and antiproton meet together, they both are destroyed. In order to exist they must be separated. In mythology the forces of creation are very often described by the god who is torn apart, by the separation of the male and the female sides of the androgynous god. Human existence is contingent upon cosmic imperfection, and it can exist only as long as it sustains an equilibrium between the plus and the minus, the good and the evil, that form the divine nature in the religious model.

Human perfection, therefore, is the state of equilibrium—the balance between good and evil. If humanity chooses to bend to one side only, we risk this equilibrium and therefore our own existence, no matter which side we call plus or minus, good or evil.

Terrorism is nourished from our belief that in the human world complete knowledge can be realized. Hence, terrorist groups believe that they know which is the "good" side and that this knowledge obligates them to destroy the evil and the unjust side. But, in fact, what results is the destruction of both sides—the entire world. The only way to combat terrorism is to destroy the gnostic model that claims that it can produce the ultimate answer, and that the real creator is but man himself. In the modern and secular world, the gnostic person arrogates to himself the role of the Almighty. A certain measure of humility not only is desirable in person-to-person relationships but also is a necessity in the sustenance of humankind itself.

NOTES

1. The term *gnosticism* in relation to modern thought was introduced by Hans Jonas, "Gnosticism and Modern Nihilism," *Social Research* 19 (1952). A revised version of the article was published as an epilogue to the second edition of Jonas's *The Gnostic Religion* (Boston: Beacon Press, 1958, 1963). Eric Voegelin uses the same term in his *Science, Politics and Gnosticism* (Chicago: Henry Regnery Co., 1968), published first in German in 1959, and in his *From Enlightenment to Revolution* (Durham: Duke

University Press, 1975). If I understand him correctly, he applies the term *gnosticism* to all forms of modern thought, excluding only the classical form of Christianity, thus negating secular gnosticism for the sake of one form of religious gnosticism.

2. For an elaborate discussion of modern ideologies as a form of myth, see Peter L. Berger, *Pyramids of Sacrifice: Political Ethics and Social Change* (New York: Penguin Books, 1974).

3. "In the mythology and folklore of different peoples, certain motives repeat themselves in almost identical form. I have called those motives archetypes and by them I understand forms or images of a collective nature which occur practically all over the earth as constituents of myths and at the same time as autochthonous, individual products of unconscious origin. The archetypal motives presumably start from the archetypal patterns of the human mind which are not only transmitted by tradition and migration but also by heredity." Carl G. Jung, *Psychology and Religion* (New Haven: Yale University Press, 1938), pp. 63-64 in the 1976 reprint.

4. In a very exciting essay dealing with the relationship between mythology, literature, and music, Claude Levi-Strauss seems to propound a somewhat similar idea. "It is exactly as if, when inventing the specific musical forms, music had only rediscovered structures which already existed on the mythical level. For instance, it is very striking that the fugue, as it was formalized in Bach's time, is the true-to-life representation of the working of some specific myths, of the kind where we have two characters or two groups of characters.... It could be shown also that there are myths, or groups of myths, which are constructed like a sonata, or a symphony, or a rondo, or a toccata, or any of all the musical forms which music did not invent but borrowed unconsciously from the structure of the myth." *Myth and Meaning* (Toronto: University of Toronto Press, 1978), pp. 50-51.

5. Michael Bakunin, *Selected Writings*, ed. Arthur Lehning (London: Jonathan Cape, 1973), pp. 112, 114.

6. (Boston: Beacon Press, 1955).

7. In an essay whose title I have forgotten, Leszek Kolakowski deals with the social role of the court jester as opposed to that of the priest, but it seems that he ascribes to the court jester exactly the same role that Arthur Koestler, in his *The Yogi and the Commissar*, ascribes to the intelligentsia.

Measures of the Impact and Appeal of Terrorism

FRANK RACKLEY

The study of methods to control terrorism has taken on an almost obsessive quality. Yet, despite the intense interest in terrorism, it would seem that we have not yet adequately defined the problem. Most current definitions stress one distinguishing element, "a challenge by a small radical group of the monopoly the state holds on the use of force."[1] Unfortunately, each time we seek an operational definition of terrorism we must make statements with regard to the legitimate use of power. The potential for conflict is clear. A result of this inability to define terrorism is the tendency of a government to identify any act that challenges its monopoly of the use of force or that causes substantial disruption to its day-to-day operations as terrorism.

We should ask ourselves these questions as a note of caution: when do the activities of any group become terroristic? What constitutes sufficient disruption or challenge to authority to warrant government investigation and possible regulation of activity? What acts go beyond the freedoms described in the First Amendment? Our studies should at the very least seek answers to these questions, since the results of our work may have great influence on possible new interpretations of First Amendment rights. In light of the Jonestown tragedy in Guyana, it is clear that an extensive effort must be made to learn more about cult behavior. We must approach our investigation with great care, by recognizing that the possibility of unwanted and unnecessary erosion of basic rights exists.

The purpose of this short paper is to examine some surface similarities among cult and terrorist groups. Current estimates indicate that about 1.5 million Americans are members of cult-type groups. At least this many, too, are members of nonconventional or radical political groups. What is the appeal of these groups? What can we or should we do about it?

I will quickly review some thoughts about the movement away from traditional institutions. As we will see, many similarities emerge as the subject of mass change is discussed. One description places the reason for such changes as

> dislocations in the communicational and orientational institutions of advanced societies—dislocations which open the way for cults to flourish. The historical record will show a rough correlation between the proliferation of cult movements and the times and places of marked cultural and social change.[2]

The breakdown of familiar institutions seems to be the culprit here.

Another somewhat similar approach was presented in Berlin in 1978 by Professor Richard Löwenthal of the Berlin Free University, who ascribes the cause to "a decline in the credibility of the binding force of basic values of Western civilization... a cultural crisis."[3] Further, he suggests that

> the main manifestation of the cultural crisis is the loss of a coherent and rational world view, with a decline of the belief in an inevitable progress in the direction of a more rational organization of society and the fulfillment of liberal and humane values.[4]

He cites war, rapid technological change, and broad social conflict as the agents responsible.

Another explanation is Anthony Wallace's "revitalization" theory which cites "continuous diminution in [the culture's] efficiency in satisfying needs." Wallace describes a sequential process that suggests that major cultural changes occur in a rather orderly fashion as a result of social upheaval. He calls these stages: (1) steady state; (2) period of individual stress; (3) period of cultural distortion; (4) period of revitalization in which occur the functions of reformulation of values, communication, organization, adaptation, cultural transformation, and routinization; and (5) the new steady state. This approach strongly resembles others in assigning communication and social orientation major roles.[5]

Each view presented generally describes the cultural crisis as the result of social and cultural upheaval along with the failure of societies to reinterpret and redesign basic values and institutions at a pace that equals the pace of change.

Anomie is usually seen as a prerequisite for the proliferation of cults and other nontraditional groups. Increasing indifference toward traditional values and systems, feelings of disorientation, powerlessness, and repeated failure in disorganized attacks on "the system" all seem to be part of anomie response. The appearance of strong leaders and movements that will offer new and reliable meanings to these disaffected and disoriented people may very well provide a convenient substitute and an acceptable reinterpretation for old, no longer serviceable meanings. The individual's perception of personal impotence and continuing failure, whether real or induced, provides substantial justification for searching out a new substitute system that offers new meanings, new power, and the opportunity to take part in the restructuring of the failing systems.

It is important not to overgeneralize the effect of the cultural crisis. Clearly, the great majority in any society is able to adapt and cope with change without seeking membership in a cult or radical group. Although adaptive patterns may vary greatly, they are usually within accepted social boundaries. Many reports dealing with types who are prone to join unusual groups tend toward identifying them as people with little power: students, minorities, the poor (but not starving), and, if we can allow such a generalization, the chronically frustrated. Although it is certainly possible and quite appropriate to study the types who join these groups, their placement in the structure and the substructure of the various groups may allow some rather important insight into the potentially violent cult or radical political group.

The broad concept of cultural crisis will require careful study. On a more immediate basis we might compare the cultural crisis response with the individual crises that we see commonly on a day-to-day basis. We might call this the "crisis intervention model."

In the crisis intervention model, crisis is a subjective response to a stressful experience, a response so strong that the stability of the individual is affected and the ability to cope is seriously compromised: Normal adaptive patterns are disrupted, and emotional defenses are confused and may be temporarily unavailable to the person experiencing the crisis. At this point a condition comparable to the anomie of the cultural crisis may be present: confusion, fear, anger, guilt, lack of insight, and feelings of powerlessness may exist. Crisis theory emphasizes the importance of early and authoritative intervention in order for the victim to cope successfully with the immediate crisis and to avoid negative long-term effects.

Pivotal in any plan to help the victim in a crisis state is the ability of the person providing assistance to recognize the symptoms of a crisis response, to minimize the threat that the incident will happen again, to provide a safe area for the victim, and to provide for the victim's immediate needs, particularly reassurance, support, and guidance. The victim must view the helper as a substitute source of strength during a period when his or her own strength is diminished. At this point in the intervention, the goal of the helper is to provide structure to a situation that seems chaotic to the victim.

Because of the real or perceived powerlessness of the victim and the unusual degree of suggestability due to the loss of normal coping mechanisms, an intense trust/dependency relationship frequently may develop. As the victim begins to recover or to adapt to the stress of the crisis and appears able to function, the helper begins gradually to return control to the victim. He or she carefully tests at each stage; the goal is to have the victim reestablish control and return to or approximate the former level of integration.

The major points in this model are the disrupted state, the failure of normal coping methods to reduce stress, the presence of a substitute source of strength, and the gradual return of control to the victim. Victim suggestability and the development of a trust/dependency relationship are vital in the successful treatment and reduction of crisis symptoms.

The appeal of groups that offer such substitute strength and new sets of meanings seems strongest during times that we might identify as cultural crises. Although this suggests a time of broad social upheaval and a gradual onset of crisis symptoms, for the individual it may very well be a *single incident*, "the last straw."

If we accept the premise that during a crisis the victim who requires outside help becomes dependent on that helper temporarily, we can clearly see that the recruiters for cults and other nonconventional groups operate in a way that might be compared with the approach of the therapist in crisis intervention. There is one major difference, which occurs at the point of returning control to the victim: the group retains control of those who will allow it. The idea of personal powerlessness is reinforced incessantly with the theme that all power emanates from the group or the cause. The idea of personal power is viewed as possibly evil. For most members newly recruited, the memory of failure and frustration is vivid, and this appeal promises some protection from a repeat of failure. In a more abstract view, the group provides support, a sense of belonging, anonymity, and a feeling of power associated with the strength of the group. Active recruiting for cults and other unusual groups almost universally involves approaching those who are convinced or who can be convinced that they cannot succeed in the traditional setting.

If we look at some of the more famous victims of terrorist activities we see that they are typically people who symbolize power and success. Schleyer, Aldo Moro, Leo Ryan, and others were clearly successful or powerful. These symbols of power in the conventional system may be attacked because they contradict the concept that personal power and success are impossible through conventional means. A common approach is to point to the symbols as pawns used to mask the inherent evil of the system. The inability of the system to protect its so-called powerful from attack is also used as an example of the basic corruption present.

The attacks on the former lifestyle of the new member tend to reinforce the guilt associated with the past. As the membership becomes more certain, the attack on traditional institutions continues unabated. The basis of the attacks may be political, social, or religious, depending on the group. The organizations do, however, have similar themes most of the time: belief in the cause, loyalty to the group, or loyalty to the leader are the only real bases for power and success. To strive for personal, individual power is to act counter to the group. The necessary action to destroy traditional institutions must be a group effort.

A further look at a few of the similarities in the appeals of some groups is appropriate. Although the groups are quite different, the statements have a similar ring. For example, consider these excerpts from standard Jim Jones sermons in the People's Temple:

> The center of the, the heart of the multinational system that creates so much misery and slavery is right here, [the self-deprecatory theme is common] as American as Rockefeller, Standard Oil. We are living in the same mess, controlled by the same people, the same interests. They only know how to exploit us until they have no more use for us and then throw us on the scrap heap to be forgotten. Wherever poor people are, we are seen as niggers to be used.

On the possibility of using violence against opponents, Jones said,

> I think they thought, well, we were pacifists. They [the American Nazi party] have forgotten certain things Gandhi said. If a mad dog is running loose (meaning a madman) you don't allow that to happen. Now pacifism does not mean that you roll over and play dead.[6]

The Weathermen gave a similar message in June 1969, in their position paper *New Left Notes:*

> We are within the heartland of a worldwide monster, a country so rich from its worldwide plunder that even the crumbs doled out to the enslaved masses within its borders provide for a material existence very much above the conditions of the people of the world.[7]

Measures of the Impact and Appeal of Terrorism 97

The Weather Underground, in their manifesto, *Prairie Fire,* state:

> Stolen wealth, not yankee [sic] ingenuity is the basis of the tremendous concentration in the U.S. of productive forces.... Monopoly/capital imperialism is an irrational system. It is not organized to meet human needs. It is run by a small ruling class whose only morality is the morality of maximum profit.... Of all the imperial dynasties and major thieves of our times, the Rockefeller family stands out. The phenomenal growth of their clan's influence and riches parallels the development of U.S. imperialism.[8]

In 1970, a California revolutionary group called the Venceremos stated a similar but less organized theme in their platform:

> Today the revolutionary peoples of the entire world surround and batter the monster of U.S. imperialism from every side. Trapped in the storms of the people's war abroad, the ruling class faces utter chaos at home. The ferocious bellowing of U.S. imperialism comes from the agony of its deathbed struggle.[9]

Another group, the Fruit of Islam sect of the Black Muslim religion, offered these questions in a test for potential converts to the sect. The list is partial but still represents the theme of the entire test:

> Q: Why does the devil keep our people illiterate?
> A: So that he can use them for a tool and a slave. He keeps them blind to themselves so that he can master them. Illiterate means ignorant.
> Q: Why does the devil call our people Africans?
> A: To make the people of North America believe that the people on that continent are the only people and that they are savages. The original people live on this continent and they are the ones who strayed away from civilization and are living a jungle life. The original people call this conti-

nent Asia but the devils call it Africa to try to divide them. He wants us to think that we are all different.

Q: Why does the devil keep us apart from his social equality?

A: Because he does not want us to know how filthy he is and all his affairs. He is afraid because when we learn about him we will run him from us. Socialist means to advocate a society of men or groups of men for one common cause. Equality means to be equal in everything.

Q: Why does Mohammed and any Moslem murder the devil? What is the duty of any Moslem in regard to the four devils? What reward does a Moslem receive by presenting the four devils at one time?

A: Because he is 100 percent wicked and will not keep and obey the laws of Islam. His ways and actions are like a snake of the grafted type. So Mohammed learned that he could not reform the devils, so they had to be murdered. All Moslems will murder the devil because they know he is a snake, and also if he be allowed to live he would sting someone else. Each Moslem is required to bring four devils, and by bringing and presenting four at one time his reward is a lapel button to wear on the lapel of his coat, also free transportation to the Holy city of Mecca to see Brother Mohammed.[10]

Each of the groups I have mentioned recruited and indoctrinated members in similar ways. The period of time before organized violent acts began to take place seems to have differed considerably. The rationale for violent acts, however, seems to revolve around a system of government which was viewed as corrupt beyond redemption. Destruction of the system immediately by any means was advocated. Violence was presented as the most expeditious means of promoting change. The Fruit of Islam sect openly advocated violence, as was demonstrated in the so-called zebra killings in San Franciso. Between November 1973 and April 1974, twelve people were killed and six others wounded, for which members of this sect were arrested and convicted. The People's Temple, with the murders of Leo Ryan and three others and the horror of the Jonestown suicides and murders, was perhaps the ultimate terrorist act. The Weather Underground involved itself in dozens of bomb attacks across the country, resulting in millions of dollars' worth of damage, as well as several deaths. The Venceremos organization, though not as destructive as the others, seems to have provided numerous trained members to several other groups, notably the New World Liberation Front.

I put to you the question of how we might adequately study the impact and appeal of cult or other nonconventional groups. As I do this I am reminded of my earlier caution: what effect will our studies have on the interpretation of our constitutional rights? What activities must we consider restricting in order to prevent the formation of terrorist groups, or can we restrict at all? What is sufficient disruption? What is a sufficient challenge to legitimate authority? When is the mind control practiced on the members of some groups illegal or immoral? The questions do not end—nor does the dilemma of scientists who must deal with them. The complexity of the terrorist question can only be approached as we are doing now, through a multi-disciplinary group willing to accept the limitations of individual specialties and to work with the strengths of others.

NOTES

1. Richard Löwenthal, "Cultural Crisis" (Unpublished paper, Berlin, Federal Republic of Germany, 1978).
2. Allan W. Eister, "Culture Crisis and New Religious Movements: A Paradigmatic Statement of a Theory of Cults," in *Religious Movements in Contemporary America*, ed. Irving I. Zaretsky and Mark P. Leone (Princeton: Princeton University Press, 1974), pp. 612, 623.
3. Löwenthal, "Cultural Crisis," p. 2.
4. Löwenthal, "Cultural Crisis," p. 2.
5. Anthony F. C. Wallace, "Revitalization Movements," in *The American Anthropologist* 58 no. 2, (1956): 176-177.
6. Jim Jones, from tape recording made by People's Temple members in Jonestown, Guyana prior to the assasination of Representative Leo Ryan. Date unknown.
7. At the SDS national convention in June 1969, The Weathermen included these comments in their position paper which was published in *New Left Notes*, an SDS publication.

8. The Red Dragon Print Collective of the Weather Underground, "Prairie Fire: The Politics of Revolutionary Anti-Imperialism," in *The Report of the Subcommittee to Investigate the Administration of the Internal Security Act and Other Internal Security Laws* of The Committee On The Judiciary, United States Senate. Ninety-Fourth Congress, First Session. (Washington, D.C.: Government Printing Office, 1975), p. 117.

9. H. Bruce Franklin, *The Platform of the Venceremos Organization* (Probably published in Palo Alto, Calif. 1970), p. 1.

10. Exhibit no. 22, testimony by Jay Rogovoy and John McKay 27 June 1974, in hearings before the Committee On Internal Security, House Of Representatives, Ninety-Third Congress. (Washington, D.C.: Government Printing Office, 1974).

Cults, Liberty, and Mind Control

LOUIS JOLYON WEST

A considerable body of material relates to this topic of cults and mind control. However, given the substance of the papers presented so far, I would like to share some more general perspectives relating to the recent increase of troublesome cults in this country and to practical issues concerning terrorists, terrorism, and terroristic organizations. I use the term *practical* in the tradition of Hippocrates, who was concerned with diagnosis and treatment. Is terrorism a social sickness? If so, how do we recognize different types of the disorder, which may exhibit the same symptoms but require different treatments or cures?

First, let us consider the cults. In historical perspective, eras of great turbulence or social change often have also been periods in which a great many cults and cultlike organizations have been formed. This is a time of flux in our society. It is estimated that between 2 and 3 million Americans belong to cults or cultlike organizations at the present. Most of the cult members are between the ages of eighteen and twenty-five, although there are of course others outside that bracket. These organizations probably number approximately 2,500. If 2 or 3 million seems like an exaggeration, consider that L. Ron Hubbard's still-expanding Church of Scientology claimed 5.5 million members worldwide in 1972, a majority of Hubbard's followers being in the United States. The Unification Church of Sun Myung Moon boasts of 30,000 members (often called "Moonies") in the United States alone. Such enterprises as the Unification Church and the Church of Scientology may seem rich, respectable, and secure, compared with the tragic People's Temple of the late "Reverend" Jim Jones, which had a membership of no more than 2,000 at its peak.

However, the Church of Scientology, the Unification Church, the Worldwide Church of God, Synanon, and a number of other organizations have recently come under investigation by government agencies for various purposes. Other large religious cults, such as Divine Light Mission, the International Society of Krishna Consciousness, Children of God, and a number of others are now also facing public scrutiny. There is increasing public alarm about some cults' methods of recruitment, exploitation of members, restrictions on members' freedoms, and retaliation against defecting members. These phenomena include terrifying threats, struggles with members' families (who may be engaged in rescue operations, including so-called deprogramming), attacks on investigative reporters, leaked internal memoranda justifying violence, and the discovery of weapons caches. More specific events stemming from cults have included the rattlesnake attack against the Los Angeles anticult attorney Paul Morantz, in October 1978, the violent outbreak against the Hanafi Muslims in Washington, D.C., and of course the gruesome suicides or murders of more than 900 of Jim Jones's followers at Jonestown, Guyana.

Some cultlike organizations such as Charles Dederich's Synanon are relatively passive regarding recruitment, albeit harsh when it comes to defections. Others, like Moon's Unification Church, are tireless in their recruitment activities. Many employ strenuous techniques in recruitment and consolidation of members, techniques that in some respects resemble the political indoctrination methods prescribed by Mao Tse-tung during the Communist revolution and its aftermath in China. These methods, described by the Chinese as "thought reform" or "ideological remolding," were labeled "brainwashing" by the American journalist Edward Hunter in 1950. Such methods were subsequently studied in depth after the Korean War by a number of Western scientists. A review of these studies is included in the monograph entitled *Coercive Persuasion*, by Edgar Schein.[1]

To understand the power of many cults, and to a considerable extent some terrorist organizations that are cultlike, I think it is worthwhile to look at the elements that go into the recruitment and indoctrination of the members. Many of these bear considerable resemblance to some of the procedures that are described by Schein. They include the following:

> 1. Isolation of the recruit and manipulation of his or her environment.
> 2. Control over channels of communication and information.
> 3. Debilitation through inadequate diet and fatigue.
> 4. Degradation or diminution of the self.
> 5. Induction of uncertainty, fear, and confusion, with joy and certainty promised through surrender to the group.
> 6. Induction and subsequent enhancement of the recruit's dependency and regression to the greatest possible extent.
> 7. Peer pressure, often applied through ritualized struggle sessions, generating guilt and requiring open confessions of past mistakes or "wrong thinking."
> 8. Insistence by seemingly all-powerful hosts or leaders that the recruit's survival—physical, spiritual, or both—depends on identifying with the group.
> 9. Assignment of monotonous tasks or monotonously repetitive activities such as chanting, copying written material, physical drills and exercises, etc.
> 10. Acts of symbolic betrayal or renunciation of self, family, previously held values, or the past in general, designed to increase the psychological distance between the recruit and his or her previous way of life.

We have learned a good deal about the psychopathology of cults, the kinds of mental and emotional troubles that are likely to develop within the membership, refugees from cults, the types of symptoms that they bring with them when they leave, and some of the difficult issues and needs for treatment that they present in trying to return to a normal life. For example, there was quite a refugee population from the People's Temple even before the disaster in Guyana. In fact, they even had an organization called the Human Freedom Center established in Berkeley, California, where they tried to set up a rescue operation for friends and relatives who were still members of the People's Temple. Congressman Ryan's investigation originated in part from the activities of these defectors, leading to the tragic dénouement in Guyana.

In some ways I have been struck by the resemblance between certain facets of the People's Temple, its organization and its demise, and the Symbionese Liberation Army. Patricia Hearst attempted to reconstitute her own persona, following the psychological damage that had been inflicted by the SLA when they kidnapped and tortured her, after she was subsequently arrested and jailed. In striving to regain a personal identity and to put her relationship with the terrorist gang into some kind of understandable perspective for herself, she frequently used the term *crazy* to describe the members of the SLA. Part of her terror vis-à-vis the group, and the group's power to force her into the desired pattern of behavior for their purposes, stemmed from her sense of an irrational fanaticism on their part that was overpowering, that couldn't be dealt with in any way except submission. Many of the refugees from the People's Temple felt the same way, and had the same things to say about the "Reverend" Jim Jones and his intimate power elite.

As I have looked at various organizations committing acts that can be termed terroristic, it has seemed to me that the larger the organization, the less sick the individual members have to be. Consider a given act that can induce terror in others, such as exploding a bomb. If a bomb is dropped from an airplane, the people who drop it are likely to be professional military officers. This means that, mentally and physically, they represent the cream of the crop of their own society. Anybody with the least mental instability, or lacking the ability to form good interpersonal relationships, is likely to be screened out of flight training. Psychopaths don't make acceptable members of flight crews. In fact, armies in general, regardless of the acts in which the army engages, tend to be made up of people selected for good mental health as well as physical health, normal or superior intelligence, the ability to form meaningful interpersonal bonds, and to contribute valuably to groups of which they are members.

At the other end of the continuum is the solo mad bomber who terrorizes a city like New York by setting off bombs in the subways or similar public places. When they are finally apprehended, such individuals almost invariably prove to be psychotic. Although their reasons for bombing may ostensibly be political or religious, those reasons almost always turn out to be delusional. However, such individuals are not to be confused with agents of large organizations such as the IRA or PLO; the latter are more like commandos in their psychology.

It is important to keep in mind that from a psychiatric standpoint, there is a difference between a delusion and a strongly held erroneous belief. One can make reasonably accurate predictions about a person's behavior, and about the characteristics of that individual, if one has clues as to whether his or her actions are based upon a delusion or upon a strongly held belief that is not delusional. It is even possible that the strongly held belief may be erroneous and the delusional belief may be correct. Accuracy is not the basis for deciding whether an *idée fixe* is delusional or a strongly held belief: there are other criteria, based on the way the mind works in arriving at a belief, that make the difference. These criteria have practical value when it comes to figuring out how to find the bomber, and also how to deal with the person or group after apprehension.

Now, looking at the intermediate zone between large organizations which carry out terrible acts as matters of national or pseudonational policy on the one hand, and crazy individuals who explode bombs at random on the other, a variety of groups can be discerned. Some are relatively dedicated and well disciplined but may have a number of disturbed members as well. Certain Weathermen cells apparently fit this description. From there one moves to smaller gangs like the SLA, or even to the Manson family, or larger ones like Black September or the Ku Klux Klan.

In clinical psychiatry we sometimes deal with groups of fairly disturbed people, who come close to functioning in the same fashion as large terrorist gangs like the Baader-Meinhof, or small terrorists bands like the SLA. Most shared delusions occur in diads (*folie a deux*). However, the literature on the phenomenology of shared delusions shows that about 10 percent of all recorded instances of shared delusion involve more than two people: delusions shared by three or more people are thus not unknown. There is a small but growing and interesting literature about this phenomenon, and there is good reason to think that it is more frequent than previously realized. *Folie a famille*, even involving families with six or seven members, is not so rare as we used to believe. The nature of these delusional beliefs may be one of three kinds, in decreasing order of frequency.

> 1. *Delusions of persecution.* The group is convinced that it is under serious and dangerous attack, as many in the People's Temple firmly believed as a consequence of Jim Jones's *idée fixe.*
> 2. *Delusions of grandeur.* A holy mission or some other type of supreme value is vested in the group by its members.
> 3. *Delusions of wish fulfillment.* For example, the group believes that a person who is dead is not really dead, but is in fact alive and well and perhaps of great social stature somewhere else, planning to return someday.

From the systematic psychiatric study of such "family" groups, in which the "family" members are not always blood relations, one finds a succession of behaviors leading inevitably to some kind of disaster extremely reminiscent of that which befell the SLA. There is pragmatic value in applying information derived from clinical studies of such groups. They may be designed as pathological even though, as a rule, the machinery of society carries them not through the medical channels to the clinic, but through social channels to the police. Those who follow a more political route are likely to assert that they are terrorists, that they have a revolutionary aim, that they have a Marxist philosophy, as the SLA did. When the time comes to discover the facts about an unknown group that is committing acts of terrorism, the experience of the clinic can be very helpful.

Now, the psychology of a group like the SLA is probably different in many respects from the psychology of commando-type units from the Palenstine Liberation Organization, which set out in boats to land somewhere in Israel and attack a settlement. The method of recruitment of members is different; the indoctrination and training are different; the motives are different; the way they see themselves is different. But there are also some similarities, which are deserving of study.

Those who would study terrorism in a scientific way should keep in mind the potential similarities and differences between individual terrorists and large international organizations that use terrorism as a matter of policy. There is terrorism that is directed primarily toward the group's own membership, but which spills over to the outside world, as in the case of the People's Temple and various other cults. There is terrorism that is aimed primarily against the outside world, but which spills over upon the membership—to insure fidelity and so forth. Thus, we need to study both the psychopathology of the individual terrorist and the group dynamics of terrorist organizations of different kinds and sizes. Such studies are needed not only to enhance knowledge but for purely practical reasons. It is necessary to understand terrorists in order to negotiate with them, if that is necessary, in order to apprehend them and render them harmless, or even in order to destroy them if that is the unavoidable outcome. Ultimately, the goal should be to prevent the formation of terrorist groups, or at least to understand the conditions that are most likely to lead to their formation, so that we might decrease in some way the likelihood that they would form.

NOTES

1. Edgar M. Schein, Enge Schneier, and Curtis H. Barker, *Coercive Persusion* (New York: Norton, 1961).

Discussion Panel IV

POSSONY: I want to congratulate Dr. West, whom I admire for his testimony in the Patty Hearst trial. I want to make two comments, the first concerning brainwashing. The SLA was using a crude form of brainwashing. If, during the last five to ten years, terrorism had been combined with up-to-date brainwashing techniques, terrorism might have been far more effective than it has been. If we remain caught up in Cold War conflicts, terrorism will continue to be a substitute for more risky forms of war and is likely to be combined with modernized brainwashing techniques. Dr. West was exposed to the potentials of this combination. Some suspicions exist that the Soviets are experimenting with technologies to affect brain waves.

Secondly, putting on my philosophical hat and going back to gnostic movements: Professor Amon identified an extremely significant problem when he argued the terrorists are the gnostic movement of our time. Unfortunately, he got stuck in the Middle Ages, with its clowns and court jesters, and with their romantic descendants. The terrorists of our epoch are taking off from a jolly joker whom we know by the name of Karl Marx. We are confronted with the first—or probably the first—gnostic movement which is atheistic, existentialist, and positivistic. The gnostic movements of the past were theistic, mystical, and magical.

AMON: I evoked the image of the court jester because I refer to him as a protecting figure. As long as we recognize ourselves in his image and as long as, by laughing at him, we are able to ridicule ourselves, there is a good chance that we will not slide onto the road leading to terrorism. When we take ourselves too seriously, we are likely to cause the death of God. This can be done very easily, as Marx and Hegel did, by introducing a model of progress, in which we presumably advance beyond the stage of a belief in God. We kill God by claiming that we no longer have any need for the idea of God. But in this process we do not become godlike creatures, but rather clownlike. If we recognize this fact, we may be saved from turning into devils. I started thinking about it when I noticed that both the clown and the devil wear the same headgear. It seems to me that this is to warn us that if we don't laugh at the one we might turn into the other.

WEST: I don't want to discuss the case of Patricia Hearst today, because it doesn't have that much relevance to our agenda. However, it does relate to one point that I wish to emphasize as strongly as possible. It is an issue that keeps coming up: blaming victims for what happens to them.

We see this in many different paradigms of terrorism. Most of the victims of Jim Jones were members of his own organization. But the public has dismissed most of them, quickly enough, as being defective or crazy for being where they were or doing what they did. Similarly, Patricia Hearst must have been a bad girl, and therefore deserved what happened to her. Former premier of Italy Aldo Moro, who was held captive by terrorists, released some statements before he was killed urging the government to cooperate in his release. Some people were very critical of him for having done that and criticized him for it from the safety of their parlors.

Again and again you see this phenomenon—rape victims are the classical example. But even everyday victims of muggers are likely to be blamed by their relatives, their neighbors, the police, and so on. "What were you doing in that neighborhood?" "Why are you carrying money on you?" "Why didn't you have a better lock on your door?" "It is really your own fault; you brought it on yourself." You see this phenomenon even in some of the most gross and vicious international examples of terrorism, like the Munich disaster. Somehow it was the fault of those Jewish athletes; they didn't handle themselves just right or provide proper security for themselves in their barracks.

Of course, there is a reason for this commonplace reaction to terrifying events. From a psychological point of view it isn't hard to understand. If anybody could be the victim, terrorism is more terrifying because it could happen to you. If someone else may have brought it on himself or herself, then that makes him or her different from you: you would never bring it on yourself. Experienced lawyers know all about this—women on the jury in a rape trial are more likely to acquit the rapist than are middle-aged men. The woman is more prone to think that "if that could happen to anyone, it could happen to me; but if that woman brought it on herself, then I am safe. Therefore, I prefer to believe that she *did* bring it on herself, so the accused man must be innocent of rape." I believe this pattern of thought contributed to the conviction of Patricia Hearst, who had been raped by her captors. It is a mechanism to put psychological distance between oneself and the victims of violence.

Even the literature on the extermination of European Jewry in the Holocaust contains manifestations of this mechanism. A prime example may be found in Hannah Arendt's treatise, *Eichmann In Jerusalem*, in which she tends to concentrate on the failure of the Jew to behave otherwise, rather than on the viciousness, cleverness, and horrible efficiency of the Nazis.

Thus, as we view the phenomenology of terrorism and its consequences, let us be very careful that we do not succumb to the inevitable temptation to blame the victim for what happens to him or her.

KNUTSON: I am very glad that Dr. West made this point, because I was also thinking along these lines. I wish to make two others. The first one is brief. I am an advocate here for the concept of diversity; thus, I am pleased someone said that there are *different types of people* serving differing personality needs and roles within the terrorist group. I am thinking of three groups of which I have interviewed several members. These members have such different psychological roles.

The analysis of my second point is potentially much more important. I feel very strongly that the glue and mainstay of terrorist groups comes from a relatively large pool of people in any given society who are fueled by what Abraham Maslow called "belongingness needs." These are people who—and it couldn't have been said better than Charles Manson did at his trial—have *never mattered to anyone.* That need is such a powerful motivating force that Jim Jones and Hitler and Charlie Manson had a powerful, easily available source of attracting and controlling members. Thus, as Frank Rackley said in one of his excerpts, "They only know how to exploit us until they have no more use for us and then throw us on the scrap heap to be forgotten." That is *so much more powerful* than Marx's language that talks in an objective way of systems and classes. I would say that probably two-thirds of the people I have interviewed so far represent what, in my clinical practice, is a very aberrant phenomenon; in a clinical situation I would expect perhaps one of these cases out of every fifteen or twenty. These are people who have had such a horrendous upbringing that they have never mattered to anyone: they have never had close friends; they have never been nurtured. I am not speaking of people who are *unable* to form relationships in psychiatric terms, but people who have never had the *opportunity.* In joining a terrorist group, all of a sudden they *matter* to someone.

Further, I think that the phenomenon you described is very interesting: I view this as a heavy door that marks the moment of joining. Up to the point that you join the group, there may be a tremendous amount of anxiety. You are being asked to give up a lot of things, much like joining a religious order and turning your back on a lot of things. But once you are on the other side, peer pressure *always* works, because at last you have an emotional home. Thus, it is irresistible when your peers say to you, "Look, you have made plans, you have driven the car to every place involved, but you have *never placed a bomb.* Do you feel you can be a good revolutionary, be in our group, be a part of our underground cell, *without doing* that?" I remarked to one subject, "In other words, they are saying to you, 'Place a bomb or get out' "? "Oh no," the person replied, "if they put it to me that way, I would *never* have done it." But, on the other hand, the message is still clear that if you have gone through this door and finally have a place to belong, there is almost *nothing* that will cause you to go back to that nothingness.

I think it is too simple to say that most terrorists are searching for some powerful identity; I think many are searching for some reparative relationship. I said to one terrorist recently, "Aren't you glad you were active in an earlier era? If you had been five years later, you would have been in Guyana." He said, "Yeah, I thought about that." There is a wide latitude of social roles which appeal to the need for "belongingness," as this subject recognized.

One final comment I would like to make is that prisons are full of such people, and a lot of them find solace in an institutional identity. Right now—again, this is just a hunch—the relatively new prison gangs (for which there is now a national task force) may well become the terrorists of tomorrow. The Aryan Brotherhood, the so-called Mexican Mafia, and other groups are giving people a kind of façade of ideology combined with very strong feelings of being knitted together. The only way that members are going to keep that "knitted together" feeling when they get out of prison is to be able to translate that ideology of the prison into the larger society. In interviews I have completed, some of the subjects have described that process happening to them over a period of years in prison.

RACKLEY: I would like to comment on two things. First of all, I do not think that we have adequately examined the membership exchange among terrorist groups. I alluded to this earlier in my reference to the Italian groups that readily exchange members and materials despite rather deep ideological variations. Rather than the strong ideological appeal of some groups, I believe that it is the *promise* of a support system provided by the power structure of the group that appeals to the majority of the followers. The support system provides for members whose loyalty and utility are relatively predictable while the power structure provides the necessary support.

A related point needing stronger emphasis is the trust/dependency relationship that develops between the provider of strength and the person who perceives himself or herself as powerless. This relationship is an extremely powerful process with effects that do not seem to go away. We see this when we look at former members. When this need for outside strength and structure is no longer satisfied, deepening depression and progressive loss of normal ability to function often occur. This condition usually resembles the former, helpless times before joining the strength-providing group. Looking at this class or level of membership I do not wish to label them "typical," but I will say that in any group, whether violent or nonviolent, these people form the majority of members. I am not ignoring the leader and other powerful people in these groups, but there will always be the basic group that can be abused, beaten, harassed, and endure highly stressful conditions as members and still remain bound by the trust/dependency relationship that attracted them.

RAPOPORT: Rackley's stress on the needs of members suggests that Dr. West has gone too far in ridiculing the notion that people may contribute to, and may even be responsible for, events which happen to them. I know this notion can be abused, but it is odd to think that it has no valid reference whatsoever.

HATCHER: I partially disagree with Dr. Knutson on two points. In my experience, a number of the individuals have experienced a sense of belonging prior to joining the group. It depends upon the degree of sophistication of the group in developing the intensity of the belongingness so that it greatly exceeds the individual's orginial, solo experience. The important thing is the degree of sophistication that has been mobilized to create an intensity of environment so different from the atmosphere out of which the person has come. The experience is almost like falling in love. The respondents describe a tranquil or intense, sexual type of experience.
 Secondly, most of the groups contain a segment of opportunists—people who are not susceptible, who are not charismatic even, but who are opportunists in a sense of using what is available. In my way of thinking, this is one of the key groups you have to differentiate when you start to deal in negotiations or try to prevent stimulations to violent acts.

KNUTSON: I think the underground cell is comparable to the cult in providing an intense sense of "we-ness," coupled with a loss of reality because of the destruction of the normal channels of communication with the outside world.

POSSONY: I have a question for Dr. Hatcher. So many perceptive observers have spoken of Hitler's extraordinary hypnotic powers. Don't you think this is the most supreme form of power exercised by a peer leader?

HATCHER: I am not sure that it is a supreme form. Most leaders have a direct pathway and use the kind of raw power you're talking about. Charlie Manson is a classic example. But there is another type which is not hypnotic, and which in experience is equally powerful. Jones probably typified this in the same way that Manson typified the other approach. Jones was very good at moving people in opposite directions. For example, he would get you involved with one of the women in the church for the "good of the church," and then he would send for your wife while you and the other woman were in one of the upstairs bedrooms. Your wife would be called at home and requested to come up to the temple and look for some records. Several doors would be opened looking for the records, until you and the other woman were found in the bedroom. There would be some pronounced embarrassment at this point, and then later down the line there would be another sermon which would argue against sexual intercourse for everybody. Soon he would get you back together again, and the same cycle would begin. This is very, very sophisticated psychology, getting these people moving constantly between two poles. If this movement is sustained in several areas, the individual is constantly kept off balance and is much more susceptible to suggestion of any kind. It is not a hypnotic process, and is far more complex than the Manson type of raw power.

International Terrorism and the Moral Structure of International Society

JAMES A. NATHAN

INTRODUCTION

The logic of terrorism appeals not only to those who groan under colonial tyranny; it also appeals to many of those who reside in the metropolis as well. When several members of the Baader-Meinhof gang committed suicide in a West German jail a few years ago, thousands of West Germans appeared at the funeral. Indeed, some estimates of the sympathies of West German students have indicated that more than 20 percent support the activity of revolutionary terrorism. For many French, American, and British citizens there has been an undeniable double standard in approaching the violence in Vietnam, Algeria, and Palestine. An undeniable aspect of the way events were determined was the sentiment that the behavior of the FLNA, the Vietcong, and the PLO has been both understandable and, perhaps, even legitimate given the circumstances.

This is a novel situation. Previously, terrorists and guerrillas actively aimed at individuals who had some visible and easily understandable link to the ruling order. Immunities for innocents were recognized by both revolutionaries and governments. But beginning in the late nineteenth century, the traditional limits began to erode and, after World War II, they seem to have all but disappeared. How, then, can we understand terrorism? Is it an anomaly of our times or is it explicable at least in terms of the norms of international society? In my judgment, the contemporary increase in terrorism and support for terrorism is part of the spread of the logic of utilitarian/pragmatic ethics.

Ethical relativism and its companion philosophy, ethical nihilism, have been the reorganizing social cosmologies of the last two centuries. A breakdown in support for natural law led to Marxist assertions that there is no morality except the interests of classes. All morality to Lenin was "deduced from the parts and needs of the class struggle." "All morality," Lenin argued, "taken from superhuman or nonclass conceptions is a deception, a swindle, a befogging of the minds of the workers in the interests of the capitalists."[1] To Lenin and his followers, ethics are relative to one's interests and those that support the interests of the revolution. However, for American pragmatics and realists, abstract morality was not relevant when national society was in danger. Since international relations are a struggle for power, a "statesman," wrote Nicholas Spykman, "can concern himself with values of justice, fairness and tolerance only to the extent that they contribute to or do not interfere with the power objective" of statecraft.[2] The philosopher Mortimer Adler would write, "So long as national self-preservation remains the dominant end for which prudence must choose means, the principles of morality cannot be reconciled with the counsels of prudence."[3]

A seemingly inevitable result of realism in American political thought has been the abandonment of our liberal enlightenment heritage for success standards in politics. If there is an absence of absolute standards, all moralities and policies are seen as relative to time, place and purpose. The backdrop of European nihilism, two wars of epic carnage, and the fact of nuclear weapons tend to trivialize morality and mock moral certitude. But without fixed and absolute standards, we become prey to moral pariahs, on the one hand; on the other hand, we risk falling victim to an incapacity to make judgment to a debilitating cynicism and immobilizing despair.

The moral problem of the American pragmatist abuts the ethical dilemma of those who see terrorism as merely an instrument of social action—useful, if it is placed properly to time and circumstances. Hence, pragmatists debate terrorists on "common terms" of efficacy. Yet, unless acts are deemed absolutely wrong, no matter what the circumstances, we will be hostage to the moral universe of those who are tempted to extreme measures because of what is felt to be extraordinary motivation.

I. Anarchism and Fascism: Individual Action and the State

Beginning in the late eighteenth and early nineteenth centuries, the array of permissible political mechanisms of change gradually expanded. To Europeans who sought justice and meaning in their lives, revolution and violence became, perhaps influenced by the successful American and French examples, increasingly favored means of finding an equitable economic and political order. But how would the revolution come to pass? Most Europeans in the early nineteenth century thought it would either arise spontaneously among the masses or come about as a result of objective conditions, aided perhaps by disciplined organizations such as unions or a cadre of intellectuals. By 1870, a new political instrument, individual terror, became a possible and permissible act. The terrorist would, in the words of Nechaev, one of its first theorists, abjure

> every possession, occupation, or family tie...[for] the revolutionary despises and hates present day social morality in all its forms—he regards everything as moral which helps the triumph of the revolution...love, gratitude, even honor must be stifled....Day and night he must have one thought, one aim, merciless destruction— we recognize no other activity but the work of extermination but we admit that the forms in which this activity will show itself will be extremely varied—poison, the knife, the rope, etc. In this struggle, revolution sanctifies everything alike.[4]

The individual of the 1870s who advocated terror could transfer whatever residual guilt he or she must have felt into self-righteousness. Teetering on the edge of self-extinction, the individual felt that only the deed seemed to matter; whatever salvation society might derive from the terrorist act, the reward of the terrorist was the joy of renouncing his or her existence, an existence that in an age without God or purpose, could find meaning in self-annihilation.

It is readily evident that this extremist strain of anarchism and nihilism cut itself away from the Enlightenment and rationalist roots of the old order. As Sorel enjoined, "We can never do enough to break the link between the people and the literature of the eighteenth century... to demolish this whole scaffolding of conventional falsehoods...."[5] While Marxists and some liberal capitalists tended to produce tight, world-encompassing theories, politically inclined nihilists-anarchists and the early Fascists repudiated the possibility of engineering or even the contemplation of the structure of the new order.

In Turgenev's *Fathers and Sons*, we are given a preview of soon-to-be-popular political programs, while the two characters do not look beyond the necessity of shattering a dismal present.

> Bazarov: At present, the most useful thing is to deny. So we deny.
> Kirsanov: Everything?... What? Not only art, poetry, but even... too horrible to utter....
> Bazarov: Everything.
> Kirsanov: So you destroy everything... but surely one must build, too?
> Bazarov: That's not our business... first one must clear the ground.[6]

Later, Mussolini was to express a similar view:

> The years which preceded the march on Rome were years of great difficulty during which the necessity for action did not permit of research, or any complete elaboration of doctrine. There was much discussion, but what was more important and more sacred—men died. They knew how to die. Doctrine, beautifully defined and carefully elucidated, with headlines and paragraphs, might be lacking; but there was to take its place something more decisive—faith.[7]

Faced with the need to recruit supporters and answer the charges of utopianism and blind nihilism, both anarchism and fascism did, in fact, produce social strategies. For the anarchists, the practical program became syndicalism: spontaneous action focusing on the strike. It became the tool through which men would change society and discover their innate sociality. As anarchism became syndicalist, i.e., wedded to the notion of workers based in democratic communes, the general strike became the defining "bed" of men of action. Bakunin's famous dictum that the "urge to destruction is a creative urge also" became embodied in the infamous program of "propaganda by the deed."[8] The notion of a triumphant assertion of will and self through grand political acts was adopted as a group program; syndicalism became a mass-based movement, appealing to "all victims of authority."

Fascism shared with anarcho-syndicalism its attraction to the oppressed and its assumptions regarding an "organic view" of humankind.[9] Humankind was no longer to be alienated by reason of class, religion, or ideology, but to be integrated by means of work. For both Fascists and anarcho-syndicalists, work and economic questions were necessarily subsidiary to the political well-being of the community. But the Fascists believed that only the state could provide sufficient organization, order, and security for the goals of community and honor to be realized. The major difference between fascism and anarchism centered not on ultimate notions of community, but on the utility of the state in providing an organizational framework for the good life. This role of the state was the central distinction between the "impractical" anarcho-syndicalists and the "pragmatic" Fascists.

Anarchists and nihilists never resolved the issue of how the fully developed powers of the state would dissolve when faced with the "collective will" spontaneously expressed in separate, isolatable locales. Yet in nihilism there was an ambivalance about the state. On one hand, Nietzsche and his followers saw the state as a "cold, cold beast," while on the other, Nietzsche would write,

> the maintenance of the military state is the ultimate means of resuming or preserving the great tradition of the

supreme human type, the strong type. And as a result, all concepts which prolong hostility and distinction of rank between states appear to be sanctioned (for example, nationalism and protective tariffs).[10]

The quintessential nihilist insisted that the state should be preserved and the war system encouraged so that eventually, a culture of "supermen" would triumph. Nietzsche's vision was, of course, only hypothetical; he himself was not a man of action. For the most part, he spoke only to men of letters, not to men of political action.

II. The Twentieth Century Embrace of the State and Power

TREITSCHKE AND THE SUCCESSFUL STATE

To the German historian Heinrich von Treitschke, lecturing at Berlin in the last years of the nineteenth century, the power of the state was not a bondage but an authentic expression of providential grace. Man cannot realize his humanity without some kind of collectivity. The state. therefore, is a "lofty necessity of nature."[11] Individuals are mortal, but, argued Treitschke, the state had a kind of permanence and personality that transcended its living membership. Nations give expression to the endless variations of cultures, he stated. The "authentic" state cannot be weak: in order to be differentiated from other collectivities and in order to effectively represent a culture, states must be sovereign. A weak state is an evolutionary mistake, a crime against the very idea of sovereignty. "If the state is power, only the state which is truly powerful corresponds to its idea."[12] "Hence there is something undeniably ludicrous in a small state. Weakness is not ludicruous in itself, only when it seeks to assume the style of power."[13]

States become powerful, argued Treitschke, by war. War keeps individuals conscious of their collective identity, and "confirms their evolutionary fulfillment."[14] The moral duty of states and statesmen is to secure the permanence of the collective personality of their state in history through the conserving of power.

> The individual can and must sacrifice himself to his country. But a state which sacrifices itself ... is not moral, [it] contravenes that which ... is the highest in the state.[15]

Statesmen, maintained Treitschke, should seek power prudently. He did not advocate an international rampage of the powerful; rather, his counsel was to seek power for the honor of the culture it represents and because the state is the imperative or the highest form of social organization. Even though a "people does not achieve self-awareness without overestimating itself,"[16] states, Treitschke posited, should seek a balance between the desirable and the attainable. The greatness of the statesman is to know how to interpret the signs of the time and be able to judge how the history of the world is unfolding at a given moment. But he should keep a becoming modesty between ends and means.

> Granted the multiplicity and complexity of real situations with which he comes to grips, he must not permit himself to be led into the dark and uncertain ways. He should seek only attainable ends and keep his objectives clearly and steadfastly in view.[17]

No matter how moderate a statesman should be in using only proportional force, Treitschke's essential argument was for a new "power politics," based on glorification of the state and of war. It was a romantic vision of collective life with which followers of Nietzsche could be sympathetic. It had even greater appeal to the more conservative nationalists in Germany, who sought to subdue Poles, Catholics, and socialists in Germany and force a more active rivalry with Britain and France. When Germany lost World War I, Treitschke's argument was not forgotten—instead, it was embellished by Fascist philosophers.

MARXISTS, ANARCHISTS, FASCISTS, AND THE EMBRACE OF THE STATE

While conservatives such as Treitschke attempted to give life to the old order by encouraging purposeful power and, when necessary, war, a plethora of attacks on the traditional consensus gathered momentum from other quarters at the end of the nineteenth century and the beginning of the twentieth. Marxists questioned the ability of the state to provide for any but the ruling class, while national minorities felt the expression of their ethnic authenticity crushed by Austrian, Prussian, and Russian power: authority was challenged at every turn for being either too oppressive or too timid. The European consensus about the nature of individuals, morals, the state, and the purpose of collective existence seemed increasingly artificial. Some hoped that the central authority of states could retain their legitimacy, but legitimate structures eroded and the European consensus began to unravel.

A major voice of philosophic irrationalism in Europe in the early twentieth century was Georges Sorel. To him, European society rested on brute force. Violence against the state provoked official repression, which more honestly reflected the true nature of social relations. To Sorel, violence united the oppressed against the oppressors and created myths, heroes, and martyrs of those who fall to "save the world from barbarism."[18]

Sorel's call to action was congruent with Nietzsche's suggestion that men should seek self-awareness through transcendent acts, though Nietzsche could also be read as suggesting support for the state. This difference between the prophets of action presented no difficulty and was not even a consideration for anarcho-syndicalists. They merely rejected the state and emphasized the "act," the strike and the "popular will." Indeed, six heads of state were assassinated in the twenty years before 1914, in Austria-Hungary, Russia, Italy, Portugal, the United States, and Serbia. Labor movements in Spain, the United States, and France were organized and given strength by anarcho-syndicalists as part of their efforts to dislodge the state as a principle of organizing property relationships and human relationships.

World War I put anarchists in a deep quandary. The great advocate of anarchism, Peter Kropotkin, came out in favor of an Allied victory against what he saw as the much greater threat of militaristic Germany, and—at the age of seventy-four—went so far as to begin rifle practice in case of a German invasion of England. The anarchist movement was ripped apart. However, Kropotkin's friends, such as

Malatesta, could not reconcile his support of the war with a philosophy that believed all governments were equally bad. For anarchist supporters, the confusion must have been as great. Young Frenchmen did not know whether to refuse to fight or (as, in fact, many did) to march to the front with their copy of *La Conquête du Pain* in their knapsacks.

FASCISM IN THE INTERWAR PERIOD

The protracted horror of World War I forced people to ask: "What kind of society do we fight for?" Anarchists had always assumed that "society" was to be equated with the entire human species, and that the morality could be found only in internationalism. But World War I required anarchists to redefine the idea of ethical community, and many anarchists came to view the nation as the fundamental social unit on which anarcho-syndicalist ideals might be realigned. Anarchists, Wilsonian liberals, and Fascists berated the state as the unit of social community. The Fascists can be understood as a panegyric to primitive instinct, the denial of intellect, the replacement of reason with pageantry, and the elevation of the dramatic as a means of self-realization. Fascism is conceivable only when it is possible to deny reason and moral truth. Fascists and Nazis alike boasted, "We represent a new principle in the world; we represent the exact categorical, definitive antithesis of the whole world of democracy, plutocracy, freemasonry; in short, the whole world of the immortal principles of 1789."[19] Thus, in Italy, the young Marxist editor of *Avanti!*, Benito Mussolini, switched his position in 1914 and came out for Italian entry into the war against Germany. After the war, Mussolini wedded Italian nationalism and the new sociological theories of elitism to the doctrines of anarcho-syndicalism.

Mussolini was deeply impressed with Sorel. He wrote a lengthy review of Sorel's work in 1919 and by the early twenties echoed Sorel's notions about the necessity of myths in organizing the dispossessed. As Mussolini told a crowd in Naples in 1922:

> We have created our myth. The myth is faith, it is passion. It is not necessary that it shall be a reality. It is a reality by

the fact that it is a goal, a hope, a faith, that it is courage. Our myth is the greatest of the nation.[20]

Fascism was not something new. It was the logical outgrowth of the movement away from rationalism begun by the nihilists and the anarcho-syndicalists, who in the nineteenth century had abandoned God, science, and formal logic for the new idols of will, power, and the future (and in the case of nihilists, the nation). Hence, it is probably more than coincidental that fascism emerged in countries where anarcho-syndicalist experiences were strong. In Italy, France, and Spain, syndicalist movements were powerful, and fascism became a dominant element of the political order. Where the Fascists triumphed, war became a great virtue by which solidarity and brotherhood would be elevated to its most lofty attainment. War became "a happy necessity of civilization," establishing the primacy of nations and individuals.[21]

THE WAR LOVERS: THE INTERWAR PERIOD

The war ethic appealed not only to Fascists: in the interwar period, much of the European elite shared with Lawrence of Arabia the yearning for "losing themselves" and a violent disgust with all existing standards. If they still remembered the "golden age of security," they also remembered how they hated it. "The elite went to war with an excellent hope that everything they knew ... might go down in storms of steel."[22] Hannah Arendt has characterized a whole generation of surviving Europeans as unrequited war lovers: "They denied their memories of four years in the trenches as though they constituted ... a great prelude ... [to] a new world order."[23] To Nietzsche, Bakunin, and Sorel—the prophets of nihilism of the late nineteenth and early twentieth centuries—destruction was a part of the great transformation: the postwar generation found these authors of continuing relevance in their rejection of science, fact, and history. To the nihilist and anarchist was added the Marquis de Sade, who replaced Darwin in parlor rooms. Crackpot historians replaced traditional history. The distinction between trust and falsehood to Europeans of the interwar period was only a system of social sanctions. Truth was relative.

A detached depression characterized many who had marched enthusiastically to the music of Mars in 1914. Before August 1914, war was thought of in Europe as a remedy for decadence and boredom. The interwar period saw a continued disgust for the extant "bourgeois morality" and an ever firmer embrace of violence. Important movements in art, such as surrealism, Dadaism, and expressionism, celebrated the absence of meaningful form and the social irrelevance of that medium. The tremendously influential writer Ernest Hemingway would write autobiographical sketches of a generation without bearings and of emasculated figures caught in the ironic pleasure of unconsummated reunions. Hemingway's endless sorrowful drinks and physical exertions were devoid of social significance: the ebullient boredom at the turn of the century had changed to a brooding ennui. A sinister, barely contained restlessness swallowed the lost generation.

This purposelessness engulfed a generation. It was mood that would have been inconceivable, however, in an earlier age of family, church, and the "rational pursuit of knowledge." Only when rationalism became suspect, when knowledge became relative, when the church could be described as a fakery, and the family could be unprotestingly "nuclearized" and made transient, could desperate and fantastic remedies be thought necessary. Reason and virtue, the ordering rules of evidence, were no longer thought to apply, or if they did, were seen as mere social artifacts. The present could be depreciated—today could be described as ordinary, trivial, and, hence, discredited. Many of the European elite viewed the present as a shadowy illusion at best, and at worst, as mean and empty.

The last twenty years of the nineteenth century in Europe saw the denial of the Enlightenment become first fashionable and then, through the experience of the Great War, demonstrable in the mud and misery of Flanders. In the backdrop of the European experience, reason and natural right no longer seemed to make much sense; the absurd superseded reason, and power displaced right. In such a climate, the notion of a European community based on a balance of power—an equilibrium in politics that mirrored the equipoise of nature—disappeared. Hence, the dominant twentieth-century ethic was neither the balance of power nor the rights of man, but rather, "necessity of state." For many European intellectuals, the most appropriate domestic organization of states could not be individualism, but some kind of corporatism. Fascism grew ascendent in European politics, and power alone seemed to characterize inter-European politics. The European community was shattered in World War I and in its aftershock, World War II. But the second disaster only seemed to underscore that belief in the triumph of reason and right, as Nietzsche had prophesied, was dead.

III. America Confronts Europe: Pragmatism

In the United States there was an analogous intellectual revolution at the beginning of the twentieth century. The American rejection of its traditional foreign policy of isolationism and its embrace of expansionism was one element of the denial of the American enlightenment heritage. Jefferson had declared, "Governments [derive] their just powers from the consent of the governed," and "that all men are created equal." But consent and equality were obviously jeopardized in Puerto Rico, Cuba, and the Philippines in the great leap outward of 1898. To be sure, Theodore Roosevelt had managed to justify this expansion by saying it was in accord with the "finest, nicest and highest" forms of morality and ethics. It was obvious, however, that these explanations were rationalizations for seamy deeds. The United States had forsaken its special isolationist heritage and had become, as Roosevelt had urged, a predatory nation. America's traditional idealism had become a cloak for its newly acquired will to power.

The symbol of America's great departure in foreign policy was the taking of the Philippine Islands in 1898. It breached a historic restraint against expansion beyond the continental U.S. and involvement in extrahemispheric politics. In reality, the imperialisms of 1898 were a movement born of what historian Richard Hofstadter calls the "watershed nineties."[24] As Frederick Jackson Turner noted in his paper of 1893, the frontier had closed. A great depression subsequently occurred in a new social/economic context of increased urbanization and diminished opportunity for individuals in business. "Radical" populist movements gained importance. American political life of the era was shaped by a dynamic group of publicists and politicians, including Theodore Roosevelt, writers

Henry and Brooks Adams, Senator Henry Cabot Lodge, and Whitelaw Reid, editor of the *New York Herald Tribune*. They, and others, argued for the drama, virtue, and opportunity of a "large foreign policy."

America's rejection of Washington's *Farewell Address* by its imperialist movement of 1898, and even more finally by the intervention in Europe of 1917, was presaged by a period of transformation in American politics dating from the 1850s. By the mid-nineteenth century, the American-European heritage was becoming a pious memory, and it was gradually replaced by an ethic shrewd in practical injunctions and uncompromising in its advocacy of success.[25] Darwinian conceptions of humankind and society gave an initial impetus to "philosophic" rationalizations of the commerical ethic, where ideas have value in a "marketplace," and where music and art are valued because they "pay" in terms of cementing the "right" social connections or commanding esteem from the "right" people.

Concurrent with the revolution in American foreign policy was the revolution in American thought. The denial of English "natural right" and "utilitarian" thought, indeed of all European rational "formalisms," was a feature of the pragmatic revolution in philosophy. In the end, pragmatism led to or at least encouraged the denial of idealism and the adoption of realism and realpolitik by a generation of American policymakers who were to lead the United States through its most assertive era in foreign relations during World War II and the Cold War.

American pragmatism was first developed by Charles Peirce in the 1870s, though it was not really noticed until it was revived and reformulated by William James in the 1890s. It was further developed and disseminated in the twentieth century by John Dewey. To James, the truth of ideas was their "cash value," that is, their efficiency; the worth of ideas was how well they worked in practice. An idea was "good" when, in James's words, it "link[ed] things satisfactorily, working securely, saving labor."[26] Truths and the "good" shared the same test, i.e., they must satisfy the query, "Do they pay?"

To Dewey, ideas only become "true" when their "draft upon existence" is honored. Hence, philosophic truth is a function of the cultural "superstructure." For Dewey and the behavioral scientists, social philosophers, and statesmen who succeeded him, reality can be described as things that are defined as real and thus have become real in their consequences. Therefore, the basic calculation of pragmatism was the consequences of instruments in action. To the pragmatist, the measure of ends and means knows no fixed proportion; the relationship between goals and methods is, instead, simply a function of circumstance. Judgments on any one social issue are not necessarily known by judgments on antecedent issues, for conditions may be changed in some meaningful particular. Philosophy cannot become, as Dewey stated, "an analysis of what is past and done with." Rather, it must look to "future possibilities with reference to attaining the better and averting the worse." The use of history was therefore instrumental—the proper use of the past was not discovery of abstract truths, but rather "useful" truths.[27]

The pragmatists did not believe there is necessarily a single social "best." Their criterion of "better" was strictly functional, so to ascertain value they asked, "Does it work?" In this way the pragmatists abjured the self-evident assertions of Locke, Jefferson, and the *Farewell Address*. In fact, they despised these assertions because, as one of the pragmatic sociologists, Thorstein Veblen, put it, the old liberal dogmas had become "in the course of time and shifting circumstances incompatible with continued peace on earth and good will among men."[28]

Walter Lippmann, fresh out of Harvard, had been deeply influenced by James and Dewey. He was very well connected, having worked as an assistant to the famed journalist Lincoln Steffens and then helping found the influential review *New Republic*. In his first book, *A Preface to Politics*, Lippmann presented the first complete political testimony of the new liberal pragmatism. "No moral judgment," he wrote, "can decide the values of life. No ethical theory can announce any intrinsic good."[29] In explaining Dewey's thoughts, Lippmann told readers of the *New Republic*:

> Once we grant that... philosophy is not a reevaluation of absolutist principles, but of a human being's adjustment of his desires to his limitations... then... the modern man asks himself: Why have I come to believe this and so?... Why are certain principles congenial?... [Are they]

a product of circumstance... or [a] justification for his material condition?[30]

Lippmann's associate at the *New Republic*, Herbert Croly, also insisted that all ideas must "be submitted to the pragmatic test of asking what economic interest is served by believing [them]."[31] Gradually, during the interwar period, liberal thought became denuded of meaning. Principles became suffused in policy. Indeed, guiding principles sometimes all but disappeared, and a kind of debilitating relativism crept in on American liberals. If all ideas reflect material interests—the political-economic conditions of individuals—an individual might easily ask why he or she should not merely advocate the program most congenial to his or her own special circumstances.[32]

If a person advocated a program for the "good of others," then that person's motives or judgment became suspect. What was in it for him? If there was no personal gain, was he or she not being a naive idealist, speaking from the airy scaffolding of remote ideals rather than from the solid bedrock of interest? And if an individual were to rely on abstract "principles" for the support of policy, then liberals like Lippmann would respond that such devices were at best "pretentious" and possibly even "monstrous."[33]

Since they believed social good was dependent on "time and circumstance" and that advocates of a policy had difficulty divorcing themselves from their own material conditions, liberals were necessarily a contentious group. They agreed that progress was possible through ingenuity and dedication. But the specific nature of the achievements for which humankind was to march was vague and variable with the advocate. James, for instance, thought war could not "solve" anything, though Dewey could see both sides of the issue. To him, "purposeful" and "intelligent" coercion is merely "energy"—simple mechanical force:

> No ends are accomplished without the use of force... squeamishness about force is not the mark of ideal[ism] but [rather of] moonstruck morals.... The criterion of value lies in the relative efficiency and economy of the expenditure of force as [a] means to an end....[34]

Some pragmatic American intellectuals were drawn to fascism for its promise of efficiency. However, pragmatic liberals were not the only ones who admired Mussolini, nor were all liberals uncritical of fascism—Dewey, Veblen, and Holmes were, in fact, extremely hostile to the Fascist program. The vehicle for most liberal accolades to Mussolini was the *New Republic*. The great historian Charles Beard, an American standard-bearer of liberalism and a close associate of Dewey, wrote in the *New Republic*:

> Beyond question, an amazing experiment is being made here, an experiment in reconciling individualism and socialism, politics and technology. It would be a mistake to allow feelings aroused by contemplating the harsh deeds and extravagent assertions that have accompanied the Fascist process (or all other immense historical change) to obscure the potentialities and the lessons of the adventure—no, not adventure, but destiny riding without any saddle and bridle across the historic peninsula that bridges the world of antiquity and our modern world.[35]

Beard was especially pleased that fascism was flexible, unfettered by any "consistent scheme."[36] Herbert Croly, editor of the *New Republic*, wrote an "Apology for Fascism" in 1927, claiming that Italy's new order was the successful demonstration of an effort

> to emancipate human life by means of the discovery and realization of truth. But truth emerges as a function of individual and corporate life, and it needs for its vindication the subordination of principles to method.[37]

Thus, as some liberal pragmatists suggested, liberalism and fascism were predicated on the same assumptions.[38] It was clear that American liberalism had begun to slide into a debilitating relativism. When confronted by Mussolini's or Stalin's rhetoric and promises, some seemed bedazzled and even morally benighted. As one chronicler of this period, Eric Goldman, has written:

> Relativism easily turns into a doctrine of expediency. Asserting the impossibility of absolute standards removes any very compelling check on the choice of means to an

end, thus encouraging a practice that usually needs little encouraging anyhow—justifying the means by the end. [But means] can change the end. They can even ... become the end.[39]

Thus, despite their liberal and democratic roots, some of the more prominent spokesmen for the liberal pragmatist perspective found themselves applauding the flexibility and "pragmatism" of fascism. Others of the liberal pragmatist persuasion stopped short of this too facile linkage of pragmatism and expediency. Nevertheless, the relativist implications of pragmatism underscored its limits as a guide to policy, especially for statesmen confronted with the chaos of the late interwar period. In time, liberal pragmatism would be incorporated into the "realism" that had been so important to American diplomacy when the latter sought to reconstruct world order after World War II. But during the years leading up to the final collapse of the old order in World War II, pragmatism could offer no compelling alternative to policies of narrow political and economic expediency in the 1930s that propelled the world into total war. Indeed, it was often indistinguishable from them.

CONCLUSION

In slightly more than thirty years, through two total wars and a great economic depression, the 300-year-old center of global political and military power—Europe—was reduced to the status of dependent. The disintegration of European primacy was overtly political, military, and economic. But no less important was a parallel disintegration of the more or less coherent conception of what constituted an acceptable and desirable world order. The rationalistic notion of order based on equilibrium, balance, and classical diplomacy that was seemingly firmly entrenched at mid-nineteenth century had been undermined by the early twentieth century by romantic nihilism and nationalism. With the First World War, whatever was left in Europe of the old notions of a benign order based on reason yielded to more primitive conceptions of international politics and morality. Notwithstanding the persistence of liberal idealism in America, many European statesmen and thinkers between the wars increasingly accepted and acted upon images of international reality that were defined by the imperatives of state interest and national aggrandizement.

In America, the older liberal conceptions were refined by the likes of Peirce, James, and Dewey. But, by the onset of the slide into World War II, their pragmatism had proved itself susceptible to a relativism that was in many ways indistinguishable from extant European ideologies. In a sense, the lack of moral certitude that has given such latitude to American policymakers since the decline of the acceptability of the old moralisms has made the acceptability of the flexibility of formerly repugnant means easier and more pervasive than conceivable in an earlier age when values were permanent and immutable.

The "success" criterion of pragmatism informed Cold War foreign policymakers. It was also the lodestar of virtually any other individual or group of people who had rejected the medieval amalgam of chivalry and Christianity with which the state system began, or the thought of the Enlightenment that gave international relations its period of greatest stablity. The nineteenth-century revolution against reason began in Europe, with the Nietzschean rejection of old values and the glorification of power. Americans turned their backs on the Enlightenment at about the same time. Pragmatism, as it denied concrete morality and enjoined an ethic relative to circumstances, was a two-edged sword. It allowed statesmen to do what they might not do as individuals, but it also allowed individuals to do against states what they might not do against each other.

In recent years, as distinctions between state and society, guilty and innocent have seemed less important, the "pragmatic" criterion of political action has grown to be virtually the only common idiom of discourse in international relations. Statesmen threaten atomic warfare—really a form of genocide—because it "works." Deterrence keeps the peace, or at least it has so far. Terrorists murder innocents regularly to "demonstrate" that governments do not effectively guarantee security and hence are not legitimate because they "don't work." Terrorists also "perform" their acts, no matter how distasteful, because it accords them access to media. Their criterion of values is just as "success" oriented as the statesmen's pragmatism.

Perhaps the most disturbing difference between Establishment pragmatism and the practice of terrorists is that even when the latter ostensibly "fail," they still "win." Say, for instance, that terrorist hostages are slaughtered, unransomed. As long as the terrorist performance was noticed and the cause goes on, in a sense it "worked." In the nineteenth century, the "deed" could be lonely, existential, and, if reasonably harmless, accorded little notice. Contemporary communications, the absence of a moral lodestar, the hunger for the sensational, all make the horrific compelling. Today's terrorist almost never fails. For terrorists, pragmatism is almost infinitely elastic. For statesmen, failure can result in electoral punishment; but for the man who would for a moment be noted, punishment is not the issue. And we, who judge all things by how well they function, may well be abetting merely by being witnesses to his acts. Ethical relativism has cheapened the character of interstate and interpersonal relations and has opened a path for the international gunman, whether he is a representative of the state or the desperate claimant of the dispossessed.

NOTES

1. Samuel Mendel, ed., "Speech to the Third All-Russian Congress of the Young Communist League of the Soviet Union," *The Soviet Government in Theory and Practice* (New York: D. Van Nostrand Co., 1967), pp. 174-175.
2. Nicholas J. Spykman, *American Strategy in World Politics* (New York: Harcourt, Brace and Co., 1942), p. 12.
3. Mortimer Adler, *How to Think About War and Peace* (New York: Simon and Schuster, 1944), p. 78.
4. James Joll, *The Anarchists* (New York: Grosset & Dunlop, 1964), pp. 94-95.
5. Georges Sorel, *Les Illusion du Progrès,* 5th ed. (Paris: M. Riviere, 1947), p. 81.
6. Ivan S. Turgenev, *Fathers and Sons*, trans. Bernard Guerney (New York: Random House, The Modern Library, 1961), p. 67.
7. Benito Mussolini, "The Doctrine of Fascism," quoted in David E. Ingersoll, *Communism, Fascism, and Democracy* (Columbus, Ohio: Charles E. Merrill, 1971), p. 102.
8. Quoted in *The Essential Works of Anarchism*, ed. Marshall S. Shatz (New York: Quadrangle, 1972), p. 221. For a first-hand account of French "propaganda by the deed," see Victor Serge, *Memoirs of a Revolutionary* (London: Oxford University Press, 1963), esp. chap. 1.
9. Unlike its mutation nazism, fascism did not require any notion of race. Hitler explained the difference between fascism and national socialism when he wrote in

Mein Kampf, "All that is not race is trash." To Hitler, race, not state, was the central issue: "The state represents no end, but a means. It is, to be sure, the premise for the formation of a higher culture, but not its cause, which lies exclusively in the existence of a race capable of culture." (Adolph Hitler, *Mein Kampf*, n.p., p. 391).

10. Cited by Ernst Notle, *Three Faces of Fascism* (New York: Holt, Rinehart and Winston, 1965), p. 445.
11. Heinrich von Treitschke, *Politik* • Vorlesungen *gehalten an der Universität zu Berlin* (Leipzig: S. Hirzel, 1913).
12. Ibid., 1:38.
13. Ibid., 1:43.
14. Ibid., 1:63.
15. Ibid., 1:100.
16. Ibid., 1:127.
17. Ibid., 1:551.
18. Georges Sorel, *Reflections on Violence* (New York: Peter Smith, 1941), p. 218. All extant editions use the "authorised trans." of T.E. Hulme.
19. *The Portable Nietzsche*, Selected and trans. Walter Kaufmann (New York: Viking Press, 1968), p. 527.
20. Herman Finer, *Mussolini's Italy* (New York: H. Holt & Co., 1935), p. 218.
21. David E. Ingersoll, *Communism, Fascism, and Democracy* (Columbus, Ohio: Merrill, 1971), p. 109.
22. Hannah Arendt, *The Origin of Totalitarianism* (New York: Harcourt, Brace & World, 1966), chapter 3, pp. 25-26.
23. Ibid.
24. See Richard Hofstadter, "Manifest Destiny and the Philippines," in *American Imperialism in 1898*, ed. Theodore P. Greene (Boston: D.C. Heath, 1955), pp. 54-70.
25. H.S. Thayer, *Meaning and Action: A Critical History of Pragmatism* (Indianapolis: Bobbs-Merrill Co., 1968), p. 438.
26. Cited by H.S. Thayer, "Pragmatism," in *Encyclopedia of Philosophy* 6 (New York: Macmillan Co., 1967): 433.
27. Cushing Straight, "Pragmatism in Retrospect—the Legacy of James and Dewey," *Virginia Quarterly Review* 43 (Winter 1967): 132 passim.
28. Cited by Morton White, *Social Thought in America: The Revolt Against Formalism* (Boston: Beacon Hill Press, 1957), p. 187.
29. Walter Lippmann, *A Preface to Politics* (New York: Mitchell Kennerly, 1913), p. 215.
30. *Early Writings of Walter Lippmann*, ed. Arthur Schlesinger, Jr. (New York: Liveright, 1970), p. 308.
31. Cited by Eric F. Goldman, *Rendezvous with Destiny: A History of American Reform* (New York: Alfred A. Knopf, 1952), p. 199.
32. Ibid., p. 200.
33. Schlesinger, *Writings of Walter Lippmann*, p. 310.
34. Cited by White, *Social Thought in America*, p. 163.

35. Quoted by John P. Diggins, "Flirtation with Fascism: American Pragmatic Liberals and Mussolini's Italy," *American Historical Review* 71 (January 1966): 487-506.
36. Charles Beard, "Making the Fascist State," *New Republic* 57 (23 January 1929): 277-8. Cited by Diggins, *"Flirtation with Fascism,"* p. 494.
37. Diggins, *"Flirtation with Fascism,"* p. 496.
38. "Liberalism vs. Fascism," *New Republic* 50 (2 March 1927): 33-35.
39. See Goldman, *Rendezvous with Destiny*, p. 200.

The Moral Factor in Interstate Politics and International Terrorism

C.E. ZOPPO

I. Defending the Moral Issues of Terrorism in International Politics

In order to examine the moral issues of international terrorism, the morality of interstate politics must be examined along with the individual's role in politics. The politically justified violence of states and of individuals in the international order is integrally related to the historical practices of nations and to the political rationales advanced to justify modern international violence. National leaders, as individuals, function in a politically defined role; so do terrorists. In both cases, their actions represent collective interests and shared political values. Consequently, the individual ordering a violent act in international politics—or carrying one out—is morally, legally, and politically responsible in terms of the rules of behavior defined by two collective entities: the state controlling the territory where he or she lives, and the states of the international system. Other moral, legal, and political systems are outside the compass of contemporary international politics.

There are important links between the domestic policy and the international system; however, a focus on the international aspects of terrorism requires a distinction between domestic and international terrorism. Of the several reasons that justify this distinction, one is compelling. International terrorism—in contrast with domestic terrorism—is either irredentist, or a covert extension of a state's national policies, or both; at the same time it may be the bearer of revolutionary ideologies. Relevant examples that contain either all three of these elements, (or at least two), are the Palestinian, Basque, and Irish terrorists. Hence, international terrorism would neither have political justification nor be capable of achieving policy goals if it could not be explained in terms of interstate politics.

Keeping in mind the importance of collective international behavior and the relationship of individual behavior to it, how may the moral issues that arise in connection with international terrorism be cogently addressed? They clearly should not be evaluated outside the norms of the international political system. Three subject areas provide an ethically justifiable basis for an analytical approach relevent to the contemporary problem of international terrorism: *international law, ideology,* and *technology.*

Custom is law, law is morality. And the rules and principles of *international law* are the only legal system available to, and recognized by, governments for defining the jurisdictions adjudicating state behavior and individuals' acts in international politics. Issues that occur under international law are human rights, war crimes, and the individual as a subject of international law.

Ideology is used in our secularized political world to justify political, social, and ethical ends, whether it appears as nationalist ideology or as one of the revolutionary ideologies of the twentieth century—socialism, Marxism, fascism, and their variants. Thus, ideology identifies the human and institutional targets for political violence and generates the justifications for its use. Crucial, in this context, is the clash between the sovereign rights of states and the right to revolutionary action to change the status quo within and among nations.

The relationship between the means and ends of politics has always been a concern of statecraft—in pragmatic as much as in moral terms. In regard to military and insurrectional means of violence, the relationship between technology and political objectives has included considerations of the distinction between civilians and soldiers: innocent bystanders and appropriate political foes. The modern technology of violence has made increasingly difficult, and at times impossible, the separation of the military from the civilian and of the potentially threatening from the innocuous. The concept of and the dedication to total war, in modern times, has tended to fuse technology and ideology, undercutting some of the constraints of traditional international practice.

This discussion of the moral issues of international terrorism will lean heavily on Western experience and Western perspectives regarding international law, ideology, and technology. The reasons for this focus are easily justified.

The original sources of contemporary international law were the natural law of the ancient Greeks and the jus gentium of Rome, combined with ethical considerations from Judeo-Christian traditions. The most important explanation for the primacy of Western influence in framing issues of morality results, however, from the dominance of the nations of European culture in the modern international system—a dominance whose legitimacy has been questioned seriously only since World War II, first politically, then ideologically, and most recently, economically.[1]

The nations of the West have not only provided the primary sources and the practices of international law, they have also developed and spread the ideologies that dominate international politics today, and have invented and developed the modern means of violence from the handgun to the nuclear bomb. Contemporary international terrorism, as we know it, is therefore predominantly a product—in its rationales and practices—of the Western historical political experience. This is not to say that terrorism is an exclusively Western phenomenon, or that there would not be international terrorism today if international politics had been dominated by nations non-European in location or in culture. It means, simply, that the analysis cannot escape from the historical role of Western civilization.[2]

The moral precepts of the world's great religions and the ethics they have generated are a part of the analysis only to the extent that they have been assimilated into the customary political behavior of modern nations. Historical illustrations regarding the relationship of morality to politics in *interstate* relations are drawn, however, mainly from the Western experience, because of the ascendancy of European culture during the formation of the nation-state system. The moral issues of international terrorism will be discussed within this framework.

II. International Law and Morality in International Politics

In what way is international law germane to the moral issues of international terrorism? International law, particularly as embodied in the charter of the United Nations, defines the legal scope of the behavior of states.

The ethical rules governing violence by individuals in national societies, especially in democratic political systems, do not generally apply to the use of international military violence. The morality of interstate politics is, therefore, substantively different from the morality of domestic politics. If international terrorism is an extension of interstate behavior, then the moral standards by which it would be judged are those that apply to the use of violence by nations in international conflict.

In the same vein, if the morality of individual behavior in the execution of a state's interstate acts is different from the individual's moral responsibility in internal affairs, the moral standards by which terrorist actions are evaluated depend on whether the terrorist is acting for himself in a domestic setting, or as a representative of a collective will that is engaged in international action.

The existence of a fundamental distinction between the moralities of domestic and international politics in the contemporary world can be made clear by reference to modern international law. Modern international law is positivist and secular. In fact, the rise of positivism in Western political and legal theory corresponds with the advent and the establishment of nation-states from the eighteenth to the early twentieth century, and their increasingly absolute claims to legal and political supremacy. This advent brought a shift toward emphasizing the voluntary law of nations built upon state practice and custom. The bulk of legal and political theory, elaborating the sovereignty of the state, has made an explicit distinction between the international law of nations, like the ancient "natural law" or "law of conscience," and the external law, or "law of action."[3]

This assertion of the national will through the legal concept of sovereignty has sanctified "raison d'état," or "sacro egoismo," which respects no higher morality than self-defined national interest, and is often not even respectful of international law. The terms of the Peace of Westphalia in 1648 established the plural, secular, modern view and destroyed the divinely sanctioned hierarchic order of the Middle Ages. Henceforth, this exclusively political view of international relations makes the state an end in itself, free of any moral rein. Politics takes precedence over morals because of reasons of state or public safety. This has tended to minimize or exclude from international politics, and even law, considerations of reason and justice,[4] hobbling individual human rights and humane values.

The supremacy of the national interest over morality is clearly illustrated in Dean Acheson's statement that

> those involved in the Cuban crisis of October 1962, will remember *the irrelevance of the supposed moral considerations* brought out in the discussions.... Judgment centered about the appraisal of dangers and risks, the weighing of the need for decisive and effective actions against considerations of prudence; the need to do enough, against the consequence of doing too much.[5]

Is this a simple matter of "realism"? One outcome could have been a nuclear war, whose horrendous consequences might conceivably raise some moral issues. There is an increasing awareness of the importance of making individuals who commit acts on behalf of the state morally responsible, but morality in international relations continues to be at best contingent, at worst expedient.

This difference between the rules for moral behavior in the international and domestic spheres of politics is apparent in individual as well as collective behavior. The order to drop atomic bombs on Hiroshima and Nagasaki given by President Truman in 1945 was not regarded as a criminal or immoral act by the governments of the time, including the Japanese government. Nor has the individual citizen of any nation who kills enemies in the course of military duty ever been considered a murderer. To the contrary, he has been decorated for being a patriot, and battlefield decorations are usually awarded for "actions beyond the call of duty." The individual's behavior is permissible under modern international law, and sanctioned by the U.N. Charter, when undertaken in his nation's defense.

Major factors in the dehumanization of international politics were the rise of modern liberalism and of modern nationalism. Liberal ideas, originally as revolutionary as those representing later ideologies, separated power from its religious foundations. By emphasizing institutions' contingent character and relative value, liberalism and nationalism destroyed the traditional solidarity of sovereigns. By the same token they relieved attacks against the state of their absolute criminality and excluded international cooperation in a domain where the moral law counts for less than the law of success. With this change in political beliefs was joined the concern of governments not to aid a regime whose national aims collided with or embarrassed their own national interests.

Liberalism's own decline was succeeded by a nationalism imbued with a new mystique of power, later reinforced by the advent of totalitarian ideologies. Authoritarian regimes have shown no mercy for political dissenters who they have regarded as criminally dangerous malefactors. For example, this state of affairs reduced the practical interest of the clauses in the 1937 and 1949 Geneva Conventions for the prevention and punishment of international terrorism, even before the current wave of international terrorism. International cooperation was inconceivable at a time when fundamental human rights were being brutally violated by Nazi Germany and Stalinist Russia.[6] The legitimate attempt to exclude so-called social criminals from the privileged treatment of political offenders implies a minimum moral as well as legal community. The inadequacy of international cooperation in repressing crimes against the safety of the state, and especially terrorist attacks, is generally admitted. This acknowledged inadequacy forms the basis, for example, of Israel's legitimization of its acts against terrorism.

It seems logical that national governments, which are the political if not the actual physical targets of terrorist attacks, would cooperate with each other to maintain the power of the state and repress not only domestic but international terrorism as well, legitimizing their actions through treaties and other legal acts. Terrorism could pose dangers to the stability of the interstate system. A clear illustration of this kind of danger has been provided by the Iranian hostages case, an action almost unanimously condemned at the United Nations for violating international law and diplomatic practices. However, the government of Iran was condemned because it failed to provide adequate protection for the Americans taken captive by the student militants. Even worse, from the viewpoint of the rules governing diplomatic immunities, the Iranian government legitimized the terrorists' actions by the policy positions it assumed officially. The condemnations spoke not to terrorism but to the issue of diplomatic immunities among sovereign states.

The Iranian situation also illustrates, in an unusually blatant fashion, the direct use of terrorism in the pursuit of national objectives. More usual has been the indirect support of terrorism by national governments through the covert aid given to terrorist groups: An example is the aid given to Macedonian terrorists by the Fascist government of Italy in the 1930s. Another form of support for international terrorists that is indirect, though ultimately legitimizing, has been the political recognition of irredentist or separatist groups who use terrorism as one of their major means of violence. The best contemporary illustration is Arab support for the Palestinian irredentists.

It is not surprising, therefore, that the United Nations has not been able to reach any agreement on what constitutes international terrorism or on what would be appropriate responses by the member states. A U.N. General Assembly resolution on international terrorism, in December 1977, while "deeply perturbed over acts of international terrorism," reaffirmed "the inalienable right to self-determination and independence of all peoples under colonial and racist regimes and other forms of alien domination." It also upheld "the legitimacy of their struggle, in particular the struggle of national liberation movements" and further condemned "the continuation of repressive and terrorist acts by colonial, racist, and alien regimes in denying peoples their legitimate right to self-determination and independence."[7] The resolution—adopted by a vote of ninety-one for, nine against, with twenty-eight abstentions—showed all parliamentary democracies voting against or abstaining, but the overwhelming majority of the members voting in favor.

Implicitly, terrorism is condoned when it is a means to national self-determination and condemned when it is state terror to prevent independence. Newly established nations, having used terrorism themselves as a tool for liberation, find condemning it in others awkward. That irredentist terrorism is a historic phenomenon can be shown by reference to the exploits of European nationalists during the nineteenth and early twentieth centuries. Terror by states, totalitarian and dictatorial governments, and substate groups has been a recurrent, and generally accepted, phenomenon of the nation-state system; it has been justified ideologically by nationalism and the revolutionary beliefs of the political right and left.[8]

The morality of the interstate system has officially sanctioned the right of asylum for political crimes since the beginning of the nineteenth century. "Political crimes" have included terrorist acts, often assassinations. A scrutiny of the international conventions, U.N. General Assembly resolutions, and even treaties especially drawn up against international terrorism during the seventies will show how strong the distinction between civil and political crimes remains for nation-states, regardless of the ideological cast of the governments.[9]

A clear example of the difference between criminal and political violence is the language of the French reservation to the European Convention on the Suppression of Terrorism of 27 January 1977. In the reservation, attached to its signature, France pointed out that efficiency in carrying out the antiterrorist struggle "must be reconciled with respect for the fundamental principles of our criminal law and our Constitution, which states in the Preamble that 'anyone persecuted on account of his action for the cause of liberty has the right to asylum on the territory of the Republic....'" Furthermore, the reservation points out, "taking action against terrorism does not absolve us from tackling the political problem of the causes of terrorism. For in many respects the real struggle against terrorism is a struggle for a just peace which guarantees everyone's legitimate rights." The U.N. Charter envisioned human rights as a source of moral inspiration and a principle of collective U.N. action, but the charter nowhere defined the rights of men and women. It does, however, forcefully define the right of self-determination. As France's reservation illustrates, the morality of the modern international system is still defined by the sovereign right of nations and their ideological commitments. Politics basically defines what is moral. There is as yet no rule in international law against either state or subnational terrorism, and the customary behavior of nations remains, in this regard, eminently political.[10]

III. Ideology, Terrorism, and International Morality

The relations between power, law, and morality have often been the subject of serious inexactitudes and misunderstandings. These relationships must not be presented in terms of a conceptual antinomy neither supported by reason nor confirmed by the observation of facts. Law finds its objective expression and its sanctions only in support of power. Power becomes precarious if it collides too openly with law. So long as the potential tension between power and law does not exceed recognized limits, concern for the status quo may hold political power within the orbit of law. The necessity for order is thus the point of coincidence where politics and justice, or morality, may meet and complete each other. So it is also in international politics. Whatever general assets basic rules of international behavior enjoy are largely due to the action of power.

This does not justify the conclusion that the action of power on law is without social direction and inapplicable to ends other than those purely political or national. It does suggest, however, that even when ends and means are not justifiable in strictly political terms, they must reflect, on the one hand, an awareness of the uses of power and, on the other, a generally held set of beliefs that legitimizes both ends and means.

In the modern world, the secularization of societies not only resulted in the nation-state system itself, but also issued in political ideologies that either sublimated the ethical considerations of religious beliefs into political values (consider the French Revolution's "droits de l'homme"), or negated them altogether (consider Nazi Germany's Aryan laws), often in domestic as much as in international relations. International morality is political morality. And political morality is ideological morality. This may not be as shocking as it seems at first sight. Unlike Buddhism, which in theory has been largely unconcerned with politics, Judaism, Christianity, and Islam have all developed political ideologies that are rationalized by religious beliefs and are directly relevant to the morality of international politics of modern political ideologies, and even terrorism, before the emergence of the modern state system.

    I will discuss succinctly only the Christian antecedents of modern ideologies underlying state behavior and international terrorism, merely noting Moses' slaughter of the worshippers of the golden calf, the ideology and actions of the Zealots when Israel was part of the Roman Empire, and the distinction made by Muslim jurists between the world of Islam or peace (dar al Islam) and the rest of humanity (dar al Harb), or the world of war. With the destruction of Judea by Emperor Titus in 70 A.D. and the ensuing Diaspora, Jewish traditions and experience relevant to morality in international politics were absorbed—often distorted—by Christian political acitivists. And although the Muslim world remained an important element of the politics among nations to the end of World War I because of the Ottoman Empire, the decline of its political power coincided with the rise of the European system's global role and its hegemony in world politics.

    Organized religions in the West, when confronted with the uses of violence for political purposes, denied their religious enemies those moral rights that they promoted among their followers—much in the manner of contemporary political totalitarian ideologies—and even permitted terrorism against the "infidels." For example, in the mind of Pope Urban II, the Holy Crusade was to be not only a great unification of Christendom against the Turk, but a magnificent and general act of repentant faith that would culminate in the moral reform and the total renewal of Christendom. The Crusade was expected to subdue Islam permanently and was considered a "war to end wars." Islam was regarded as the incarnation of all the forces of evil, so whereas killing an enemy Christian soldier would earn a Christian soldier forty days' penance, killing Muslims became the "epitome of all penance." There was no "Truce of God" in killing Turks. In the words of St. Bernard, "I call blessed the generation that can... be alive in this year of God's choice."[11] There was a terrible moral risk for anyone who refused, rather than took, this opportunity. It is surely significant that in the Middle Ages this conception of Christian virtue became a struggle to death with pagan adversaries, who were wickedly standing in the way of one's divinely appointed goal. What was intended as a remedy of sins of violence became a consecration of violence. So, too, it was in the Muslim world.

In the antechamber of modern political times, revolutionary ardor and morality joined the eschatological thrust of Christian militancy; the best example is furnished by the Puritans of England, in the days of Cromwell. There is no higher political morality than that of the revolutionary. Seven years before the Peace of Westphalia created the modern state system, Stephen Marshall spoke these words before Parliament: "All people are cursed or blessed according as they do or do not join their strength and give their best assistance to the Lord's people against their enemies."[12] The indiscriminate slaughter of Irish Catholics gave grim reality to this ideological viewpoint, while the auto da fé of the Catholic monarchs of Spain provided the historical counterpoint. When the tension of the foreign battlefield was carried into domestic politics, the number of "false brethren" was automatically increased. It was no longer possible for men to be neutral; permanent warfare was the central myth of Puritan radicalism. And the distress of their "brethren" abroad was a prime consideration. Though the Catholic Suarez wrote "if the end be permissible...the necessary means to that end are also permissible... and hardly anything done against the enemy involves injustice, except the slaying of the innocent," the Puritan Bernard went further than this and managed to suggest the nightmare of total war: "In a just and necessary war, the conquered are in the hands of the conquerors... the State cannot otherwise be weakened but in its subjects...." Puritan casuists, like Bernard, who were examining the problem of means and ends, seemingly adopted some religious version of "reasons of state." Puritans did not accept the Catholic insistence that war was essentially a secular affair—of fallen human nature, of limited response to a specific violation of peace and order. Bernard exemplifies the Puritan campaign for military intervention on the Continent and a revolutionary ideology certainly more like modern secular ideologies than ancient moralities of international politics, pagan or Christian.[13] The fanaticism of religious ideology in Europe exhausted itself with the political formula of *cuius regio cuius religio.**

Once the French Revolution ushered in the era of modern nationalism and planted the seeds of the modern political ideologies on the Left and (later with Napoleon some of the Right), the judgments of religion in regard to the legitimate uses of political violence were supplanted by those of "Goddess Reason" in domestic as well as international relations. The individual's behavior in the politics of international relations was henceforth to be judged almost exclusively by the morality either of the state, or of the particular political ideology that he or she represented or of which he or she was the victim. For interstate politics, nationalism became the secular religion.

Nationalism has been so powerful an ideology that it has successfully resisted encroachments by such a universalist ideology as Marxism and its variants. Even when the ostensible rationales for armed international terrorism have been defined in revolutionary, rather than irredentist, terms, the dominance of the nationalist commitment is unmistakable. An ETA (Basque separatists) manual, *Insurrection in Euzkadi,* says that revolutionary war to achieve national liberation for national independence cannot be conservative and must have a revolutionary ideal. Nevertheless, the basic rationale for action is clearly nationalistic.[14] Similarly, an el-Fatah pamphlet, *The Revolution and Violence: The Road to Victory*, redolent with revolutionary terminology, speaks of "a war of annihilation" of one of the rivals, either wiping out the national identity, or

---

*"Of his region, of his religion." The phrase refers to time before religious toleration was acknowledged in the 1648 Peace of Westphalia, during which citizens were supposed to adopt the religion of their sovereign.

wiping out colonialism...and asserts that "violence will have a unifying influence on people, forging one nation for them."[15] Palestine has become the independent nation of Israel, cemented by the Zionist nationalist ideology and armed conflict. The Palestine Liberation Organization has succeeded in blurring the distinction between irredentists, who have no autonomous territory, and a sovereign state, by being allowed to represent itself at the United Nations and in many countries as if it actually had become a sovereign state.[16] Armed terrorism has evidently been a legitimizing political tool for the PLO.

When the same ideology motivates international terrorists who are fighting the leaders of nations already in existence in order to establish a state, the morality of terrorism can hardly be made to depend on the motives that lead to the political use of terrorism in international relations. Hardly a modern nation was born without terror.

IV. Terrorism, "The Slaying of the Innocent," and Technology

Perhaps moral factors operate uniquely in the violent methods and the human targets of international terrorism. These too must be compared, however, with the violence used by the sovereign nations of the interstate system. For the technology of international violence does relate to the moral aspects not only of international terrorism but also of war.

Military technology, itself a product of political values, is relevant to the moral concerns regarding distinctions between soldiers and civilians, between the politically responsible and citizens at large, between the aggressor and the guiltless.

Insofar as conflicting relations among states are concerned, moral considerations have become either archaic or largely irrelevant. Even before the first atom bomb was dropped in 1945, the airplane combined with dynamite was making discrimination between civilian and military, culpable and innocent, practically impossible. The German raids on London and the Allied raids on Dresden hardly spared women and children, and the napalm used on Vietnamese villages was similarly haphazard. Modern military technology makes it difficult to discriminate among human targets.

With the advent of nuclear weapons, napalm, and other means of modern military violence, the moral issues of warfare have become the subject more of debates among the advocates of various arms deterrence doctrines than of genuine moral concern. The few texts that have addressed the morality of nuclear weapons have either vindicated their conclusions by outright ideological rationales or have walked the tortured road to legitimization of such weapons as defensive, deterrent measures, justified by the morality of nationalist imperatives. Arguments justifying nuclear weapons resemble the religious rationalizations against the infidels.[17] On nonpolitical, nonideological grounds it is very difficult to argue in favor of the morality of strategic military technology, for its ultimate targets are the populations of whole countries. The so-called limited options of the U.S. limited nuclear war doctrine (a counter-force doctrine) have to explain the humaneness of 8 to 20 million collateral, or civilian, casualties, in the United States alone. Although conventional weapons have more limited effects, and in theory could be used more discriminatingly, it has been at times difficult to apply such limits on the battlefield.

It is suggestive that whereas the total weight of bombs used by all national combatants for both strategic and tactical purposes in the Second World War and the Korean War combined was 3.1 megatons (one megaton equals 1 million tons of TNT), the total weight of bombs dropped on Indochina between 1965 and 1971 was 6.3 megatons. Nevertheless, political will can curb modern, nonnuclear battlefield technology. The recurrent military conflicts between Israel and its Arab enemies have caused very few civilian casualties, notwithstanding their intensity.

The technology of modern war, exemplified by nuclear weapons, has changed the expectations of nation-state leaders about the use of violence so that they resemble the expectations of terrorists. Nuclear weapons have made war less military. "Victory is no longer a prerequisite for hurting the enemy."[18] The distinction between the civilian homeland and the military battlefield has disappeared. Terror is the key to political effectiveness. The threat to do violence has become as important as its execution. These tenets have always been in the classical lexicon of terrorists.

In contrast to the governments of nation-states, international terrorists have not sought to maximize the casualties of their adversaries nor have they resorted generally to indiscriminate violence. The first step in irredentist terrorism may seem indiscriminate. Random bombings, arson, assassinations conducted in as spectacular a fashion as possible, by concentrated, coordinated and synchronized waves were the first acts of the Algerian nationalists against the French *colons*. But this was done to gain publicity for their cause. Once this was achieved, selective terrorism became the operational mode, the killing of government officials, such as policemen, mayors, councilmen, and teachers.[19] And, indeed, very few acts by terrorists have been wholly indiscriminate. Sometimes terrorists have not been particularly concerned about who gets killed or they have taken innocent travelers as hostages, but nonetheless they have been selective in choosing the actual physical targets, like a national airliner. Thus, their violence only appears to be indiscriminate.[20]

One limitation on terrorist violence has been the monopoly in the development and the production of weapons enjoyed by the nation-states. Actually, a few technologically advanced nations hold a monopoly of manufacture in regard to most other states as well. Consequently, the kind and quantity of sophisticated weapons available to international terrorists are a direct consequence of the actions of national governments making this technology available abroad. So far, no weapons of mass destruction have fallen into terrorist hands. With the spread of nuclear technology, this may change.

In the total wars between states in this century, with their indiscriminate bombings of enemy populations, there has been little recognition of the principle of innocence. Most political terrorists, like most national leaders, have a strong sense of moral outrage, an absolute conviction in the righteousness of their cause.[21] Neither for national leaders nor international terrorists is "the slaying of the innocents" morally reprehensible, and this is the result of political decisions, not the inevitable consequence of modern technology.

V. In Search of a Morality

As Raymond Aron has so aptly pointed out, nations constitute a unique kind of society that imposes norms on its members and yet tolerates the use of military violence. As long as international society preserves this contradictory character, the morality of international action will also be equivocal. "To declare that force is intrinsically unjust is to decree the original injustice of all judicial norms, inconceivable without the existence of states. Hence, the ultimate alternative: Either there is a right of force, or the whole of history is a web of injustice."[22] To preserve a nation or to establish one are but two aspects of a single historical process. Resource to force is an expectable event when people possessing the means of violence lack alternative means to satisfy legitimate aspirations. It must be acknowledged that force has played a central legislative role in world politics, often changing situations of oppression, injustice, and decadence.[23]

Liberal democracies have been capable of satisfying legitimate nationalist aspirations. The ethnic autonomy and identity that form the basis for the Swiss democratic state have successfully withstood separatist tendencies. The terrorist irredentism in the Sud Tyrol of the postwar period disappeared as the result of the grant of effective autonomy by the Italian state. French Canadian irredentist terrorism is heading toward the same solution. In the newly established democratic state of Spain, the grant of political autonomy to Catalonia and Euskadi has undercut the popular support for nationalist terrorists, and may eventually bring an end to terrorism without evoking state terror.

The cases of Northern Ireland and Palestine, where tragically two different nationalities claim the same territory, lean in the other direction. However, precisely because territorial options do exist for the Palestinians, their nationalism may achieve legitimacy, thus undercutting the incentives for terrorism.

The record of parliamentary democracy with regard to groups seeking self-determination is quite good, and there is no moral case for irredentist terrorism. But parliamentary democracies are rare, and totalitarian dictatorships do not recognize the legitimacy of self-determination claims. Moreover, parliamentary democracies will use terror against those who would overthrow them whether those people are citizens or foreigners.[24] On this level at least, the morality accepted by governments and terrorists alike is that "the cost of enslavement...can be higher than the cost of war, even atomic war.[25]

NOTES

1. In international law the emergence of independent new states in Asia, Africa, and the Middle East has not basically affected the system of interstate relations. The new states have generally accepted the traditional norms of customary law. The single, extraordinary case is that of Iran's treatment of the U.S. hostages, which combined insurgent with state terrorism in defiance of accepted international diplomatic behavior. Wolfgang Friedmann et al. *Cases and Materials on International Law* (St. Paul: West Publishing Co., 1969), pp. 9-10.

2. Although Marxist doctrine challenged the nation-state and its legal system, which is generally thought to be an instrument of exploitation of the working class by the capitalist bourgeoisie—a theory still influential among the philosophical approaches of Soviet communism—the Soviet Union, as a nation-state, has generally practiced the rules and customs of modern international law.

3. For a discussion of Richard Zouche and Emerich de Vattel as influential exponents of positivism and their influence on modern international law, see Friedmann et al., *International Law*, pp. 5-7.

4. Charles de Visscher, *Theory and Reality in Public International Law* (Princeton: Princeton University Press, 1957), pp. 3-11.

5. In an address given at Amherst College, as reported in *The New York Times*, 10 December 1964.

6. De Visscher, *Theory and Reality*, pp. 244-5.

7. The U.N. General Assembly set up an ad hoc committee on international terrorism by resolution on 18 December 1972, to study first the underlying causes of terrorism and then to recommend practical measures to combat it. The General Assembly resolution referred to was one outcome. Yonah Alexander et al., *Control of Terrorism: International Documents* (New York: 1979), p. 147.

8. The constitutions of the U.S.S.R., Yugoslavia, and most democracies grant the right of asylum to foreign nationals wanted for their activities "in the interest of the working class or of *national liberation*" (italics mine). De Visscher, *Theory and Reality*, n. 36, p. 244.

9. Alexander, *Control of Terrorism*, p. 94.

10. For an unusual approach to international law focused on international societal development, see Wesley L. Gould and Michael Barkun, *International Law and the Social Sciences* (Princeton: Princeton University Press, 1970).

11. Thomas Merton, *Mystics and Zen Masters* (New York: Dell, 1969), p. 104.
12. Michael Walzer, *Revolution of the Saints: A Study on Origins of Radical Politics* (New York: Atheneum, 1968).
13. Ibid., p. 281-83, 293.
14. Walter Laqueur, ed., *The Terrorism Reader* (New York: Times Mirror Co., 1978), p. 143.
15. Ibid., pp. 149-150.
16. David Carlton, "The Future of Political Substate Violence," in *Terrorism: Theory and Practice*, ed. Yonah Alexander, David Carlton, and Paul Wilkinson (Boulder: Westview Press, 1979), p. 204.
17. An extended discussion of the various moral approaches to modern warfare may be found in Paul Ramsey, *War and the Christian Conscience* (Durham: Duke University Press, 1961).
18. Thomas Schelling, *Arms and Influence* (New Haven: Yale University Press, 1966), p. 22.
19. David Galula, *Counter-Insurgency Warfare: Theory and Practice* (New York: Praeger, 1964), pp. 58-60.
20. Brian Jenkins, *International Terrorism: A New Mode of Conflict* (Los Angeles: Crescent Publications, 1975), p. 8.
21. Ibid., p. 6.
22. Raymond Aron, *Peace and War* (New York: Doubleday, 1973), pp. 331, 335.
23. Richard Falk, "Historical Tendencies, Modernizing and Revolutionary Nations, and the International Legal Order," in *The Strategy of World Order*, ed. R.A. Falk and S.H. Mendlowitz (New York: World Law Fund, 1966), pp. 172-173.
24. Aron, *Peace and War*, p. 321.
25. Ibid., p. 361.

Arab Terrorism and Israeli Retaliation: Some Moral, Psychological, and Political Reflections

EDWARD BERNARD GLICK

I don't really know where to draw the lines between the moral, psychological and political. Perhaps there are no lines to draw outside of the unreal world of academic separatism. Perhaps the three categories are fused together in an undifferentiated mass, an undelineated whole.

Whatever the case, I want to make a set of statements. These statements will, I hope, paint an accurate picture of how Israelis view Arab terrorism, how and why they react to it, how they react to the world's reaction to it, and especially how they react to the outside world's usually negative response to Israeli military retaliation. In other words, I want to discuss the reciprocal relationship between *teror* and *tagmul*, the Hebrew words for "terror" and "retaliation" or "reprisal."

First, let me say something about the emotional stress caused by the ever present danger of being killed or injured, either at home or abroad, by an Arab terrorist attack. It is not very pleasant for Israelis serving their country in an overseas diplomatic post generally to be forbidden by their government to live in detached private homes with gardens and grounds about them. For security purposes, they are usually forced to live in multi-level apartment houses. This is much more of a psychological deprivation than Americans may realize. For, unlike many Americans, the majority of Israelis in Israel live in what we would call condominiums or housing cooperatives, with relatively little space and privacy. The symbolic proof of this is that, to an Israeli, almost any dwelling that has no outside walls connected to any other dwelling, and no ceilings or floors below or above any other dwelling, is, regardless of its size, usually called a villa.

It is neither pleasant nor cheap for Israeli diplomatic and commercial establishments overseas to be saddled with security precautions and paraphernalia that their counterparts from most other countries can dispense with. Similarly, it certainly is not pleasant to have your purse or bag searched upon entering almost any large store or building, as happens within Israel itself. And if you enter such a store or building twenty times a day, your purse or bag will be searched twenty times a day. It is just not relaxing to have to be always on the lookout for the unattended package, the unaccounted-for suitcase. Nor is it fun to be subjected to body and baggage searches each time you travel by air in, to, or from Israel. And it is not the most pleasing part of parenthood to be faced with newspaper pictures and descriptions of buttons, pins, pencils, pens, marbles, etc. that are really explosive devices in disguise. I remember that at the end of one school year, the Israeli press published pictures and descriptions with such large type headings as: *"Parents, study these pages carefully with your children and make sure they know their contents." "Parents, now that school is out for the summer holidays, make sure that your children do not pick up objects such as these from the streets or from the fields."*

My second point has to do with the words Israelis use to refer to Arab terrorists. At least until recently, the outside world used to call them guerrillas or commandos. The Israelis never do. They remember that *guerrilla* comes from the valiant efforts of the Spaniards to free themselves from Napoleon's domination in the early 1800s and that those efforts were directed against French soldiers, not civilians of whatever nationality. As for *commando*—and thousands of Palestinian Jews served in the British armed forces during the Second World War—they consider that a very honorable word, associated with daring military exploits by military men in uniform against military targets or other military men in uniform. To Israelis the term *commando* conjures up memories of British or Canadian or

American units doing the kinds of military things that the laws of war permit and about which the lords of Hollywood sometimes make exciting movies. Since the hijacking of civilian aircraft, the shooting up of schoolhouses and schoolchildren, the massacre of passengers at airports, or the extermination of athletes at Olympic games are not the kinds of things that real commandos do, or should do, the Israelis, in referring to Arab terrorists, *always* use the Hebrew words *mekhablim* or *teroristim* ("saboteurs" or "terrorists"). Never anything else.

Third, Israeli soldiers have great respect for the fighting abilities of their uniformed Arab counterparts whom they meet in battle. But they have nothing but scorn for irregular Arab terrorists trying to "do their thing" on civilians, be they Israelis, Arabs, or foreign visitors and tourists.

Fourth, Israelis resent the Arab terrorist claim that everything in Israel—including every single Jewish man, woman, and child—is a legitimate military target. This point is very often overlooked by outsiders or by casual visitors to the country. The thinking of Arab terrorists who feel this way and act accordingly is as follows: Israeli men go into the army and serve in the reserves every year until their fifties. Israeli women also are drafted into the army. And since every child is either male or female, he or she, upon growing up, will also enter the army. So, if a person is not in the army now, he or she will someday be in it—or the border police, or the civil guard, or the reserves. Therefore, all Jews living in "occupied Palestine," which to the terrorists means every square inch of both 1947 and 1967 Israel, are present or potential military targets.

Israelis perceive and therefore resent even more that many foreign governments and journalists in the democratic world appear to be letting the Arab terrorists get away with this military target claim. So, too, do they resent what they believe to be the double standard being applied to their situation by the outside world.

The double standard goes something like this. Everyone knows that innocent people get killed in wars. If innocent Israeli men, women, and children get killed in the Ma'alot school or in Jerusalem's Zion Square or Makhanei Yehuda market, that's the terribly unfortunate result of, in this case, a Palestinian Arab war of national liberation. But if, on the other hand, the Israeli army attacks Lebanon and shells, bombs, and blows up terrorist arms caches and bases that have very deliberately been placed in the middle of Arab refugee camps, villages, or homes—often against the wishes of the inhabitants of these camps, villages, and homes—well, here is another example of the bloodthirstiness of those trigger-happy, arrogant Israelis.

In other words, when the outside world does react to Arab terror and to Israeli retaliation, it does so in the most two-faced fashion. And it is this double standard that the Israelis resent most bitterly and most of all.

Fifth, the tactical purpose of terror is to terrorize. If its strategic purpose in the case of Israel is to frighten Israelis, to disorient them, to widen existing socioeconomic cleavages, and to turn them away from their government, their patriotism, and their commitment to the renascent Jewish state, that purpose is simply not being achieved. In fact, the opposite has happened: Arab terror brings disparate segments of Israeli society closer together than might otherwise be the case.

Sixth, the Israelis warned the world years ago that the terrorist virus in the Middle East, if left unchecked, would spread to other causes, countries, and continents and to their cities, planes, and people. They begged for international cooperation against it. Now that the warning has come true, the Western countries, at least, are trying to do something about it. But the more cynical in Israel say that that is because Christians are now being killed—before, it was only Jews and Moslems.

Seventh, while Israelis take Arab terrorism very seriously and take every possible precaution to prevent or minimize it, they are not intimidated by it. They distinguish between a threat and a thorn: terror is a thorn—a terribly bloody and costly thorn—but it is not a real threat to their security and survival. They believe that, given that the terrorists have killed many more Arabs—from peasants to prime ministers—than they have Jews, they are a far greater danger to the Arab governments that spawn, supply, and shelter them than they are to Israel.

So much for terror. What about retaliation?

Hard data are hard to come by because they are secret. But the total number of Israelis who have been killed by all kinds of terrorist activity in the three decades of modern Israel's existence seems to be a little more than 600. That number is not much greater than the annual number of Israelis killed in automobile accidents on the nation's streets and highways. Why then does Israel retaliate? Certainly, retaliation will not change the demographic imbalance between Israel and its neighbors. We already know, and the Israelis freely admit, that they cannot stop terrorism. Nor can they be sure about their degree of deterrence against terrorism. For how can anyone measure how many terrorist attacks there would be both with and without retaliation? Are there fewer attacks because the terrorists know that the Israelis always retaliate? Would there be more attacks if they knew that Israel's reaction would be erratic or completely absent?

I have been pondering these questions for many years in an attempt to find *the* answer. Obviously, Israel's desire to attain some military and political leverage in southern Lebanon is one part of the answer. The duty of any government to protect its citizens from internal and external violence is another part of the answer. *Eiyin takhat eiyin* (the Biblical "eye-for-an-eye") and Israel's origination from and location in the Middle Eastern, Mediterannean milieu in which revenge and vendetta are part and parcel of the regional culture are also parts of the answer. But even when added together these are all only partial answers.

To the extent that I can correctly fathom the matter, *the* answer lies elsewhere. Israel's political and military leaders know full well that when they retaliate against a terrorist attack, they bring upon themselves the verbal condemnation of the United Nations (which by now they don't give a damn about) as well as the wrath of some individual governments and nations they do care very much about—the United States, for instance. They also realize that each Israeli military response weakens the position of those Arabs, including Palestinians, who really want an accommodation with Israel. But domestic psychopolitical pressures and the historical memory of the Jewish people leave them no choice. For since the Nazi Holocaust, within Israel itself and within the range of Israeli response in the Middle East and elsewhere, the era of unarmed Jews being killed and maimed with impunity is over!

That is the textual imperative, and everything else that can be said about Israeli retaliation is secular Talmudic commentary.

As best I can determine, this is the reason of reasons for Israeli retaliation against Arab terrorism. And I leave it to others to measure and decide just how much of what I have had to say lies in the specific realms of morality, of politics, and of psychology—if that is really necessary and if that is really possible in the real world.

Morality of the Use of Violence: A Conceptual Dichotomy in the Indian Perspective

NEMAI SADHAN BOSE

Perhaps more than any other country and people, India and Indians have been associated with the concept of nonviolence *(ahimsa)*, both in theory and practice. While this has lent a kind of halo to Indian culture and civilization, it has also been responsible for misunderstandings of Indian history and the Indian attitude to life. While some have been inclined to hold that the "history of Indian culture is the history of the growth of ahimsa,"[1] and that the dominant purpose of Indian culture has been to develop *daiva prakriti* ("divine nature in man") and remove *himsa* ("violence") from the heart of man,[2] there are scholars who assert that this is not historically true and that the Hindus have used violence in the same way as other people.[3] The two views seem irreconcilable. But an analysis of the Hindu views through the ages on *ahimsa*, or "nonviolence," and on the morality of the use of violence will facilitate a better understanding of the complexities involved in the issue.

The supreme importance of practicing nonviolence has been emphasized since the earliest period of the Vedic civilization. This was hundreds of years before Gautama Buddha and Mahavira made it a dynamic creed and a great force transcending the territorial limits of the Indian subcontinent. In the *Rig-Veda* there is the *shanti mantra* ("hymn of peace"), which evokes peace within ourselves, with neighbors, with society, with the elements, and with the whole universe.[4] The very special significance attached to this hymn is clear from its recitation by the priest at the end of all religious ceremonies, for the benefit of the householders and all others present. It continues to be so in millions of Hindu homes today.

The idea of nonviolence came to be increasingly valued in the Vedic Age. Moral justification of animal sacrifice was sought in the interpretation that it was really a symbolic sacrifice of the animal instincts in men. It aimed at the realization of one's self. *Ahimsa*, along with self-discipline, generosity, straightforwardness, and truth in speech, is mentioned in the *Chandogya Upanishad* as an essential virtue, which is to be cultivated by the votary seeking self-realization.[5] The *Vedantasara* refers to three states on the way to absorption (*samadhi* or "union," "completion") required of a Vedantic candidate. The first of these three is *yama* ("general discipline") of which, again, the prime element is *ahimsa*. This implies renunciation of the intent to injure other beings by thought, word, or deed, with special emphasis on the prohibition against taking a creature's life.[6]

Both the Indian epics, the *Ramayana* and the *Mahabharata*, as well as other Hindu religious texts and mythology, assert, *Dhigvalam Kshatriyavalam Bhramatejovalam Valam* ("Fie on brute force; soul force is the real force"). Later, with the tremendous impact of Buddhism, the dictum *Ahimsa Paramadharma* (nonviolence is the greatest of religions) became an article of faith with innumerable Hindus. The widespread vegetarianism of the Hindus bears testimony to the influence of this doctrine in personal life. It is often overlooked that even the *Bhagavad-Gita*, generally viewed as containing the most articulate and persuasive moral justification of the *use* of force, enjoins that a man should not hate any living creature. He should be friendly and compassionate to all; a man who neither molests his fellowmen nor allows himself to become disturbed by the world is dear to God.[7]

The high pedestal on which the creed of nonviolence was installed in Hindu religious thought and the value attached to it as a code of conduct in personal life often posed problems and raised questions that appeared insolvable. The sharp contradictions between these values and the demands of a practical life often left an individual in the midst of confusion, symbolized admirably by

Arjuna on the battlefield of Kurukshetra. The problem has confronted Indians intermittently throughout history, right down to the present day.

While looking for an answer to this question, it is important to note that Hindu religion is a mosaic of values and moral codes, nonviolence being a principal value. Thus, while extolling the virtue of nonviolence, Hinduism lays no less emphasis on the necessity of resisting and, if necessary, fighting evils and evildoers. Nonviolence does not imply total inaction and indifference to the practical requirements of life. There may be occasion when the use of physical force is deemed more virtuous and desirable than inaction, for the use of violence is not always reprehensible. The purpose for force and the spirit in which it is applied are the criteria for judging its morality. The great war of the *Mahabharata* was necessary for the triumph of right over wrong, of *dharma* upheld by the Pandavas against evil or wickedness represented by the Kurus. God had incarnated Himself as Krishna "to deliver the holy, to destroy the sin of the sinner, to establish righteousness."[8] Arjuna was an instrument in the hands of God in his mission, and was presented with a righteous war from which he could not turn aside without being considered a sinner and disgraced.[9] Personal qualms of nonviolence, or affection for friends and relatives, were secondary to the greater need to destroy the evil. The decision might be sad and painful, as Arjuna found for himself, but there was no second choice for him. It was not a simple defense of militarism or class system,[10] but a philosophical and logical interpretation of man's obligation to himself and to society to punish evildoers.

The philosophy of the *Gita*, undoubtedly, was contrary in some respects to the strictest observance of nonviolence in personal life. Not surprisingly, the question has often been raised in the two epics. When young Rama is asked by Visvamitra to accompany him to kill demons who are harming the sages dwelling in the forests, Rama is hesitant to indulge in killing. But Visvamitra tells Rama that for the protection of the subjects a king or prince has to commit violent or cruel acts that may even appear to be sinful. Persuaded by Visvamitra, Rama kills the demons, much to the relief and rejoicings of the *rishis*. Later, when Rama and Lakshmana in the course of their wanderings in the forests with Sita are killing demons, the latter tells Rama that she has never seen him angry or committing acts of violence. She chides her husband that perhaps it would be better for him to return home; Rama replies that he is killing the demons to protect the *rishis*. He has been bound by the promise to deliver them from the evil demons and there is no other way out. Similarly, on another occasion Rama defends the killing of Bali on the grounds that the latter had deviated from the path of *sanatan dharma* ("time-honored religion").[11]

When the Pandavas and their allies debate the wisdom of waging war to regain their kingdom from the Kurus, Krishna remarks that a person acquires *punya* ("virtue") by annihilating *dasyus* ("robbers"). Thus, it is a righteous duty of the Pandavas to fight for the recovery of their kingdom. The consort of the Pandavas, Draupadi, urges her husbands to fight for the recovery of their lost kingdom. She reminds them that men who know the paths of religion say that one commits the same amount of sin by not killing a man who deserves to be killed, as by killing someone who ought not to be killed. In another episode, narrated in the Mahabharata, Bidula pleads with her son, who has been dispossessed of his ancestral kingdom, to gather courage and fight for recovery of the lost realm, whatever the price and consequences may be.[12] Obviously, there could be no better exposition of militant nationalism and moral justification of the use of force.

The unique position of the motherland is epitomized in the maxim *Yanani Yanmabhumischa Swargadwapi Gariyasi* ("the mother and motherland are greater than heaven"). At the same time, the religious sanction for violent means to achieve even a righteous cause did not entirely remove doubts about the method from the minds of many. The unhappiness of Sita, the hesitation of the Pandavas led by Yudhistira (revered as the embodiment of religion), and the depression of Arjuna only reflected the strong doubts about the use of violence even under compelling circumstances.

Contrary to a popular notion, Hindus have been quite pragmatic in their attitude toward the realities of life. Hindu lawgivers and religious writers have sought to draw a line between private virtues and public obligations. Similarly, a sharp line has been sought between personal morality and sense of values, and statecraft. It was clearly understood that the practice of pure nonviolence, the highest virtue in a man seeking self-realization, was not a practical proposition for statesmen and administrators. An individual could live, if he wished, in a world of his own, but rulers and public figures had to cope with a world conditioned by factors and forces that were far from ideal. This is why nonviolence did not lead to the end of war or abolition of capital punishment in India.[13] There was even a moral justification of revolt against an autocratic, oppressive king. The fate of the legendary king Vena, who was ultimately slain for misusing his power and refusing to mend his ways,[14] was a reminder of the people's moral right to rise in revolt against repression.

In spite of numerous wars of conquests, border wars, personal feuds culminating in armed conflicts, and wars of succession, politics and society in ancient India were comparatively free from acts of terrorism and cruelty. The conspicuous absence of religious wars and persecution indicates that the influence of the doctrine of nonviolence and concern for a peaceful life did not remain confined to vegetarianism in personal life. In fact, assassinations and organized acts of terrorism or cruelty are very few and far between in the history of ancient India. This is in sharp contrast to the experience of contemporary civilizations in other parts of the world. The contrast is more evident during the medieval age in India (1200–1700) when violence, acts of terror, and shocking cruelty became normal features of life. The practice of nonviolence lost all meaning and validity for men of power and position.

The message of peace and love was, fortunately, not totally lost. The ideas of nonviolence, religious harmony, and fraternity found abode in the religious reformers and crystallized in the form of the Bhakti Movement which began in the fifteenth century. The lives and teachings of Ramanand, Kabir, Namdeva, Sri Chaitanya, Eknath, and Nanak, along with those of Sufis such as Khan Musn-ud-din Chisti, Khar Nizam-ud-din Aulia, and Sha Jalal taught the people to live in peace and amity. But the effectiveness of such noble ideas depended heavily on the existing conditions of life and policies of the rulers. The remarkable transformation of the Sikhs from an essentially peaceful community to a militant sect provides an example of how, under pressing circumstances, the use of violence could be sanctified and viewed as a religious and moral obligation.

The founder of Sikhism, Guru Nanak, preached the gospel of love, fraternity and harmony between Hindus and Muslims. Believing in the equality of men, Nanak sought to bring about a new social order in which there would be no invidious distinctions. Sikhism continued to grow as a religion of love and good will until Guru Arjun was executed by the Mughal emperor Jahangir, who became suspicious of the guru's involvement in political intrigues. This changed the course of Sikhism, which henceforth took a militant path. The senseless execution of Guru Tegh Bahadur by Emperor Aurangzeb in 1675 was the signal for the emergence of the Sikhs as a powerful military race, determined to resist religious persecution and challenge Mughal rule in the Punjab. Tegh Bahadur's son and successor, young Govind Singh, revolutionized the religion and organized the Sikhs as warriors. The use of violence was not only given a moral approval, it was also made the sacred duty of all true followers of the religion. Govind Singh identified God, "the punisher of the wicked," with the sword. In his autobiography, Guru Govind wrote that he had been born "for the purpose of spreading the faith, saving the saints and extirpating all tyrants."[15] This, unmistakably, was an echo of the message of the *Gita*. Thus, in Sikhism the use of violence against evil and evildoers was sanctified. On the one hand, a Sikh was to bear no malice or enmity to anyone (as preached by the order's founder, Guru Nanak) and on the other, he was to be a Singh (a lion), striking terror in the hearts of the wicked. This was not easy to accomplish or practice for an ordinary person. Yet, the task of blending the two opposites was imposed on the Sikhs by the harsh realities of life.

The conceptual dichotomy of the morality of violence became more intense and complex during the freedom movement in India. The struggle against British imperialism essentially followed the path of nonviolence laid down by M.K. Gandhi, and India achieved independence without any large-scale adoption of violent means. The Indian image of being a generally peace-loving people with an ingrained aversion to violence owed much to Gandhi and his political philosophy. *No* political leader of Gandhi's stature had ever made nonviolence an article of faith in a mass movement involving millions of people. But this unique feature of the movement led by Gandhi often makes historians and political scientists overlook the role of the revolutionaries, earlier called the "terrorists," in the freedom struggle. It is significant that the Indian people who followed and venerated the saintly Gandhi also had great respect for the revolutionaries. This apparent paradox continues and is a feature of modern Indian mind and politics today.

To the Indian revolutionaries, the freedom struggle was a symbolic contest between *devas* ("gods") and *asuras* ("demons"). The main object of the revolutionaries was to strike terror in the hearts of the foreign rulers and cause disruption by resorting to assassinations, sabotage, attacks on government buildings, etc. Almost from its inception the terrorist movement was given the character of a righteous war for the deliverance of the motherland. It was a person's highest religious duty to sacrifice his life at the altar of freedom; men had no doubt that their actions, free from personal motivations, had divine sanction. Madanlal Dhingra, who assassinated Sir Curzon Wyllie in London (1 July 1909), resented being called a "murderer," because he felt his action was fully justified. He argued, "the English would have done the same thing had the Germans been in occupation of England." In a written statement at the time of his execution, Dhingra said that his action was dictated by his own conscience. As a Hindu he had felt that the wrong done to his country was "an insult to God."

> Poor in wealth and intellect a son like myself has nothing else to offer to the Mother but his own blood.... The only lesson required in India at present is to learn how to die and the only way to teach it is by dying ourselves. Therefore, I die and glory in my martyrdom. My only prayer to God is that I may be reborn of the same Mother and may re-die in the same sacred cause till the cause is successful and she stands free for the good of humanity and to the glory of God.[16]

Dhingra's spirit of sacrifice and intense patriotism impressed even Winston Churchill, then undersecretary for colonies, who remarked that Dhingra's statement was the "finest ever made in the name of patriotism."[17]

A few years earlier, Damodar Hari Chapekar, the assassin of Walter Rand, chairman of the plague committee in Poona, justified his action as necessary for the sake of Hindu religion. A fanatical orthodox Hindu, Chapekar urged the people to take up arms and slaughter the wicked English.[18] But other Western-educated Hindu revolutionaries, who were far from being religious fanatics, also justified terrorism as a moral obligation of a true patriot.

Revolutionary activities in India had reached the peak in the first two decades of the present century. The revolutionaries knew that their methods were totally opposed to the Indian National Congress's policy of peaceful agitation, which, in spite of its limitations enjoyed widespread popular support. Moreover, the religious tradition, moral code, and ethics of the Hindus were not congenial to the widespread acceptance or approval of violence. It was essential to put forward a convincing argument in defense of the cult of the bomb and revolver that did not offend the Hindu's concept of love and peace and his generally passive nature. Consequently, time and again, the revolutionaries came forward with justifications for the course they had chosen.

Militant nationalism and acts of violence were spurred by the Swadeshi movement in Bengal, touched off by the partition of the province by Viceroy Curzon in 1905. The ranks of the revolutionaries began to swell. Madam Cama, a noted Indian revolutionary in Europe, wrote:

> Three years ago it was repugnant to me even to talk of violence as a subject of discussion; but owing to the heartlessness, the hypocrisy, the rascality of the Liberals, that feeling is gone. Why should we deplore the use of violence when our enemies drive us to it?"[19]

Madam Cama was obviously arguing that the total failure of the British government to respond to the just demands of the Indians and the hollowness of the promises made by the Liberals, exposed in the Morley-Minto reforms, had made her lose all faith in the efficacy of any further constitutional agitation. Madam Cama, being a Parsee, was not concerned about Hindu religious dictums as most of her fellow revolutionaries were.

But a different approach to justification for violence was to be found in Aurobindo Ghose and Bal Gangadhar Tilak. Aurobindo veiwed revolutionary activities as "an intensely spiritual movement," which did not aim at mere political and economic freedom. Its real purpose was "emancipation, in every sense of the term, of the Indian manhood and womanhood."[20] He had few qualms about the morality of the means to attain this goal, even the use of violence, if necessary.[21] In earlier issues of his journal *Bande Mataram*, Aurobindo had described the freedom struggle as a battle between *devas* and *asuras*, between good and evil, light and darkness. Politics, he stressed, was especially the business of the *Kshatriyas*, "the warriors." While enunciating the doctrine of passive resistance, he did not rule out the necessity of aggressive resistance and armed revolt. The path was to be dictated by the nature of the pressure brought upon the freedom fighters. When violent pressure seemed to suppress all chance of breathing, "any and every means of self-preservation" became right and justifiable.[22] Aurobindo had explained his views more explicitly in a letter (30 August 1905) when he wrote:

> I regard my native land as my own mother, I adore her, I worship her. What does the son do when an ogre sits on the mother's breast, ready to drink her life blood? Does he quietly sit down to his meal...or rush to rescue his mother?[23]

Aurobindo also found in the *Gita* justification of armed struggle against the British rulers. The destruction of British rule was inevitable because it was the will of God; God had decreed the destruction of the British in India and his will will be carried out even if men like Aurobindo refused to be his instrument.[24] He thus visualized himself and his fellow revolutionaries in the situation that confronted Arjuna on the battlefield of Kurukshetra; as Arjuna did, he decided to follow the command of the Lord.

Similar justification of the use of violence was offered by Tilak. Writing in defense of Sivaji's assassination of Afzal Khan, Tilak wrote in his journal *Kesari* (15 June 1897) that great men were above the "common principles of morality." No blame attached to a person who acted without being motivated by a desire to reap the fruits thereof. Tilak urged, "Do not circumscribe your vision like a frog in a well; get by the penal code, enter into the extremely high atmosphere of *Srimat Bhagavad Gita* and then consider the actions of great men."

The religious and moral justification of violence sought in the *Bhagavad-Gita* by Aurobindo and Tilak did not entirely remove the doubts of many people who had a deep-rooted inhibition against causing physical harm to any living creature, not to speak of human beings. Hindu scripture and religious men had been teaching for centuries that God resided in every living being. So, the taking of life or an act of violence against men, or even animals, was irreligious and undesirable, if not positively sinful. The argument that the freedom fighters in India, seeking to destroy the British, were really fulfilling divine will could also mean that the British rulers were only doing God's work. They also were merely his instruments. This thought dominated the mind of Aurobindo Ghose when he came out of prison after the Alipore Bomb Trial. By now, the fiery revolutionary had undergone a metamorphosis. He had seen the divine light, and now saw *Narayan* ("God") in everyone, including the British magistrate. He openly denounced terrorism and expressed his conviction that "it is for the *dharma* ("religion") and by the *dharma* that India exists."[25] In this Hindu religion, to which he was referring, there is no place for violence, for everyone is engaged in God's work. But such philosophy or consciousness only heightened the dichotomy without offering any realistic solution to the Indian problem. What was the alternative? For the militant nationalists the path of constitutional agitation, followed for decades, had led nowhere. Complete inaction or submission to foreign rule and tyranny without resistance would be cowardice, which was reprehensible, sinful, and irreligious. The doctrine of passive resistance had by now been formulated by Bipin Chandra Pal, Aurobindo Ghose, and others. But at that time it had little appeal to the Indian nationalists searching for a worthwhile alternative to both ineffective agitation and acts of violence. M.K. Gandhi's *satyagraha*, or the use of "soul force," was a very effective technique and philosophy that appeared to reconcile happily the two seemingly opposite dictates of religion.

The emergence of Gandhi and the nationwide impact of his *satyagraha*, with its complete abjuration of violence of any sort, made it imperative for the militant nationalists to make their own philosophy and position clear. They sought to clarify that they did not believe in indiscriminate acts of terror. Lala Lajpat Rai said in 1919 that Indian nationalists did not advocate the use of the bomb or the revolver, but that they might approve of their use against "individual tyrants or against people who insult Indian manhood or womanhood" and could not be brought to justice. But Indians, stated the extremist leader from the Punjab, did not like using bombs and revolvers for general political purposes or for terror.[26]

Significantly, the Indian revolutionaries took great pains to assert emphatically that they were not "terrorists." Their objection to that word was understandable: the word *terrorist* is "an emotive term, used to describe people seen as making an unjustifiable use of violence."[27] The militant Indian nationalists could legitimately oppose the use of the term *terrorists*, which has always carried a stigma for causing senseless and indiscriminate bloodshed and hardship. In the first place, Indian nationalists never indulged in acts of terror against the British people either in India or abroad. Second, they were not seeking to attain political objectives by the use of violence against a "democratic government working under the rule of law." The latter situation, in which modern "terrorists" are often criticized,[28] did not exist in British India. This point was made in a leaflet published by some Indian "terrorists" in 1925 when, after the suspension of the nonviolence-noncooperation movement, they had again become very active. It said:

> Chaos is necessary for the birth of a new star and the birth of life is accompanied by agony and pain. India is also taking a new birth, and is passing through that inevitable phase, when chaos and agony shall play their destined

Morality of the Use of Violence 171

> role.... A few words more about terrorism and anarchism. These two words are playing the most mischievous part in India today. They are being invariably misapplied whenever any reference to the revolutionaries is to be made because it is so very convenient to denounce the revolutionaries under that name. The Indian revolutionaries are neither terrorists nor anarchists.... Terrorism is never their object.... They do not believe that terrorism is for terrorism's sake, although they may at times resort to this method as a very effective means of retaliation.[29]

This leaflet revealed the psychology of the Indian revolutionaries, who were apparently concerned about the lack of popular response and the misunderstanding of their course of action that they suspected in others. They were aware that acts of violence and terror were considered abhorrent by most people; this was even greater because of Gandhi's doctrine of nonviolence, which had cast a magic influence. It was imperative for the revolutionaries to offer a rationale that would answer the religious and moral objections to the use of force. To them the most plausible rationale was that the British had successfully terrorized the Indian people. So, the revolutionaries argued, "official terrorism" was to be met by counterterrorism. The leaflet explained,

> A spirit of utter helplessness pervades every strata of our society and terrorism is an effective means of restoring the proper spirits in the society without which progress will be difficut.[30]

The emphasis was on fearlessness. The revolutionaries were out to show that Indians were not "terribly afraid" of their British masters. The stress on fearlessness was significant, for while Hindus abhorred violence they also abhorred cowardice and spineless passivism.

Gandhi's use of "soul force" and his experiments with truth were novel and unprecedented in their magnitude and impact. Yet, it should not be overlooked that Gandhi himself had to wrestle continuously to keep the demarcation clear between nonviolence and cowardice-germinating inaction. This was essential both as political expediency and as a religious injunction; for, according to the same authorities, while nonviolence was of great spiritual and moral value, cowardice was sinful. Seeking to make his own position clear on the issue, Gandhi said, "A nation that is unfit to fight cannot from experience prove the virtue of not fighting. I do not infer from this that India must fight. But I do say that India must know how to fight."[31] This philosophy was very difficult to comprehend even for the closest associates and followers of Gandhi, many of whom found a lack of consistency in his policy.[32] His calling off of the Anti-Rowlatt Acts agitation as a "Himalayan blunder" and sudden suspension of the Non-Co-operation movement at its height were considered by his detractors acts of betrayal, and confounded his staunch followers like Jawaharlal Nehru. It took several years of apprenticeship under Gandhi before Nehru came to grasp the complex concept.

In 1938 Frances Gunther and author John Gunther were riding to Kohat in the North-West Frontier Province, accompanied by Jawaharlal Nehru. The North-West Frontier Province, with an overwhelming Moslem population of 92 percent, most of whom were Pathan frontier tribesmen, was the stronghold of Abdul Gaffar Khan, known as the "Frontier Gandhi" for his total loyalty to Gandhian principles. He had formed an organization of nonviolent Pathan warriors, named Khudai Khidmatgars ("Servants of God"). Because of their uniforms they became known as the Red Shirts. On their way to Kohat the Gunthers were startled by shots fired by Red Shirt volunteers who were lined up on both sides of the road. The parallel lines of soldiers and shooting of guns in salutation of the honored guests continued at intervals all along the five-hour drive. On enquiry the Gunthers learned from Nehru that it was an old tradition among Pathan tribesmen to make and carry their own guns. Frances Gunther, apparently puzzled, asked Nehru:

> But how does this fit in with your theory of nonviolence? Abdul Gaffar Khan here is supposed to be Gandhi's most devoted and disciplined follower. Why, then, all these guns?

Nehru replied:

> It is true that one of the reasons that we have adopted nonviolence as our weapon in our fight for independence is that we have no other weapon. We have been totally disarmed since 1857—it is a criminal offense for a man to possess a big knife in India. But that reason is only one of expediency, and is not the basis of Gandhi's principle of nonviolence. Gandhi believes that even [if] we possessed the greatest weapons in the world, the biggest tanks, planes, and guns, still we should not use them. He believes that justice and love and reason are more powerful than the strongest mechanized forces. That is why Abdul Gaffar Khan trains his men to shoot—and then disciplines them to have the power not to shoot.

Frances Gunther remarked that this philosophy was hard for a "Western mind" to understand. She asked Nehru whether he himself believed in it. Nehru remarked,

> I do believe in it, but I also know that Western minds can create situations in which even we may be forced to shoot—and we must be prepared for that too.[33]

One cannot fail to notice a distant echo of the revolutionaries' rationale in Nehru's remarks. He, too, was suggesting that a nonviolent people may be compelled to use violence under compelling circumstances. In such a situation, use of force might not only be necessary but also morally justified. Gandhi, while aware of this problem, had sought to resolve it in his own unique way. He was realistic enough to recognize the validity and usefulness of the application of force to oppose evil. Commenting on the comparative merits of *satyagraha* and armed resistance, he had said in 1917,

> *Satyagraha* and arms have both been in use from time immemorial.... Both these forms of strength are preferable to weakness, to what we know by the rather plain but much abused word *cowardice*.... We can, with the help of *satyagraha*, win over those young men who have been

driven to desperation and anger by what they think to be tyranny of the Government and utilize their courage and their mettlesome spirit, their capacity for suffering, to strengthen *satyagraha*.[34]

Gandhi was always aware that his message of nonviolence and the technique of *satyagraha* might easily be misconstrued as total immobility or inaction. This made him repeatedly emphasize the role of "action." He wrote in his weekly English magazine, *Young India* (12 May 1920): "Never has anything been done on this earth without direct action. I rejected the word *passive resistance* because of its insufficiency and its being interpreted as a weapon of the weak." The dilemma confronting a pacifist, as Krishnalal Sridharani, an ardent Gandhian, points out, involves either going to the camp of the men believing in the use of force, or joining the "ranks of inactive pious wishers" who bolster the pillars of status quo.[35] Hindu religion essentially has disavowed such immobility, which impedes progress, spiritual as well as material. In spite of the dominance of the concept of *ahimsa* and universal love, Hindu scripture, literature, and tradition have often eulogized men who had trod the paths of violence inspired by patriotism and idealism, completely free from personal motivations.

This dichotomy has for centuries tended to blur the Indian attitude towards violence and terror. It became evident during the Naxalite movement of the recent sixties and seventies; the widespread reign of terror created in West Bengal and other parts of Eastern India by the young radicals was viewed with horror and dismay by most people. The ultimate decline of this radical movement was largely due to its failure to win popular support for its methods and policies. Yet, there was undoubtedly considerable admiration, sympathy, and compassion for many of the fiery, "misguided" young revolutionaries. Even Jaiprakash Narayan, the Sarvodaya leader acclaimed as the inheritor of the Gandhian technique of nonviolence, expressed appreciation of their revolutionary zeal and appealed to them to devote it to the success of his "total revolution."[36] Jaiprakash Narayan and other Gandhians expressed support for the ideal behind the Naxalbari movement because it wanted to "do something for sharecroppers." He hoped that he would be able to persuade the Naxalites to give up violent means, but at the same time he expressed his doubt as to whether the social revolution could be achieved by democratic means.[37]

Jaiprakash Narayan's sympathetic view of the Naxalites, his absolute faith in and dedication to Gandhian principles and techniques notwithstanding, is reminiscent of Gandhi's own admiration for the militant nationalists. Gandhi, too, had hoped that the revolutionaries would see the efficacy and wisdom of *satyagraha* and give up the path of violence to strengthen his movement. The hope never materialized. Narayan also entertained such hopes with similar results. He voiced India's age-old conceptual dilemma of whether the end justified the means when he said that he was willing to take the path of violence, if he was convinced that there was "no deliverance of the people except through violence."[38] One like Jaiprakash Narayan possibly would never seriously doubt the wisdom and effectiveness of nonviolence. To his preceptor Gandhi it was an article of faith, a way of life and thought from which he could never deviate, even under the most compelling and adverse circumstances. His *satyagraha* was, as Heinrich Zimmer writes, "potentially a vastly powerful modern experiment in the Hindu science of transcending the sphere of lower powers by entering that of higher.... Nonviolence—peaceful protest—is the first principle in the religion *(dharma)* of the saint and sage. One who succeeds in attaining such a power and steps again into the material world is "literally a superman."[39]

Gandhi was possibly a superman by this yardstick, and in his quest for truth he endeavored to resolve the quandary that had confronted Rama in the *Ramayana*, the Pandavas in the *Mahabharata*, the Sikhs against the Mughals, and the Indian revolutionaries against the British. Whether he succeeded will remain a neverending controversy. But no country can possibly produce too many true Gandhians, not to speak of a Gandhi or even Jaiprakash Narayan. The conflict between the concept of *ahimsa* and faith in the existence of God in all living creatures, on the one hand, and the religious and moral injunction to resist or fight evil, on the other, has been going on in India for centuries. The borderline between "sanctified" and "plain" violence has also been often blurred,[40] especially in the present day, causing much confusion and frequently generating mixed responses varying from total support to veiled admiration. Yet Indian history has been comparatively free from outbreaks of violence and terror. By and large, the Indian mind essentially abhors violence and acts of cruelty. But in India, as anywhere else in the world, the cult of violence is sure to acquire much wider appeal and acceptance unless the conditions that breed terror and violence and generate sympathy for such acts are removed.

NOTES

1. Krishnalal Sridharani, *War Without Violence* (New York: Harcourt, Brace and Company, 1939), p. 166.
2. M.A. Ayyangar, *Indian Culture and Religious Thought* (Calcutta: University of Calcutta, 1962), pp. 10, 11.
3. K.M. Panikkar, *Asia and Western Dominance* (London: George Allen and Unwin, 1959). See also Saleem Qureshi, "Political Violence in the South Asian Subcontinent," in *International Terrorism*, ed. Yonah Alexander (New York: Praeger, 1976). Qureshi writes: "However, both in terms of sources of attitudes, such as religion and mythology, as well as in terms of recorded history, violence occupies a respectable position in the Hindu religion. Hindu behaviour and mythology glorify virtuous men, gods, and demons who do not abhor violence; who resort to terrorism, such as kidnapping, deception, and extortion; and who take to war readily" (p. 154).
My article will show that this view is unhistorical and untenable.
4. Ayyangar, *Indian Culture*, p. xvii.
5. *Chandogya Upanishad*, iii.
6. Heinrich Zimmer, *Philosophies of India* (Princeton: Princeton University Press, 1974), p. 433.
7. Swami Prabhavananda, trans., *Bhagavad-Gita* (New York: New American Library, 1972), p. 99.
8. Ibid., p. 50.
9. Ibid., p. 39.
10. A.L. Basham, *The Wonder That Was India* (London: Sidgwick and Jackson, 1954), p. 342.
11. Rajsekhar Basu, trans., *Valmiki Ramayana* (Calcutta: M.C. Sarkar, approx. 1279 B.C.) pp. 23, 155, 221.
12. Rajsekhar Basu, trans., *Mahabharata* (Calcutta: M.C. Sarkar, approx. 1287 B.C.) pp. 319, 331, 337, 351, 352.
13. Basham, *The Wonder That Was India*, p. 123.
14. Ibid., p. 87.
15. A.C. Banerjee, *History of India* (Calcutta: A. Mukherjee & Co., 1974), pp. 498-499.

16. Dhananjaya Keer, *V.D. Savarkar*, p. 55. See also Bimanbehari Majumdar, *Militant Nationalism in India* (Calcutta: General Printers & Publishers, 1966), pp. 144-147.
17. Quoted in E.M.S. Namboodripad, *The Mahatma and the Ism* (Delhi: People's Publishing House, 1958), p. 14.
18. Majumdar, *Militant Nationalism in India*, pp. 72-73.
19. Ibid., p. 148.
20. *Bande Mataram*, 11 May 1907.
21. Amales Tripathi, *The Extremist Challenge* (New Delhi: Orient Longman, 1967), p. 128.
22. *Bande Mataram*, 11-23 April 1907.
23. See Tripathi, *The Extremist Challenge*, p. 42 n. 39, p. 230.
24. Ibid., pp. 136-137.
25. *Karmoyogin*, 27 November 1909, *Dharma*, 12 Paush, 1316 B.S., and Tripathi, *The Extremist Challenge*, p. 138.
26. Lala Lajpat Rai, *The Call to Young India* (Madras: Ganesh & Co., 1929), p. 213.
27. Conor Cruise O'Brien, "Liberty and Terror: Illusions of Violence, Delusions of Liberation," *Encounter*, October 1977, p. 34.
28. Ibid.
29. Jagadesh Chandra Chatterji, *In Search of Freedom* (Calcutta: Panesh Chandra Chatterjee, 1967), p. 346. See also Sukhbir Choudhary, *Growth of Nationalism in India*, vol. II (New Delhi: Trimurti Publications, 1973), pp. 162-173.
30. Chatterji, *In Search of Freedom*, p. 348; Choudhary, *Growth of Nationalism in India*, pp. 168-170.
31. *Collected Works of Mahatma Gandhi* (New Delhi: Publications Division, Government of India, 1958) 77 vols., vol. 14, pp. 462-463.
32. See Erik H. Erikson, *Gandi's Truth* (New York: W.W. Norton, 1969), pp. 373-378.
33. Frances Gunther, *Revolution in India* (New York: Inland Press, 1944), pp. 83-84. The dilemma confronted Nehru time and again when he was the first prime minister of independent India. His firm faith in peace and nonviolence and his commitment to peaceful solution of all international disputes caused much misunderstanding and evoked sharp criticism, when the Indian army marched into the Princely State of Hydrabad to put an end to the Nizam's rule and atrocities of the Razakars and, years later, liberated Goa from oppressive Portuguese rule, when patient negotiations for more than a decade had failed.
34. *Collected Works of Mahatma Gandhi*, pp. 517-520.
35. Sridharani, *War Without Violence*, p. 273.
36. See Lahiri, Probosh Chandra. *Amrita Bazar Patrika* (Calcutta), May 24, 1975.
37. See Marcus F. Franda, *Radical Politics in West Bangal* (Cambridge: M.I.T. Press, 1971), p. 163. Asish Kumar Ray, *The Spring Thunder and After* (Columbia, Missouri: South Asia Books, 1975), p. 251.
38. Franda, *Radical Politics in West Bengal*, p. 163.
39. Zimmer, *Philosophies of India*, p. 171.
40. Alexander, *International Terrorism, Introduction*, p. xviii.

A Courtship with Terrorism: The IRA Yesterday, Today, and Tomorrow

THOMAS E. HACHEY

The Irish Republican Army, or the IRA as it is more commonly known, orchestrated the strategy for Ireland's war of independence between 1919 and 1921. In doing so it established a model for future wars of national liberation that directly influenced the thinking of such nationalist revolutionaries as Mustapha Kemal, Jawaharlal Nehru, and Gamal Abdel Nasser.[1] More than half a century later, there is still an IRA fighting British authority in the six counties of Ireland that remain a part of the United Kingdom. But the IRA of today is a very different organzation from that of 1919, in terms of both tactics and political philosophy. The reason for these differences can only be fully understood, however, in the context of the IRA's historical experience over the past six or more decades.[2]

The 1916 Easter Rising provided a significant object lesson for the IRA, one which has not been forgotten since by that organization, irrespective of the leadership or ideology that has guided it. On the occasion of the Easter Rising, the self-styled Irish Republican Army was led by poets and visionaries who sought victory in defeat, and emancipation in a "blood sacrifice." Even the socialist James Connolly believed that the IRA's defiant challenge to British authority on Easter Monday would almost certainly prove suicidal, but he also agreed to the necessity of adopting so desperate a course in order to polarize national opinion against English imperialism. What

Connolly did not anticipate was that the capitalist enemy would, in a classic display of governmental or institutional terror, destroy private property in a furious bombardment that not only crushed the rebellion but also left much of central Dublin in ruins and an indeterminate number of innocent bystanders dead or wounded. To avert further hardship and suffering on the part of the civilian populace, the Irish revolutionaries surrendered. The IRA had used such uniforms as they could obtain, as well as other identifiable insignia intended to distinguish them as belligerents. Moreover, they had also observed the rules or traditions of conventional warefare, engaging the vastly superior British military in a firefight rather than in hit-and-run guerrilla tactics.[3] Despite these considerations, however, the London government refused to accord the captured IRA insurgents the status of prisoners of war and instead charged them with treasonable insurrection. Fourteen leaders of the Rising were promptly tried and executed, and over a thousand other participants were deported to internment camps in England and Wales. That experience has been cited ever since by IRA spokesmen as one justification for guerrilla campaigns and acts of terrorism against what they contend is an unprincipled and illegal authority.[4]

In much the same way as latter-day political groups like the Vietnamese National Liberation Front have worked in tandem with guerrilla forces like the Viet Cong, the self-proclaimed Sinn Fein Government in Ireland established itself as the political arm of the IRA paramilitary forces during the Anglo-Irish conflict that ensued between 1919 and 1921.[5] The goal of both groups was an Irish republic, and their strategy included a guerrilla campaign to make the island ungovernable by traditional British methods while simultaneously establishing shadow institutions to replace those existing under British law. The IRA military effort carefully balanced small, evasive guerrilla strikes in rural areas with selective assassination in the cities, in what became an intensive and unrelenting offensive against British rule in Ireland.[6] But the armistice of 1921, and the subsequent Anglo-Irish treaty that formally acknowledged the partition of Ireland, indisputably showed that neither side had achieved a "total victory." The Irish had not won, but neither had they lost; and Britain could not triumph without resorting to methods that were anathema to many citizens of the United Kingdom.[7] The compromises, however, split the IRA into treaty and antitreaty factions and plunged the country into a violent civil war. Terrorism and assassination were met with repression and executions, as the level of violence in the fight between former IRA comrades exceeded anything practiced on or by the British during the preceding conflict.[8] The unregenerate republicans were forced to abandon the fight in about a year's time, but many of them went underground and began to espouse a social radicalism that moved the IRA toward the ideological left. During the 1930s, 1940s, and 1950s, the Marxist antecedents of the contemporary IRA "Officials" could be found in Saor Éire ("Free Ireland"), the Socialist Clann na Poblachta ("Children of the Republic"), and the Workers' Revolutionary councils, all three of which supported the IRA's call for the socialist republic envisioned by James Connolly.[9]

First established in January 1970, the IRA Officials are committed to an all-Ireland, thirty-two-county socialist republic in which the Catholic and Protestant working class of both North and South would live in harmony. Hence, in the view of the Officials, the IRA Provisionals' campaign of terrorist bombings and murders of British or Irish Protestant targets will only sustain and enhance divisive sectarianism. Because the Provisionals, or the "Provos" as they are more commonly known, divide as well as kill workers and thereby reinforce rather than weaken British imperialism, the Officials contend that such a misguided strategy is calculated to produce the very antithesis of a workers' republic.[10] To underscore their opposition to the Provo bombing campaign, the Officials announced a self-imposed cease-fire with Ulster authorities in May 1972. Three years later, when there was every indication that Catholics in Northern Ireland were wearying of the destructive violence and that the Official IRA was gaining strength in Ulster's republican strongholds, the Provos turned on their rivals. A savage intra-IRA battle followed, involving both assassinations and bombings.

Unlike the Irish civil war of 1922, the intra-IRA war of late October and early November 1975 lasted less than a fortnight and ended inconclusively. The Officials accused the Provos of having conducted a "Fascist pogrom," while the Provos charged that the Officials' alleged strategy of waiting for the "right time" to strike for a workers' republic was a sham intended to disguise their capitulation to the enemy.[11] Both organizations, however, recognized very early that the cost of their internecine struggle was prohibitive to themselves and helpful only to their common foes. The armistice that followed has been respected to this day, but the bitter rivalry between the two groups also endures.[12]

The IRA Provisionals, like the Officials, formally emerged in January 1970 with both political and military commands. And, also like the Officials, the Provos regard themselves as the true heirs of the Irish republican tradition that has long sought to unite Ireland and terminate the British connection. But the Provo manifesto, *Eire Nua* ("the new Ireland"), illustrates the dissimilarity between the two IRAs. Unlike the Officials, who seek a thirty-two-county socialist republican Ireland, the Provos advocate a federal solution and a federal constitution for Ireland. Their plan would allow for regional governments in the four historic provinces of Connaught, Leinster, Munster, and Ulster, and would provide for an Ulster with nine—as opposed to a six—counties. An all-Ireland parliament would administer the federation and, although a place would exist for the Roman Catholic Church in the new state, the political and economic system would be an amalgam of the best from East and West, an Irish variant of Alexander Dubček's "capitalism with a human face."

Ever since the Provos were defeated by the security forces in the shooting war in Belfast in the early 1970s, the organizations' tactical reliance upon bombing has increased. The Provo leadership's stated objective for such terrorist activity is to secure Irish sovereignty and weary the British of Ireland. Moreover, a calculated campaign of random terror is useful in that it engages enormous manpower reserves of police and troops in preventive efforts, while simultaneously crippling industrial output physically and by frightening away investment capital.[13] The Provos are inflexible and uncompromising and refuse to accommodate other groups or to accept strategy, tactics, and solutions other than their own. They are prepared to keep on bombing and shooting until their proclaimed goal is achieved.

The IRA Provo prefers, as do most terrorists, to think of himself as a soldier or guerrilla fighter. That designation legitimizes his role, at least in his own eyes and in the eyes of his defenders. The latter will argue that guerrilla warfare is a mode of military operation with a history of sufficient length and distinction that it cannot with any plausibility be subsumed under the heading of terrorism. But guerrillas often *are* terrorists, and that is no less the case in the instance of the Provos.[14] Of course, it is also true that terrorism of this kind differs little in its consequences from the conduct of modern wars, which almost always involve the killing of noncombatants and innocents. The pertinent question is whether terrorism is in particular circumstances justified, and the answer will depend upon one's view of the legitimacy of the state or regime against which terrorism is directed.[15] From the Provo perspective, the British government turned a deaf ear and a blind eye to the outrages and abuses of the Northern Ireland Stormont government for the roughly fifty years of its existence. Protestant Unionist groups terrorized the Catholic nationalist minority at will, particularly through Stormont's infamous paramilitary B-Specials, which had no equivalent in any other part of the United Kingdom. Throughout recent history, Ulster's Roman Catholics have shared a plight similar to that of blacks in the United States, as they have been routinely denied their civil rights and have been discriminated against in education, housing, and jobs.[16] Not surprisingly, the IRA took full advantage of the Protestant backlash to the 1967 Northern Ireland civil rights movement that helped focus the world's attention on the Ulster skeleton in John Bull's closet. The reactions which followed, both within the United Kingdom and internationally, ultimately led to London's abolition of the Stormont government and to the substitution of direct rule in 1972.[17] But by this date the terrorist tactics of the Provos had displaced the passive resistance methods of the civil rights movement, because an increasing number of Catholics saw violence as their only means of obtaining victory.

And the Provos today still believe that their terrorist strategy is working and that they are gradually winning the war. Although the British government continues to claim that it will never agree to the unification of Ireland without the consent of the majority in Ulster, in England there is a growing sentiment of opposition to this view. It is a climate of opinion directly fashioned by terrorism, with IRA atrocities being met with UDA (Ulster Defense Association) reprisals, all of which have contributed to a profound sense of revulsion on the opposite shore of the Irish Sea. The British people are sick of Ireland and they "want out," as they wanted out of Palestine; it will not be easy for any British government to ignore that feeling. In Ireland itself, the failure of the Ulster authorities to protect their Catholic citizens from Protestant militants bent on revenge for IRA outrages has prompted such Catholics to welcome help from anyone who would provide it. Very often it has been the Provos who have accommodated that need.[18]

In attempting to understand the IRA terrorist's own perception of the moral world, or to comprehend the Provos' insistence that a guerrilla war can have different standards of justification from those of a conventional one, it is useful to remember that which he seeks to defend. During the first four years of intensive terrorist activity in Ireland, over 1,000 people were killed, 14,000 were wounded, property loss and damage exceeded $200 million, and many neighborhoods and whole towns were gutted. Yet, it was only with grave reluctance that the Provo leadership authorized operations in Britain. In other words, the selected targets of IRA terrorism were part of a discriminate strategy.[19]

A bomb was detonated in the cellar of the Tower of London in July 1974, killing one and injuring forty-two. In November of the same year, two Birmingham pubs were bombed, killing twenty-one persons and injuring 184, many of them teen-agers. In August 1975, however, the IRA shifted its attack from London pubs and other lower- and middle-class points of congregation to the elite clubs and restaurants of the West End. One bomb was set off in the London Hilton and another outside the Belgravia home of Edward Heath, Conservative prime minister from 1970 to 1974. Other bombs killed scores of people in restaurants in the posh Mayfair and Chelsea districts of London. Outraged, Ross McWhirter, publisher-editor of the world famous *Guinness Book of World Records,* announced a campaign of counter-terrorism and put up a personal contribution of $100,000 for a start. The Provos responded by shooting him dead on his doorstep.

Britain stepped up its police surveillance of the IRA in both England and Ireland, but the London government also agreed on 5 December 1975 to end its detention of terrorist suspects without trial, a practice that had been in effect since August 1971. The last forty-six detainees were freed from the Maze Prison at Long Kesh in time for their Christmas shopping and family reunions.[20] IRA terrorism diminished in the months that followed, but even the IRA's fiercest opponents grudgingly conceded that it had won a victory. Throughout its program of violence since 1970, the Provos have sought to impose certain limits on their terrorist activities; those limits have been rather consistently observed. The IRA campaign in Ulster, therefore, operates within real parameters. It usually avoids, for example, such violent variants as the airport massacre at Lod. As a result, dreadful as they may be, IRA operations often reveal a definite structure in contrast to the spontaneous vigilante campaigns of the UDA.

Indeed, the Provos have most frequently struck against economic targets, such as electrical plants, businesses, etc. and, in a great number of instances, they have telephoned a warning in order to avoid or minimize civilian casualties. On a number of occasions Provos have telephoned to accept responsibility for unintended deaths when either ineptitude or miscalculation resulted in premature detonations.[21] This is not to suggest, however, that such action is reasonable or justifiable. Nor can it be argued that the Provos are without the sadists and psychotics who inevitably gravitate to such organizations. There is a criminal element within the Provos, as evidenced by the IRA's own account that one-third of the $42,000 stolen in robberies from Belfast banks in 1973 was embezzled by Provo officers for their own private use.[22] Just as there is no honor among thieves, there is little integrity or principle among the crazed anarchists and greedy opportunists who doubtlessly have infiltrated the Provo ranks. It remains to be seen whether their number is yet sufficient to compromise the control of what to date has been a comparatively disciplined terrorist organization.

There is, of course, another and equally tragic dimension to the legacy of violence in Ulster today. It is the psychological impairment of a society under an interminable siege.[23] Alcoholism among adults has risen sharply and drug addiction in Ulster has increased dramatically. In 1969, for example, there were 480 known addicts in Northern Ireland, but within four years that number had risen to 8,000. Moreover, the victims of violence include more than the maimed and the dead. Hospital wards are filled with people who have developed nervous disorders, amnesia, and any number of undertermined mental illnesses. Children of all ages have been traumatized, and many suffer from psychic scars and emotional handicaps inflicted by the conditions of life in which terror has become a part of daily existence.[24] This latter circumstance is particularly ominous in the implications it contains for the generation approaching adulthood, and hence for the future of Ulster society itself.

Despite the concessions that IRA and UDA terrorism has wrung from the British in Northern Ireland, it seems precipitous to predict this as a part of an irrepressible tide. There is, after all, the real possibility that the escalation of terrorist atrocities may yet produce another result. Perhaps the uncompromising separatist and the unyielding Unionist may yet learn that a common humanity is more important than religious creeds, and that their neighbor's civil liberties are the safeguards of their own freedoms.[25] But whether or not such a reconciliation can be reasonably expected, the strong likelihood is that when and if the unification of Ireland is accomplished, it will happen in a manner different than the IRA intends. Terrorists are very rarely the beneficiaries of their terrorism.[26] Meanwhile, IRA terrorists very probably will continue for a time to achieve their more immediate goal of political disruption. Aside from accomplishing that end, however, terrorism faces an uncertain future in a society in which the capacity to feel shock or horror has been so muted by the barbarism of recent years that the effect of violence is substantially neutralized. It remains to be seen how IRA terrorists will respond to the challenge of finding alternatives to violence if their stock in trade loses its value.* This time it may be the IRA that must confront the issue of survival. As with the execution of Robespierre at the end of the French Reign of Terror, the revolution in Ulster may indeed begin to consume its own children.

---

* Professor Hachey's paper was written before the hunger strikers' campaign in Northern Ireland. His comment seems quite perceptive in retrospect.

The Editors

NOTES

1. Giovanni Costigan, "The Anglo-Irish Conflict, 1919-22: A War of Independence or Systematized Murder?" *University Review* 5, no. 1 (Spring 1968): 66.
2. A recent and popular analysis of the IRA is: T. P. Coogan, *The IRA* (New York: Praeger, 1970).
3. The Hague Convention of 1899 and 1907 had stipulated four conditions that combatants must observe: (1) to be commanded by a person responsible for his subordinates; (2) to have a fixed distinctive emblem recognizable at a distance; (3) to carry arms openly; (4) to conduct operations in accord with the laws and customs of war. Hague Convention, 18 October 1907, Annex, Section 1, Art. 1, *Carnegie Endowment for International Peace,* Washington, D.C. (1915).
4. For a representative commentary on the IRA perception of British institutional terrorism, see Sean Cronin, "Internment in Ireland: Everyone But the Terrorists," *Commonweal* 94, no. 20 (17 September 1971): 470-471.
5. Although the Sinn Fein government admitted as early as April 1919 to working closely with the IRA, the former did not assume public responsibility for IRA military actions until March 1921. *Dáil Eireann: Minutes of Proceedings* (Dublin, Ireland: (Eire) Parliament, n.d.), 10 April 1919, p. 47; and Coogan, *The IRA,* p. 25.
6. One of the more authoritative accounts by an IRA participant is: Ernie O'Malley, *Army Without Banners; Adventures of An Irish Volunteer* (Boston: Houghton Mifflin Co., 1937).
7. British Prime Minister David Lloyd George recognized this fact by the summer of 1921. Lloyd George to George V, 21 July 1921, *Lloyd George Mss.,* F/29/4/57.
8. This phase of the civil war is ably told in Calton Younger, *Ireland's Civil War* (London: Muller, 1968) pp. 240-523 and (New York: Taplinger Publishing Co., 1969).
9. The definitive study on the evolution of the IRA throughout this era is J. Bowyer Bell, *The Secret Army: A History of the IRA, 1916-1970* (New York: John Day Co., 1971).
10. For an instructive analysis of how the end result of such IRA strategy is counterproductive to the original political intent, see William F. May, "Terrorism as Strategy and Ecstasy," *Social Research* 41, no. 2 (Summer 1974): 283.
11. Tom Bowden, "The IRA and the Changing Tactics of Terrorism," *The Political Quarterly* 47, no. 4 (October 1976): 433-434.
12. "The Officials today accuse the Provos of being committed to terror for its own sake, arguing that the latter have become so blinded by their hatred for Protestants that they cannot understand that they are making Protestants believe that no compromise is possible." See David Rapoport, "The Politics of Atrocity," in *Terrorism: Interdisciplinary Perspectives,* ed. Yonah Alexander and Seymour M. Finger (New York: John Jay Press, 1977), p. 54.
13. Bowden, *The Political Quarterly,* pp. 435-436.
14. This view is pursuasively argued in Conor Cruise O'Brien, "On Violence and Terror," *Dissent* 24 (Fall 1977): 433-436. See also John Ellis, *A Short History of*

Guerrilla Warfare (New York: St. Martin's Press, 1976).

15. Of course, as one author has shown, the various concerned disciplines have been to date unable to agree on any common definition of terrorism. See J. Bowyer Bell, "Trends on Terror: The Analysis of Political Violence," *World Politics* 29, no. 3 (April 1977): 481.

16. Lawrence J. McCaffrey, "The Catholic Minority in the North," in *Divided Ireland*, ed. Francis William O'Brien (Rockford, Illinois, 1971), pp. 48-49.

17. Thomas E. Hachey, *Britain and Irish Separatism: From the Fenians to the Free State, 1867-1922* (Chicago: Rand McNally College Pub. Co., 1977) pp. 305-308.

18. Moreover, the Provos are seen by many as being the champions of the proletariat, clearly representing the frustration of thousands who have not shared in the post-World War II prosperity of Western Europe. Ioan Davies, "Violence and Political Impotence: Europe in the Seventies," *The Canadian Forum* 58, no. 683 (August 1978): 14.

19. For a thoughtful examination of this policy of selective terrorism by the IRA, see J. Bowyer Bell, *Transnational Terror* (Washington, D.C.: American Enterprise, 1976). Three other related studies that deal with the concept of selective terrorism are Richard Clutterbuck, *Living With Terrorism* (London: Faber, 1975); Edward Hyams, *Terrorists and Terrorism* (London: Dent, 1975); and (New Rochelle, N.Y.: Arlington House, 1976); Paul Wilkinson, *Political Terrorism* (London: Macmillan & Co., 1974) and (New York: Halstead Press, 1974).

20. Albert Parry, *Terrorism: From Robespierre to Arafat* (New York: Vanguard Press, 1976) pp. 378-391.

21. A recent and dramatic departure from that policy was the deliberate and wanton killing of Earl Mountbatten of Burma, his fourteen-year-old grandson, and another teen-age boy, on 27 August 1979, at Mullaghmore, Ireland. Political observers in Britain and elsewhere, however, concluded that it was too early to judge whether these killings, which resulted from a bomb exploding on the Earl's boat, signaled the advent of a new and more indiscriminate IRA campaign of terrorism.

22. Parry, *Terrorism*, p. 379.

23. For an extensive study of this subject, see Rona M. Fields, *Society Under Siege: A Psychology of Northern Ireland* (Philadelphia: Temple University Press, 1977).

24. Harvard psychiatrist Robert Coles is currently engaged in researching and writing a study on the anxiety reactions of children in Northern Ireland.

25. Hachey, *Britain and Irish Separatism*, p. 310.

26. It was the Irish nationalist moderates, not the Irish republican extremists, who were made the heirs to the new order in Ireland after 1921, just as the *Irgun Z'vai Le'umi* drove the British from Palestine only to make way for the more moderate Jewish Agency and the Haganah. Anthony Arblaster, "Terrorism: Myths, Meaning and Morals," *Political Studies* 25, no. 3 (September 1977): 419.

Discussion
Panel V

FIELDS: Not only were the early IRA revolutionary tactics models for the development of revolutionary theory in India, but Menachem Begin said that these strategies and tactics were also considered and applied by the Irgun. There are many parallels in the British occupation of these three places—India, Ireland, and Israel. Even now there are some rather startling parallels between the contemporary situation in Northern Ireland and the situation during the two years of the Palestine mandate. In fact, there was even a kind of "exchange of personnel" among these three revolutionary societies during the 1940s. These historical facts tend now to be overlooked and minimized while we attempt to destroy the collaboration of revolutionary or terrorist groups in the 1970s. I think a reexamination of the tactics and connections between these groups in the 1940s can be fruitful to understanding and even coping with the current situation.

Most recent developments in Northern Ireland have again highlighted some of these parallels. The Provos, for instance, have now consigned themselves to seeking out military targets and targets with particular symbolic implications, rather than randomly bombing and shooting people presumed Protestant or otherwise not of their persuasion. On the other hand, the Official IRA has altogether put aside their military existence, becoming instead Sinn Fein—the Worker's Party. The Protestant paramilitary, the UDA, has also turned towards a marginally socialist political objective, organizing towards a six-county statelet. Now one of the important issues I would like the panel to address is the effect of the current international situation on these movements and current developments in all three countries. For instance, between 1945 and 1948 in Palestine, it was the response to British colonialism and its tactics that stimulated the development of terrorist and revolutionary organizations. What kinds of currents are presently stimulating revolutionary and terrorist development?

GLICK: I really don't know how to answer that question. My top-of-the-head reaction is that I don't see *much* similarity. There is, of course, some similarity: the three countries were under British rule, but I really don't know whether the fact that the British ruled in each case suggests that a common response must have occurred.

My second point is to remind you that Begin and the Irgun were a deviant group within the organized Jewish community of Palestine. Begin and his followers were against the original Palestine partition resolution of 1947. That makes Begin's present position a really tremendous turnaround personally and politically. Thus, it is very difficult for me to do more than just draw a connection between the three places, the time periods, and the colonial power in question.

BOSE: I would just like to add that as far as the Indian situation was concerned, there was considerable interest in and sympathy for the movement in Ireland among the Indian nationalists. It can be traced back to the time of Raja Ram Mohun Roy, regarded as a pioneer in the growth of Indian political consciousness. He was very sympathetic to the revolutionary movements taking place in different parts of the world after the Congress of Vienna in 1815. The revolutionary or terrorist movements started in India towards the end of the nineteenth century, reaching their peak in the first two decades of the present century. It was during this period that the Irish example had some influence on the Indian revolutionaries, although there was not much direct contact. The influence was in the realm of ideas and modalities. After the emergence of M.K. Gandhi in 1915, that particular revolutionary phase ended. The Indian people watched with interest and great expectations the practical application of the technique of *satyagraha*, or "soul force." It was again in the late twenties that revolutionaries became active in India. My personal view is that during this period the Indian revolutionaries were looking towards the Soviet Union for inspiration and for a model. The Russian revolution exercised a great influence on them—here was a revolution that appeared to have succeeded and ushered in a new era in the struggle against imperialism. However, after the enactment of the Government of India Act of 1935, revolutionary activities in India faded.

SISSON: Two additional points: when reforms were instituted in the Indian case, there was a pattern of diffusing revolutionary activity. In the 1919 Government of India Act and the 1935 Government of India Act, substantial participation in legislative matters was extended to the Indian population, in the early instance provincial governments being recruited exclusively from the directly elected provincial assemblies. Each of these acts was seen as a step toward ultimate self-government and was enacted after intense pressure for reform was aroused. Secondly, there was a pattern of terrorist strategy to choose targets only among the governing colonial elite. Their targets were not so much British citizens who might be there for whatever time and with whatever purpose, but rather those who were a part of the colonial state. In those cases where "innocents" were killed, usually unintentionally, the public reaction was critical.

HACHEY: I will keep this very brief so as not to preclude opportunities for the audience to ask questions. But I must frankly say that I do not see any essential relationship between international currents and terrorist activity in India, Palestine, and Ireland. I would argue that neither the character of the revolutionary organizations in these countries nor the particular terrorist tactics which they embraced are uniquely indentifiable as institutional products of British colonialism. In expanding upon an observation made earlier by Professor Glick, I would suggest that there is yet another dimension to these three particular societies which warrants our attention. Specifically, it will be recalled that India, Palestine, and Ireland all endured both a war of national liberation against an imperial enemy from without and a divisive sectarian struggle from within. While the latter included widely differing circumstances, and such diverse adversaries as Catholics against Protestants, Jews against Arabs, and Hindus against Moslems, the British response to all three situations was the political expedient of partition. Perhaps, therefore, there is also more commonality than I can currently perceive among the terrorist organizations in each of these countries, but at the moment I am at a loss to say what that might be.

SISSON: The British rule and divide!

RAPOPORT: I'm unhappy about Professor Glick's insistence that *everything* Jews do derives from the elementary fact that they are Jews. This is a particularly misleading way to perceive the Israeli retaliation policy, especially retaliations against terrorist incursions from foreign soil. When capable of responding in kind to such acts, sovereign states normally will do so. The French crossed the Tunisian border to get at the FLN, we went into Cambodia, and the Rhodesians for the last few years have been making life miserable for neighboring African states that support the rebels.

Fields's question is interesting. Begin certainly alludes to the Irish experience, and he cites observations of Irish rebels concerning salient features of the British character. But contrary to Fields's suggestion, he never discusses Irish influences over his strategy and tactics, and I believe he never discusses them because they are not significant.

Consider the following facts. When the Haganah turned Irgun members over to the British, when it seized Irgun arms in the Altalena incident, when it fired upon the Irgun, and even when it murdered a kidnapped Irgun officer, Begin refused to retaliate. I know of no comparable instance of restraint in the history of revolutionary movements, and I am certain that the history of terrorism contains none. Begin was willing to accept defeat rather than permit a violent conflict between Jews. He compelled the Irgun to accept the partition plan, knowning that the only alternative was civil war among Jews. For purposes of comparison, we might recall that civil war did occur in Ireland when some rebels refused to accept British peace terms for partition in the 1920s. Finally it should be remembered that the Irgun never sought to govern; how many rebel groups can make that claim?

The restraint of the Irgun was manifested in other ways, too. Arms were held in armories and released temporarily only after an operation was authorized by the high command. As you know, many terrorist groups give their cells autonomy to choose targets, and the consequences for "easy, defenseless, innocent" victims are enormous. The Irgun, I believe, was the first to employ a warning system so that civilians could be evacuated. The Irgun's principal operations were conducted against *military* targets, armed personnel, and bases. Government offices were attacked and civilians working in them harmed, but as far as I know other civilians were not. Captured British soldiers were normally released at the first opportunity. Several military captives were hung, but that was in reprisal for the British decision to hang Irgun captives, and when the British changed their policy, the Irgun did too.

Begin wanted to avoid atrocities which might inspire counter-atrocities; in this respect, his strategy has been quite different from that of most modern terrorists, including the Irish. Begin even discouraged passive resistance sometimes, because when the unarmed are pitted against the armed, atrocities are bound to occur and the struggle will get out of control.

What is the rationale for this peculiar restraint? Begin cites precedents not from modern *Irish* but from ancient *Jewish* history; precedents, furthermore, that are not examples to be emulated but mistakes to be avoided. The only historical experience he refers to—and he refers to it over and over again—was the struggle against Rome that led to mass suicide at Masada, the loss of the homeland, and the Exile itself which lasted for 2,000 years. The struggle began as a passive resistance effort and ended in a furious terrorist campaign. A strategy to provoke latent hostilities governed that struggle, leading to a civil war among Jews, forcing the Romans to fight an unwanted total war, and providing magnificent opportunities for the other local residents—the Greeks—to join the Romans. The potential for repeating history was enormous, and Begin was determined to avoid it. Parenthetically, his efforts to make sure that the local residents, the Arabs (the counterparts of the Greeks in the Roman Empire), were not provoked into aiding the British were extraordinarily successful. Fields's note that, after all these years, the Provos have finally concluded that massacring Protestants only strengthens the survivors' loyalty to Britain indicates that if the Irgun learned this lesson from IRA history, the IRA itself waited thirty years to learn it from the Irgun's history.

I want to make a final brief note on the relationship between pacificism and terror to supplement Bose's fascinating discussion. The ancient Jewish experience represents the first historical example of a pacifist campaign, and it also may be the first example of a terrorist campaign. Gunther Lewy's *Religion and Revolution*, moreover, discusses a number of Christian confessional groups which move directly from pacifism to terror. While nothing seems more opposed than the pacificist and the terrorist, they are alike in rejecting the common belief that violence can be legitimate when regulated by rules. Also, passive resistance, like terror, is often designed to provoke atrocities which morally disarm the strong and gather sympathies for the weak.

QUESTER: One thing that all three countries inherited is the British notion of "state of emergency," and that's very troublesome. The British constitution in many ways doesn't prepare the world very well for possible tensions between civil liberties and terrorism. My question to Dr. Glick is whether he wouldn't concede that Israel is badly served by his moral comparison of the (World War II) commandos and the Arab terrorist, especially when you take into account the Irgun, and the fact that the head of the Irgun is now the head of Israel. Some of the same casuistry, by which every woman and child in Israel is a military target for the PLO, was used by the Irgun, which gave "military reasons" for hitting all kinds of targets in the British mandate. I disagree somewhat with what was just said about Irgun policy in 1944 and 1945. The Irgun's policy explicitly was not to hit military forces, because they were involved with the struggle against Hitler. The Irgun instead did hit police forces and magistrates and civil offices, which were in an intermediate category between the military on the one hand and women and children on the other. But occasionally they got women and children in the process.

SISSON: Would you like an opportunity for a response?

GLICK: One of the great ironies is that Begin came to power not because of his foreign policy views but because of domestic political considerations. And within a matter of months, because of Sadat's visit to Jerusalem, he and the entire cabinet spent 99 percent of their time on foreign policy. Because Begin has been thrust into the foreign policy arena and cannot spend much time on internal problems, people are now romanticizing and overstating the importance of the Irgun within the prestate Jewish community in Palestine. I have to remind you that in its day the Irgun was a deviant minority group within the country. Occasionally, the Haganah (the official armed forces of the organized Jewish community in British Palestine) fought the Irgun, Jew against Jew. There were times when the Haganah actually communicated information to the British, especially when they found out the Irgun was going to try something which the Haganah and the Jewish Agency felt was reprehensible. So I think the circumstances that Begin is now the prime minister of Israel and has signed the peace treaty with Egypt have put the Irgun and its role in the struggle of the Jewish community against the British and the Arabs all out of historic proportion. Other than that, I would agree with you. But don't overlook the overemphasis upon agreement with your question—because it is an overemphasis, it is somewhat incorrect.

LIEBSTONE: The cases we have talked about have brought something to mind: what makes our subject so difficult is that in many instances terror has served good causes. This is rather frightening, and is difficult to accept. It makes me wonder, if this is so, if terror has served good causes, then perhaps it is not to terror that we must attribute morality or immorality. Perhaps it is to *the cause of terror* that we must attribute morality or immorality.

SISSON: Let me suggest a distinction between the Indian and the other cases as they have been presented here. In the Indian case there is a very strong emphasis on personal liberation through the eradication of inequity, and the emphasis derives its moral justification from religious orthodoxy. Religion provides morality, because the act can provide personal salvation. In the other cases the act and its justification are more exclusively political. It is also intriguing that in the religious case we find a limited institutionalization of terror, whereas in the other cases it has been pervasive and pronounced.

HATCHER: Professor Bose, as you are aware, there is a substantial minority party in India, the RSS, which has a very military orientation, including drilling the children. How do you see them fitting into the political scene and how does the majority view them?

BOSE: The RSS (Rashtriya Savaimsvak Sangha) started as a very orthodox, militant Hindu organization that felt that the interests of the Hindus were not being fully protected by the Congress Party, the ruling body in India after independence. The government of India seemed to them to be making a lot of compromises and conceding unjust Pakistani demands. That was the origin of the RSS. The RSS had no terrorist program as such. Their contention was and is that the Hindus must defend themselves and their religion. They must be ready to stand their ground, firstly, against attacks from Muslim communal and religious fanatics, and secondly, against their own leaders' policy of appeasement. Many people suspected that the RSS was involved in the plot that led to the assassination of Gandhi, although the RSS has denied the accusation. A lot of things have changed since then. The RSS insists that it does not believe in violence or acts of terror, but it does believe that the Hindus must be strong, self-disciplined, and trained to use force when necessary. However, there are a large number of people in India who are apprehensive of the RSS program and objectives and are inclined to view the RSS as more than a Hindu communal organization. RSS, as you may be aware, has a large following in certain parts of India. Taken as a whole, the RSS is not powerful. The leaders of the RSS strongly deny any political ambition, and they dissociate themselves from politics. Still, there is a suspicion that they exercise political influence through the Jan Sangh, a major constituent of the Janata Party. This is a very controversial issue in India today. I cannot give any conclusive answer as to whether the RSS really has political objectives. This is the present situation.

SISSON: Are there not severe strains within the RSS right now with respect to who shall succeed to what position of power? At the national level the organization has traditionally been controlled largely by Brahmins, of course, a large proportion being of the

Chitpaven caste from Maharashtra. As a consequence of the organization's effort to expand its social base, activists from non-Brahmin groups have started to demand power in high councils. Division has also been induced by the participation of the Jan Sangh party, which the RSS staunchly supports, in the government as a function of its membership in the Janata coalition.

POSSONY: I want to make a comment on what's wrong with the eye-for-an-eye doctrine. I do *not* mean the principle of retaliation. The principle of retaliation is an indispensible requirement of defense. What is wrong, and even childish, is the idea of an eye for an eye. Why should you take an eye because someone took yours? You may want to take something entirely different. If you adhere to the eye-for-an-eye doctrine, you don't select your target, you attack the target the enemy selected for you. If you counter a terrorist attack with similar terrorism, you are compelled to ignore psychological, economic, political, and other options. This terrorism of defense appears to have little value as a deterrent against offensive terrorism. "Eye-for-an-eye" is not strategy, it is a reflex.

GLICK: I said that the "eye-for-an-eye" was a very small part of it in my view. You may argue that retaliation is just a modern word for "an eye-for-an-eye," but that's a definitional question. What I was saying is the eye-for-an-eye concept obviously is much, much older than the Holocaust. Between the eye-for-an-eye injunction in the Torah and the Holocaust, there is a whole history of the Jew as a nonviolent, nondefensive individual. If there's a pogrom there's a pogrom. Jews don't resist or fight back. I will say one thing that is in absolute agreement with you and has nothing to do with terrorism: I believe that the Israeli public relations campaign, what you're calling psychological warfare, leaves much to be desired. I don't even think the Israelis understand psychological warfare; and if you can't understand it, how can you wage it?

POSSONY: Terrorist as well as military operations that aim only at firepower effects are particularly silly if they are linked to a defensive strategy. Whenever warfare is reduced to firepower, the strategist is intellectually incapacitated.

SISSON: I cannot perform my duty to respond to all the hands. The hands are terrorizing me.

HACKER: Without promising to be quick, I will be quick. We are indebted to Professor Glick for the very rich detail in describing the particular situation in his country in which, as some of you know, the terrorists themselves sometimes used to call themselves by different names, like patriots or counter-terrorists. The early Zionist settlers committing acts of terror against the British regime conceived of themselves as counter-terrorists, i.e., they felt that their acts were protests and retaliation against terrorism directed against themselves. Terrorists always feel that they have been unjustly victimized and that their own religious, national, or otherwise noble cause excuses all the means used in self-defense or counter-terror. That's not only par for the course, that is the terrorist mentality as it has been described over and over again. Now Professor Glick was very clever in guarding himself against any accusation that what he says is not new, which indeed it wasn't and need not have been. He knows, of course, that not only his own argument but also the complementary Arab counterarguments are by now so well known that they are performed almost like a ritualized dance, which is so well rehearsed that neither this nor any other informed group needs any repetition, because they have heard and seen it all before.

But the only really important point I want to address myself to is the claim that this or, for that matter, any other conflict is sui generis, because this is a striking example of what I call the particularistic fallacy. Of course, everything is in a sense sui generis. Any people is different from any other people. Any country is different from any other country. Every individual is different from any other and therefore could claim to be sui generis. Undoubtedly there are individual, national, and religious differences in any situation. In fact, the strong emotional conviction that an individual's case is so much sui generis that nobody else can understand or judge it is quite universal and indicative of this particularistic fallacy. As long as this misconception exists it is an effective impediment to any conflict resolution. The claim of it being so sui generis as to be removed from any evaluation, judicial or otherwise, for anybody else then becomes an immunizing factor, a conscious or unconscious strategy that prevents resolution of that particular conflict. When it is asserted that only the experts, namely, the ones emotionally involved, can understand the conflict, then nobody can resolve it. Under the circumstances, judgment is made by and appeals are directed to exactly the same biased opinion that is the breeding ground for terrorist and any other such activity. With full appreciation of the obvious differences between various countries and conflict situations, it must be stressed in the name of general morality that there are also systematic similarities among all these conflicts. It is the overriding morality and emphasis on structural similarities that make conflict resolutions possible. The denial of that human universality and the nonrecognition of similarities (analogies, isomorphisms, etc.) makes every conflict unsoluble, escalating it into violent confrontation. The exclusive concern with any specific experience, no matter how gruesome and extraordinary (Holocaust, Hiroshima, or Jonestown), prevents the contemplation of alternatives to violence, and removes that conflict from reasonable and just solutions by promoting the kind of terrorist mentality that it is supposed to combat and remove.

GREGOR: The identification of various terrorist revolutionary groups with British occupation has something to do, I suspect, with the *negative* correlation between terrorist revolutionary activities and essentially nondemocratic governments. There is a surprising absence of rebel terror in the Soviet Union or Communist China or even Idi Amin's Uganda that suggests that in democratic states terrorists are sufficiently shrewd to realize that measures taken against them will always have to be confined by law. I'm reminded of professor Rapoport's remark that the Provos would send children out to retrieve wounded comrades because they knew the British wouldn't shoot down children. Now it seems to me quite clear that the British, for example, may yield to passive resistance. If you lie down on a track, the British are not going to run over you. But don't try it with anybody who's a little more ruthless, otherwise there will be a lot of maimed Indians. It seems quite clear that you pick your strategies in accordance with your environment. Don't be a terrorist in Nazi Germany; your life will be short, brutish and nasty. You can be a terrorist in Israel, because they still defend so many elementary civilities of government. The best evidence I have that Israel is a democracy is that terrorists can function there. I'm sure that the CIA would underwrite terrorism anywhere, because the CIA is disposed to do that. The fact is that you can't get a terrorist into the Soviet Union to try to assassinate a state minister: they just don't have much opportunity to operate. If the question is why these campaigns took place in a British environment, it seems to me that we must remember that the British are democratic and sensible to moral appeals.

NATHAN: I wanted to ask Ed Glick something. There was a question raised by George Quester that wasn't really dealt with, and I'd just like to push it further for a moment. If I understand that question, it concerns who began the attack on innocents. Earlier forms of terrorism were directed at agents of the state, but the terrorism of the post-World War II period is different. It is aimed against absolute innocents in any normal sense of the word, and the people who began this, if I understand Professor Quester's question correctly, were the Israelis. Hence, to give a defense of Israeli action/reaction as sympathetically and as compelling as you did, and as eloquently as you did, seems to me to leave out an ingredient which is at the genesis, perhaps, of the whole lamentable process: the liberation struggle begun by the Israelis in 1944, using rather extraordinary and novel techniques, albeit due to extraordinary and novel circumstances. The moral issues here warrant a response in an otherwise very helpful and compelling talk.

SISSON: I presume you want to stick to *your* question regardless of whether your interpretation of Professor Quester's question is *correct*.

QUESTER: My sense is that it is very difficult or impossible to settle who was the first to cross the terror line. I am not arguing that the Israelis were first, but possibly that no one could prove now that the Arabs were the first either. It's a mistake of the Israelis to reconstruct history. A typical example is the mailing of bombs so that children have to be warned not to pick up things. The way I remember it, Israelis were mailing bombs to German scientists in Cairo back around 1952 or 1953, and this was thought to be a very good action, because German scientists were going to be building advance copies of V-2s for Nasser. Terrorist methods get copied very, very quickly, and if they are useful for your side they unfortunately can often be as useful for the other side as well.

GLICK: I'm rather pleased to have been very cleverly attacked by Professor Hacker because it proves objectivity on my part. In Israel and in some sections of the American Jewish community, there are people who consider me a member of the PLO. Why? Because on November 17, 1977, a few days before Sadat's visit to Jerusalem, the *New York Times* asked me to write an article outlining what I in this room will call the Glick Plan for Peace. One of the items in that plan is the acceptance of a Palestinian state *roughly* within the 1967 borders, provided that that state will accept and live in peace with Israel. So, the fact is that at a meeting such as this, I am accused of being blindly pro-Israel while the Israelis have accused me of being blindly pro-Arab.

But I will take exception with you on one point. I do believe that terrorism against Israel is sui generis. When the Indians were fighting against the British, they were not out to destroy the existence of the British state. I don't particularly think that most Irish Republican opponents really want to see the end of Britain as a sovereign state. They just don't want to see Britain in Ireland. But at the risk of repeating what you all must know, the essential difference between the Arab terrorists and moderate Palestinians is that for the Arab terrorists it is not a question of just establishing a state. They want to establish one state by destroying another.

ZAWODNY: There is a predisposition on the part of some people in the Western world, particularly some elements of the media, to feel that the people of the state of Israel are actualy responsible for the Arab terrorists. If Israel did not exist, Arab terrorism would not exist, and we would have a peaceful world and live in peace. I have been studying the organizational dynamics of terrorist movements for the past thirty-six years, and I have found it to be empirically validated that terrorist movements have about seven cross-cultural sources of frustration, stemming from internal organization. In order to preserve the cohesion of the organization, the movements are compelled to perform violence *externally, outside of their own organization*. That is, the violence of terrorists is not related as much to the external world as to their "internal" problems, problems within the organization. Therefore, I personally think that the Arab nations would undoubtedly be in disagreement among themselves over some issues other than Israel, and once these organizations are in existence, there would still be violence related to Israel because the *internal* dynamics of terrorist organizations secures survival by external violence. So violence would be here, Israel or not.

If you accept that I might have a point in my analysis, then this is a further complication concerning passing judgments about the morality of terrorists. One's hero is somebody else's bandit. I know from experience.

Finally, I would like to assure you ladies and gentlemen that even the most outrageously violent, if not mindless, terrorist group have internal codes policing themselves, codes that they consider to be highly "moral." These are very rigidly enforced. They are totally different from ours, of course, but there is such a thing as an internalized system of rules and regulations, written and unwritten, which these subgroups create to police themselves. They serve as the steel belts of integration and are also the moral beacons of these organizations.

If we reject these "internal codes" completely and superimpose the moral judgments from our own cultures on these organizations, we will never understand them. Moreover, we will never be able to combat them in a sophisticated fashion. The nature of this internal code is, in my judgment, the key to their peaceful manipulation. Such codes, as a rule, reflect the culture in which the terrorist operates. My feeling is that if we want to deal effectively with these groups, the first thing that we ought to do is not to bomb them out of existence, because it cannot be done, but to attempt to manipulate them, to defuse them peacefully. One can only do so by discovering these operational, internal codes, listening to terrorists' aspirations (remember, they do have a concept of what is just), and then attempt to diffuse the violence if possible.

AMON: A few short comments about the Israeli situation and one question of method. We should remember that since 1920 the British government and governors supported the Arabs wholeheartedly; therefore the Israelis considered the British not only foreign rulers but enemies. Accordingly, some of the Jews understood their role not only in terms of liberating the country from British rule but also as inflicting punishment upon an enemy who had inhibited the immigration of Jewish refugees from Europe and therefore shared in the responsibility for their deaths in the Nazi Holocaust. This point was in the minds of many people.

My second comment concerns the Israeli acts of retaliation. I would translate the Hebrew term *gmul* as retribution, rather than retaliation, putting less stress on revenge and more on just deserts. My reason for this is that Arab society in the Middle East still functions under the traditional custom of vendetta. The act of retribution, therefore, fits well within their frame of reference. The question I would like to raise is whether the Israelis are right in imposing retribution on wide sectors of the Arab population. It seems to me that it would be much more effective to seek out those individuals who are personally responsible for the acts of violence. In the terms of Middle Eastern mentality, such acts would be effective, justified, and maybe ethical.

Concerning the Holocaust, I remember a question raised by the late Israeli politician, Eliezer Livneh—I think it was in 1965. As the Western powers failed to do anything to stop the extermination of Jews in the Nazi concentration camps, why did not the Jewish Agency send people like myself, trained by the Palmach, the striking force of the Jewish underground in Israel, to mine the railroads and stop the stream of trains on their way to the concentration camps? I don't think that anybody ever raised the question before, but once it was raised, it gave rise to guilt feelings. Since that day this question has haunted me, as I know that we were well trained for exactly that kind of action. We may assume that it is such feelings of guilt that motivate the Israelis, nowadays, to strike back so severely each time Jewish blood is spilled.

Coming now to the question of method, I feel somewhat uneasy with the fact that here we regard each movement that spreads feelings of terror by violence as a terrorist movement. Following such a rationale, I may be justified in adding my mother-in-law to the list and supervising a dissertation about her mode of action.

Considering the three countries discussed in this session, it strikes me as interesting that there was no contact between the movements fighting to liberate those countries, although they all were under the same rule. Terrorist movements do have mutual relations, and therefore it seems to me that their rationale for action is much broader than mere liberation from foreign rule. In the case of Israel, some groups, like the Lechi (the Stern Group) and the Irgun, did indeed have contacts with Italy, Poland, and even Germany, but they dealt with governments and not with the undergrounds opposing those governments. I think that we should differentiate between terrorist movements and all other kinds of violent movements.

WEINBERG: Acts of nonviolent resistance produce effects similar to acts of terror—demonstration effect, publicity, and so on. Assuming nonviolence to be infinitely preferable to terror, the question we should attempt to answer, I think, is: how can we encourage and spread this nonviolent approach to making one's grievances known?

Another point: Jim Gregor says that nonviolent resistance worked in India because the British were self-restrained. Presumably such an approach would not have worked against, say, the Japanese in China during World War II. On the other hand, there are instances in which the British were confronted by anticolonial opposition, in Kenya and Palestine for example, when they do not seem to have exhibited much self-restraint.

Approaching the same problem from a different angle, in the late 1960s the authorities in Northern Ireland were confronted by a civil rights movement, derived from the American civil rights movement, that was led by Bernadette Devlin, and that sought to employ

Gandhi's principles to improve the situation of Catholics in the region. The nonviolent approach here was quickly overtaken by IRA terror tactics. The question then becomes: what circumstances will yield success for a strategy of nonviolent resistance? Was India somehow unique? In addition to self-restrained authorities, does nonviolence not also require a disciplined opposition and leaders who can continue to maintain popular support while counseling a course of nonviolent confrontations for their followers?

SISSON: That is a very important question, which I will not even attempt to answer. Unfortunately, I will not invite the panelists to attempt to answer it either, since I've been informed that the hour has come to a close.

Eliminating the Terrorist Opportunity

GEORGE H. QUESTER

The biases of the author should be made clear at the outset. Some portions of the phenomenon of terrorism are clearly to be explained by the frustrations and injustices of our society and by the sociology or psychology of the individuals then driven to enlist in terrorist groups. Other portions of terrorist activity stem from technological or social changes which make such activity easier or more difficult.

I am more interested in the latter than the former. This may simply reflect my own interests (some people find sociology fascinating, while others are more intrigued by economics or psychology.) But my contention is that opportunity plays an underrated role here, while the values and grievances of the rebel have drawn disproportionate attention. At a slightly different level, the working premise, regardless of whatever *causes* terrorism, is that the opportunities provided by technological change as more manipulable and controllable than the plane of value preferences; it will be easier to lock up the boarding areas of airports than to change the feelings of the would-be skyjacker, or to attend to his grievances which sometimes are quite bizarre. Moreover, whatever the current significance of personal motivation or physical opportunity in the explanation or controlling of terrorism, the trend over time may have to be toward control, as some very significant and dangerous avenues of attack are opening by which terrorists can make their mark on society.

What Is the Problem?

Most of us are appalled by terrorism. Yet our reasons may differ substantially when we are forced to explain them. Some would be quick to note the unnecessary human suffering caused by attacks on airliners or by the dynamiting of tourist attractions. Yet the human suffering caused by terrorism has not yet even begun to match that caused by automobile accidents, accidents whose frequency might be substantially reduced if a still-lower speed limit were legislated and enforced.

Others might then state a much more serious objection to terrorism, in the threat it poses to all of law and order and legitimacy in society. If felons can be released from prison simply because their friends have seized an airliner, is there any end to all of this? Or will all of society be compromised and forced to submit to a blackmail of the most fundamental sort. Most of us thus share a sense of dismay and humiliation at seeing bank robbers leave the scene of a crime with hostages as their shield, having been given safe conduct to some unknown destination. Even when the hostages are released unharmed, the worry of how in the future we will ever be able to deter or apprehend bank robbers assails us.

The novelty of some terrorist tactics has suggested open-ended possibilities of success, and it may be this open-endedness in particular that dismays the ordinary citizen. It is one thing for such forces occasionally to get away with the holding of a hostage and the dictating of terms to a government, as long as one can see some definite limit to how much the state is willing to concede in such a case. If a period of time must elapse, however, before this limit is identified, doubts will arise as to whether the state will ever be able to thwart physically such attacks to reject them when they have become contests of resolve.

If ambassadors are the objects of kidnapping attempts abroad, is there anything that the government can do to shield them more effectively against such imprisonment in the first place? Or will all bodyguard arrangements ultimately be breached? If such important persons are taken hostage, will there be any circumstances in which the state can at last reject the demands made in exchange for the hostages' release, so as to avoid encouraging still more such kidnappings?

A "solution" of simply tolerating and "living with" such terrorist tactics will not strike most citizens as bearable. If we simply decided to "grin and bear it," huddling out of the line of fire of terrorist offensives, life might become altogether constricted, and "law and order" too confined. Rather, the sense of most people is to look for as early a reassurance as possible that such terrorist attacks are being hemmed in and contained.

Society could, of course, reduce the incidence of terrorism by simply giving up the parts of technology that have proven most vulnerable to the attacker. Yet the price of this would also strike many as altogether too great in terms of material sacrifice.

Additionally, we could consider a redistribution of wealth and political influence so that the grievances of society were more evenly spread, so that the poor would not feel driven to such tactics by their resentment of the rich. Again, the vested interests would oppose the material sacrifice, but this is not the only problem; I believe that such redistribution could not by itself stamp out terrorism. Deprivation is not the only motive that through history has driven people to try to impose their will upon the rest of society by threats of physical violence—the recourse to terrorism undeniably reflects a combination of motives and opportunities.

The motives thus might never be totally eliminated no matter what the reform of society; the opportunties for terrorism, if anything, would threaten to increase. And as if the array of weapons currently at the terrorists' disposal is not fearsome enough, a future wave can be visualized that may be a quantum jump more terrifying. What will the world be like if nuclear weapons slip into the hands of groups with similar motivations? Even short of this, what can we expect when modern precision-guided missiles (PGMs) appear more and more in the catalogs of weapons sold to substate political movements? It is on these possibilities that an individual might perhaps want to base his or her bet that opportunities, rather than intentions, may be more determining in the future than in the present.

Is there any society in the world that even today would not have to fear the uses to which dynamite, letter-bombs, high-powered rifles, and hand grenades might be put if they were not forbidden or countered? As one ranges from the United States to Sweden to Albania to Cuba to Vietnam, or to anywhere else, the threat of terrorism that springs from such simple availability of weapons remains. The police states of this world (some of which also purport to be the most egalitarian of societies) in the end solve their terrorism problem by making the possession of guns and bombs more difficult.

Why then have we seen a particular upsurge of terrorism since 1960? An observer of a theoretical bent different from my own would point to the boiling over of the frustrations and social injustices that had remained from before World War II, indicating that the world was overdue for revolution. The approach here, in explaining the current wave of terrorism—as well as some earlier waves—would point rather to the increasing fragility of many of the physical arrangements upon which we depend. The mere invention of dynamite facilitated and set the stage for the earlier waves of terrorist attack, and the dissemination of the pistol made assassinations easier. Airplanes today are more fragile and vulnerable than buses, and thus lend themselves more to hijackings and seizures of hostages. The improvement of rifles with telescopic sights, and the continued development of smaller and smaller explosive devices, deliverable by mail, continue the trend. The increasing dependence of society on electricity generated in fragile power plants and transmitted on vulnerable lines offers a further target for the attacker.

The vulnerability of society is also expanded by social and political developments, as the respect shown for human life has indeed increased for much of the Western and industrialized world. The greater investments we make in medical devices keeping patients alive illustrate this, as does the abolition of the death penalty in large segments of our society. This concern for human life obviously handicaps a regime when bargaining with anyone threatening such life. The new ability of the news media to transmit a direct view of the plight of such hostages, and of the anxiety of their relatives, makes it all the more difficult for a state authority to pretend to be indifferent to hostages' safety. And the absence of the death penalty conversely suggests that a convicted terrorist will always then serve as an incentive for his comrades to capture new hostages somewhere else in a campaign to release him.

Some Issues of Definition

Most discussions of terrorism thus far have pertained to individuals and underground groups, operating from the position of guerrillas against a more powerful state authority. Yet many students of the subject would see moral or definitional reasons to expand the term to include state terror as well.

What would be the advantages, or disadvantages, of including "state terror" in our concept of "terrorism"? Some advantages are clear. We do not wish to seem morally disapproving only of underground terrorism, while sanctioning the activities of the Gestapo in Nazi Germany. The word *terror* (as apart from *terrorism*) has indeed been used quite often to refer to the techniques used by the Nazi regime, or by Stalin in the same years, or by Pol Pot or the Brazilian regime in more recent times, or by Robespierre almost two centuries ago. Terror is a straightforward enough word denoting fear, and political movements, government or underground, are prone to apply fear. The American and British bombings of World War II, and the earlier German bombings, were widely interpreted as intended to instill such terror.

Yet it will be argued here that terrorism is something more special. If a friend had asked me a short time ago for the principle news item of the day and I had wanted to tell him that the feature story concerned the techniques of the Pol Pot regime in Kampuchea, I would have been misleading him by responding that "there's a lot of terrorism in the news," for he would immediately have concluded that something else had happened, something involving an underground group rather than a regime in control. This would not have reflected any moral judgment on his part, for we both might have disapproved more of the Pol Pot performance than of any underground bombings or skyjackings. It would simply have shown that we had identified a discrete phenomenon, one that has its own reasons for increasing or decreasing in volume, one that should not be confused with some other things that also worry us.

The following stricter and narrower definition is proposed, as indeed according with our intuitions. It will be aligned with two distinctions.

All of warfare, of any form, can usefully be characterized by what is attacked, on a spectrum from "counterforce" to "countervalue" operations. The former are operations solely or primarily intended to cripple an enemy, to attack and eliminate his ability to fight. The latter are, rather, primarily intended to inflict pain on an enemy, to make him sorry he is in the war and reluctant to continue, even if his physical ability to fight is in no way impaired by the attack. The distinction between counterforce-countervalue applies currently to targeting doctrines for a nuclear war, has applied to land and naval warfare in the past, and will tie in with what we now mean by terrorism.

All of warfare can also be distinguished by whether something is being *defended*. Ordinary warfare sees a military force throwing up a line and declaring that the enemy "shall not pass," so that what is behind that line will be kept under one's own sovereignty, with its economy functioning along normal lines. Guerrilla warfare, by contrast, dispenses with this defense, thereby losing the ability to maintain a national capital, to receive a diplomatic corps, to maintain hospitals and power plants, but gaining the advantage that the enemy does not know at whom to shoot. At sea, submarine warfare has been of the guerrilla mode, as were privateering and piracy in the past.

What, then, is terrorism in terms of these distinctions? It is the confluence of the two, being a countervalue campaign in terms of what is attacked (things that hurt rather than things that incapacitate), and a guerrilla campaign in terms of what is being defended (for the moment, nothing).

Of course, guerrilla operations can be conducted in a rural or in an urban environment. Some people believe that guerrillas are tempted to shift more and more into countervalue attacks (into terrorism) as they move into the urban sector. The guerrilla ambush in the countryside can often have counterforce success in suddenly outnumbering and incapacitating a government battalion, etc. In the built-up areas of an industrialized society, however, the opportunities to win such *military* results in a guerrilla campaign are more limited. Assassinating a president or a key police chief or blowing up an army munitions dump would belong in this category, crippling the regime's ability to function, but success will more often go to the guerrillas by attacks designed to inflict pain rather than to disable, to inflict pain and thereby win concessions from the regime.

In implying a criticism of such tactics, we always risk sounding as if we were morally endorsing the law and order of all existing regimes. Without writing a continually balanced essay on "eliminating the terrorist opportunity and the tyrannical opportunity," it is hard to avoid such accusations.

It should be clear, however, that some of the examples of terrorism to be cited have been carried out by forces with which the author or the reader indeed sympathizes, whether they comprise individuals trying to escape the USSR or Cuba by hijacking an airliner, or showing their disapproval of a tyrannical government elsewhere in the world by detonating a bomb to discourage tourism. Consequently, terrorist tactics are hardly limited to the service of causes of which we disapprove. Yet the difficulty may also be that they are not limited to the causes we favor.

One kind of objection to terrorist methods would thus pertain to any form of military operation that threatens to be, or is, countervalue, in that the damage to bystanders and "nonmilitary" targets in such a campaign is substantially increased. It is hard to know how much to make of this objection, however, for it applies equally to a great deal of warfare, to aerial bombing campaigns, to blockades, etc.

A second objection might be more serious, namely, that terrorist methods may become materially too easy, may require too little in the way of national backing or popular support to be deployed. If too many different groups can use such approaches, sometimes with two or more opposed groups applying such techniques quite effectively in the same space at the same time, we then have a mode of violence which enfranchises even the most marginal group that is discontent with the peace or the status quo.

As is also true with guerrilla warfare more generally, even the types that are more typically counterforce out in the countryside, it might be a great mistake to exaggerate the degrees of popular backing and popular discontent that are required for (and thus proven by) such terrorist campaigns. To leave a bomb in LaGuardia

Airport may show little or nothing about how the residents of New York feel about their government, and it may mainly show that bombs are becoming too easy to acquire or make.

Somes Hopes for Containment

Bombs left randomly in market places, diplomats held for ransom, and airliners hijacked all basically fall into this countervalue terrorist category. The concessions we make to free hostages, or to put an end to bombings, may sometimes seem minor, but they may indeed become quite major *if* they help erode the entire structure of society's commitments to rules and regimes.

Yet even as things stand, the picture for our society may never be quite as hopeless as all this sometimes suggests. The terrorism of hostage taking does not sweep all before it, outmoding all laws and taking over governments. There are definite limits to how much society must give in to these tactics as they are introduced. The goal of the remainder of this essay will thus be to explore the nature and explanation of these limits as they take effect.

Some of such tendencies toward terror clearly stem from example, as the first group to use a new tactic demonstrates to others how it is to be applied. The past waves of bombings or of assassination attempts on statesmen, and the more recent waves of skyjackings, may consequently not really show any particular groundswells of discontent, because the incidents were obviously not independent of each other—stemming from a single basic source—but rather were inspired in a series as the example of the first was reported around the globe.

It is important that we in the West remember when the precedents for some terrorist tactics were set. The first bombs dispatched by mail in the Middle East conflict were not directed against supporters of Israel, but were mailed *by* supporters of Israel to German scientists working for Nasser in Cairo. The first skyjackings involving Cuba did not come from people wanting to go to Havana, but from those wanting to escape Castro's regime who forced Cuban airlines to come to New York.

Once the idea for a good terrorist approach is broadcast, it can be applied anywhere on the globe where similar situations of vulnerability exist. It will then take some time for counter-ideas to be developed to blunt such attacks and to be similarly spread around the world.

As social scientists, we may even have occasionally felt an injunction to hold back speculation about techniques in this area, lest we create a problem without first having thought of an antidote. Some arms control analysts in the 1950s apparently hit upon the idea of skyjacking, and decided to avoid publishing discussions of it lest their analyses become self-confirming. Discussions of terrorism through nuclear weapons were under a similar sort of injunction until about five years ago.

As the new technological possibilities of terrorism spread, with the prospect that any successful attack will be publicized and soon replicated elsewhere, where is the counterwave of innovation to come from? It is probably not beyond reach.

We are hardly alone in worrying about the possibilities of terrorism. Whatever the faults of any particular society, there still are enormous numbers of people within it who welcome some regularity and law and order in their lives, who also have a vested interest in seeing these tactics of the terrorist offensive not become so powerful.

Not the least of the persons with a vested interest in blunting this offensive are, of course, the police officers of the world, whose horror at the prospect of terrorism is reinforced by the bureaucratic career-promotion incentive. The police in effect sell a service, called law and order. To sell it, they must demonstrate that it indeed can still be delivered. We allocate tax monies to those segments of the public sector that seem to have demonstrated and proven themselves. Whatever ingenuity the terrorists put into their campaigns will at least call forth some counteringenuity by those whose whole professional status and way of life are threatened.

If we have established that we will hardly be alone in our alarm about the potential power of terrorist blackmail, what assurance do we have that the counterterror coalition will have any means of containing this menace? After viewing one blatant example after another of terrorist or guerrilla tactics embarrassing the government forces, of terrorist demands being cravenly surrendered to, we indeed wonder where are the lines of the new firebreak, the lines to which we can retreat for some security.

Ordinary Physical Precautions

The first part of a logical response to terrorism might of course simply be to fall back on the physical structures that make kidnappings and assassinations and skyjackings and bank robberies less possible. The police have all along been urging us to install better locks, as have the companies producing the locks, and we as consumers may feel impelled now to accept this advice. Terrorism and criminality may come and go in waves, matched by waves of defensive investment and relaxation, but some kinds of protection, once installed, will remain in place for good. As a most dramatic illustration of this straightforward "physical" approach, we see the devices now installed at airports to keep weapons from being brought on board aircraft. Another example is the Secret Service protection given American presidents, reluctantly accepted at first, now a standard procedure.

Beyond better locks and barricades, of course, police forces have also been investing in better "offensive" weapons for the hostage situation. They have particularly devoted more effort to training sharpshooters who might, when the opportunity arises, kill or incapacitate the hostage-taker with relatively low risk to the hostage. Hostages are thereby exposed to some undeniable danger, but the danger is still much less than if the police were simply to take no notice of the hostages' plight while apprehending the criminals involved.

Such physical safeguards may work imperfectly, but they will still impose uncertainties on potential attackers that will often deter the terrorist attack. Can terrorists know for sure that there will be hostages they can seize in a bank robbery if the police should appear? Enough can still go wrong with this possibility so that bank robberies will not become ridiculously simple, so that the entire financial and political structure will not be toppled. Similarly, kidnappers still inevitably run some chance of being caught, even when the police are bound not to begin their pursuit until after the victim has been released. Part of our prescription for a response to terrorism will thus just be "more of the same" in police protection and physical safeguards. This will hardly eliminate terrorism altogether, but it will serve as part of the explanation as to why terrorism is not simply an open-ended ticket to financial or political success.

Psychological Toughening Up

But our hopes are not limited to the random possibility of something going wrong in a terrorist plot, for we have not yet really begun to probe the inherent logic of the kinds of blackmail that we now see plaguing society. Society cares a great deal about human life; the political kidnapper plays on this by pretending to be indifferent to the welfare of the diplomat or bank patrons or planeloads of passengers he or she holds.

Can society simply eliminate this advantage for the terrorist by quickly "toughening up" and brainwashing all of us to become more indifferent to the lives of innocent persons? The answer, happily, is no. Most of us would worry about a society in which the regime could so easily reverse major moral trends. Our increasingly human concerns for the welfare of helpless individual hostages may be a problem in repulsing terrorists, but these concerns nonetheless reflect a trend toward greater decency in general, a trend we would not want reversed.

Yet again the outcome is not that society is endlessly vulnerable to the exploitation of its decency. Even if we at times cannot see the limit, there is most probably a limit to the political concessions any society will be willing to make for the safety of hostages. As the demands of terrorists increase, the public begins to attach more significance to precedent and less to the safety of the immediate victim.

We are all human beings, humane, but we are also subjective and fallible. We grieve more about a hostage than about someone already murdered, if only because our attention is captured for a longer time in the continuing case of the hostage. Even here some of our moral concern is less logical than psychological. A part of our attentiveness, moreover, also depends on the sheer novelty of the hostage situation. What if such crimes occurred with the frequency of auto accidents, which also often cause death, which also often are the direct result of crimes? Our attention, and the attention of the news media that reflect our attentiveness, would fade soon.

Moreover, long before a society's willingness to capitulate has been exhausted some other basic strategic steps tend to be taken. Societies, like individuals, can cultivate a false impression that they are together and less susceptible to pressure than they really are. If the regime and the police force cannot brainwash the general public into becoming truly indifferent to the plight of hostages, there can nonetheless be a societal conspiracy to make the concerns less obivous, to match terrorist threats and terrorist bluffs with societal threats and bluffs.

Police officials can, moreover, be clever and innovative in setting up new sets of alternatives, so that the hostage-taker can no longer be so sure that society will always want to make concessions. For a first illustration of all such tendencies, one can look at the practice of a number of American police departments in hostage situations. The practice now is neither to attack the building in which the hostages are being held nor to allow the criminal to depart with them, but merely to wait out the criminal in a state of siege. Hostages held by terrorists or bank robbers are then, in effect, a wasting asset. Do the terrorists dare let the cumulative damage, physical and psychological, to their hostages become so great that the terrorists lose the ability to deter the police? Or must they surrender before that, to escape the hail of bullets of a final police assault on the building? The police assuredly are taking risks and playing games with the safety of the hostages in these circumstances. Yet the public tolerates it because of its incremental nature, because there is no clear police initiative in itself posing a direct threat to the hostages' well-being.

Managing the News

Because we are fallible, we grieve more for hostages, we are most "humane" about their welfare, when the taking of such hostages is more definitely "news." As in the case of political demonstrations and urban riots, some would blame the news media for inducing the events in the first place by serving as vehicles for winning attention. Suggestions have been offered for forbidding the publication of news on politically inspired kidnappings and hijackings. In a nation priding itself on freedom of the press, such restrictions would be a very heavy price to pay for the reduction of terrorist leverage over society. A free press cannot remain free if it is used by terrorist groups to convey their antigovernment slogans. However, a free press is not likely to *become* a tool of terrorist policy: perhaps the public's and press's attention can *now* be exploited in twenty hostage situations a year, but it cannot be exploited in sixty. Familiarity breeds disinterest. On the basis of press coverage alone, one might consequently predict a stable but contained level of political violence, beyond which the returns of attention or political influence would quickly begin to diminish.

One sees a powerful argument for an unhampered press in the experience of some Latin American countries: diplomats have been kidnapped simply to force the government to publish the revolutionary manifestos that could not have been put into print otherwise. Where criticism of the government is more generally legal and possible, the incentive to resort to terrorism for this specific purpose fades considerably.

Society's resistance thus rebuffs terrorist attacks by exploiting the real limits of its concern for hostage safety in some cases, and by feigning an indifference to such safety in others. A valuable example can be extracted from the construction of a new bank in southern California, after a series of bank robberies exploited the hostage techniques. All communication between customers and tellers in the new building is now by closed circuit television. For all the depositor or would-be bank robber knows, the tellers could be in a different building miles away, hence making the dynamiting of a bank a less potent threat because no bank personnel are obviously at hand to be threatened by the explosion. But what if the threat is simply redirected at some innocent depositors unfortunately in the bank at the time of the robbery? The bank has an answer for this, too. As soon as a robbery is announced, all the lights and television screens are turned off, creating the impression that the management has lost all interest in, and information about, what is occurring at its bank. If in truth the cameras are still recording the fate of the innocent hostages, the hostage-takers for the moment have no way of verifying this.

Quite apart from bank managements, the political leaders of countries have historically proven themselves adept at "tuning out" in a similar way when their concern would prove to be a bargaining handicap if visible to the opponent. New York Governor Rockefeller's decision to stay some distance away from the prison riot at Attica clearly was an effort to avoid strengthening the hand of the prisoners holding the prison guards as hostages. Kaiser Wilhelm's decision to go ahead with his yacht cruise in the summer of 1914 may have been a similar ploy during the crisis prior to World War I.

If we all disapprove of any state efforts to control or suppress the information media during a terrorist maneuver, the state thus can at least avoid allowing itself to become a tool of the terrorists via the media. News should not be suppressed, but it should not unnecessarily be made, either.

The Contest of Momentum

An important part of any such contest of resolve between government and terrorists depends on who will most demonstrably be bluffing. Each side may, for the short run, have to do things it would prefer not to do, to avoid giving the other the opportunity to exploit preferences to its advantage. Not only will there be pretenses of indifference to the costs of the contest, but even retaliations in the form of "cutting one's nose off to spite one's face," to impose the desired responses on one's adversary. An important part of such a game will thus depend on whether either party can communicate a sense of momentum, a sequence of some earlier steps that prove malicious retaliatory propensities in the latter stages.

For example, holding a plane full of hostages on the ground may give terrorists much more leverage than planting a radio-controlled bomb to be detonated when the plane is in the air. In the latter case, if the terrorists' bluff is called, the game is over either way: they can carry through with the threat to blow up the plane, and collect no ransom, or they can fail to carry through with it. In the former case (as happened once with a plane sitting on a runway in Tunisia), the terrorists might kill one passenger first to prove their resolve, and then a second passenger, and so forth, still leaving enough hostages unharmed to continue as the focus of the government's anxieties.

As a parallel case, it might do little good for a terrorist group to acquire one atomic bomb; having several, though, it could detonate one if the government had decided to take its chances by ignoring the demands, and then presumably could begin winning concessions when the government saw the inexorable trend of events. As a demonstration of the reasoning that may make a repeat-capacity crucial for this kind of nuclear terrorism, apparently there have already been a number of nuclear threats directed against various cities in the U.S. In every case, the demand for a cash ransom payment was ignored. In every case, apparently the threat was a hoax. One might also recall that two atomic bomb attacks were required to drive Japan to surrender in World War II, not one.

Yet it is obviously not the terrorist who might be capable of aligning some resources to present a continuing and repeatable threat, i.e., to develop some momentum. All in all, the state will be far more capable of this, having more resources to deploy. Law, after all, may be nothing more than the state doing for the short run what is doesn't want to do, as part of developing a pattern of predictable responses that deter for the longer run.

When this process has been carried out in an orderly manner, the credibility of the state in this mode of behavior has been fairly high. The state is not always being simply vindictive, of course, for to lock up confirmed criminals is to shield oneself against further crimes, and to collect traffic fines may help balance a small town's budget. Yet many of the penalties imposed amount to an immediate loss of public utility, as when a father of five children must be sent to jail after having been convicted of embezzlement. Here there is no need to jail the individual to protect society, and society would draw greater material profit if the man were allowed to take on some other job to support his family. Rather, the state is acting punitively against the man and against itself as a way of establishing a deterring precedent for future crimes.

The Thresholds of Resolve

Recent events have produced expressions of nostalgic fondness for an earlier day when states supposedly displayed a steely moral resolve and never paid blackmail to shield privileged humans. Frederick the Great's instructions were indeed quite categorical that no ransom was ever to be paid if he should be taken prisoner, a practice in striking contrast to the concessions made to the Baader-Meinhof Gang after the 1974 kidnapping of the CDU candidate for mayor in West Berlin. Japan's attitude toward the fate of any Japanese soldiers taken prisoner during World War II may have approached this, again in contrast with the much greater and more obvious concern for the safety of Japanese diplomats falling into terrorist custody today.

Perhaps this simply shows that rulers and diplomats are more valuable today than before, as the election process results in persons with mandates clearer than that of Frederick the Great. Governance in the days of monarchy was by proprietary right, with a well-established succession following the terms of the proprietary arrangements; taking one's chances under such circumstances might simply reflect fulfilling obligations to the family, with little damage to the workings of the state. Quite apart from this, of course, Germany has become more generally a humane place in the era of Baader-Meinhof, and Japan confronting the Red Army Faction in 1975 has become more humane than it was in 1941. At the same time, kidnapping and associated terrorist tactics have become more prevalent than at any recent time; as a relatively "new thing," such kidnapping may not yet have betrayed the counters to which it is vulnerable.

One country attempting to maintain the older standard is of course Israel, which has repeatedly, and fairly consistently, risked the lives of hostages to set the grander precedent of giving no encouragement to the hostage-takers. Israel may be more humane than Frederick's Prussia, but at the same time it is more clearly threatened on the foreign policy front, with the final outcome producing the same state tactic.

Some commentators have similarly proposed the passage of general laws forbidding anyone to pay ransom to kidnappers, no matter what the situation. Not all laws are enforced, of course, and the risk is great that the first violation of this law in seemingly compassionate circumstances would go unprosecuted. However much such a statute might contribute to discouraging kidnapping, the costs of seeing worried parents punished in such a case would probably be too much for society to bear. But surely, if the number of "ordinary" kidnappings for simple monetary ransom were to double or triple, society's attitudes on a law would change quickly enough, such that payers of ransom would indeed begin to be prosecuted. There is a finite and limited amount of kidnapping that society will tolerate before it begins to strike a new balance in its humanistic equation.

Society has long faced similar problems in combatting the technique of the hunger strike, in which the political activist in effect uses himself as the hostage. In some instances, the state has been clever or diabolical enough to devise methods of force-feeding, which keep the adversary from committing the suicide he seeks and turn the technique of political endurance totally around, as the hunger striker is shown to be incapable of fulfilling his threats. When such force-feeding techniques are not possible, the state, of course, might yet steel itself to the "sacrifice" of letting some hunger strikers die, in hopes that the precedent would discourage the tactic soon enough to keep the losses from becoming politically and socially unbearable.

A parallel choice appears in the all-night gas stations where employees immediately deposit all receipts in vaults that cannot be opened until morning. If a gunman threatens to kill the attendants unless money is handed over, there will still be no way for anyone to give in to the threat. Perhaps a few attendants will be killed as the gunmen vent their frustration and rage, but not many will be, and the number of holdups goes down.

Pacts Not to Be Honored

A substantially different range of tactics for the state emerges when one begins to question the state's obligation to keep any pledge it makes while under the duress of the hostage situation. We normally wish our governments and rulers to keep any promises they offer in public; much of what is regular in law and order depends on this.

What the state can nonetheless do is to announce in advance that, without exception, it will never consider itself bound by any promises made under the kinds of duress implicit in the hostage situation, i.e., that it will make every promise demanded but not necessarily keep any of them. If thus denied the option of relying upon the government's habit of keeping its word, the hostage-taker will be forced to hold on to his hostages in all situations until he can receive "payment in advance" on his demands; this will increase the discomfort and peril to the hostages in many situations, but at the same time it makes it less likely that the technique of hostage-taking will seem effective. As noted earlier, the hostage is a wasting asset while held in captivity, in a position of deteriorating health and well-being. In some cases, this technique will produce an earlier surrender by the kidnappers, lest the fate of the hostages come so much into doubt that the police no longer are deterred from storming the captives' place of imprisonment.

When we revert to discussing the status quo, many might note that police behavior is already employing this type of deception. In the tragic incident of the Israeli athletes at Munich, for example, the German government had brought sharpshooters to the Fürstenfeldbruck Airport despite an implicit promise that the Palestinian terrorists would be allowed to make their escape holding their hostages. Yet the position of the state on these matters might well be clarified in both directions. Rather than having the public think of their police in general as increasingly duplicitous, it might be well for the state to delineate clearly the ordinary circumstances under which its word is to be taken seriously, and the terror-hostage situations in which it will not feel bound. The police should establish a clear precedent and habit of "promise them anything" in the hostage situation, with no link between this and the seriousness and solemnity of the ordinary true promise.

As with the other techniques discussed, this avenue will complicate the task of those who care only about saving the lives of the hostages; yet the point here is again that more complicated motives will take hold soon enough, indeed have already taken hold, with the likelihood that the impact of terrorists' tactics will be circumscribed.

Forcing Symmetry on the Terrorist

Some people argue that the terrorist group can counter the "broken promise" ploy easily enough simply by demanding secure access to the ultimate point of sanctuary before releasing the hostages. Yet even here the state will win some important points, if it in the process constrains the terrorists to identify the territory to which they must "belong." Simply disappearing into the depths of a city is much safer than having to find a home in Cuba or Libya or Yemen. The country that offers sanctuary must accept that its territorial identity lays it open to various kinds of retaliation, not excluding terrorism, as a counterweapon. The absence of a populated territory with which one is identified (the absence, in effect, of some vulnerable hostages for counteraction) has always been an important asset for guerrillas and terrorists. When they are forced to fall back on the prop of the sanctuary, some of this asset has been whittled away.

When groups want only to win the trappings of statehood, as may be true with the Palestinian desires for sovereignty over "Palestine," we can hope that the terrrorists might thus be domesticated soon enough, as a consequence of winning their major demands. It is less clear, however, what "sovereignty" groups like the Baader-Meinhof Gang aspire to. Granting them access and control over any piece of territory might not end their felt need for terrorist activity, and it might indeed be an embarrassment for them. It is precisely this kind of embarrassment that state tactics most profitably can try to impose on such groups, not by granting them territory, but by forcing them to need the amenities and protections that only territory can offer.

Some might argue that the concessions currently made to convicted PLO terrorists simply amount to the "exchange of prisoners of war" or "diplomatic immunity" to which we are accustomed in the normal international scene. Yet the exemptions and privileges of formalized diplomacy are much more symmetrical in style and impact than what we seem to be witnessing between the British army and the IRA, or between the French government and the PLO. When both sides have territory there will be symmetry. If Libya repeatedly offers itself as comfortable sanctuary for those seizing diplomats, Libya after all has some diplomats of its own out on the international circuit. One would not have to see the Jewish Defense League as a conscious arm of Israeli policy to conclude that terrorism against Arab or Cuban officials is not an impossibility.

Transfers of Money

Anonymity has generally helped the guerrilla and the terrorist, while any need for openness and publicity hurts. Terrorists have been interested largely in acquiring money, and here again the forces of society have begun to make some changes in regular practices that can frustrate terrorist activity and diminish its appeal as a tactic.

Even when the leverage of the terrorist seems enormous, there may still be problems, for example, merely in delivering the huge ransoms. If the ransom is in cash, the payment may simply be too bulky to facilitate anonymity and escape. Much more clearly this is true if any resort has to be made to banking systems as the mode of payment. The classic anonymity of the Swiss bank account was introduced in the 1930s to help Jewish refugees escaping from Hitler's Germany. More recently, such accounts have been used to shield the holdings and operations of criminal syndicates such as the Mafia. Whether the Swiss would long tolerate this criminal use of their system should organized crime begin operating within Switzerland itself, is open to doubt. Similarly in doubt is whether the Swiss would tolerate the use of such accounts by political terrorists in the wake of the operations that have plagued the world's airports, and whether outside powers would allow Switzerland to maintain such a system.

The terrorist organization can of course dispense with trying to collect monetary ransoms for itself, instead demanding a transfer of wealth to some worthy charity or to the poor at large. This was the approach of the SLA (Symbionese Liberation Army) after the kidnapping of Patricia Hearst, and it has also been used in the case of Argentinian kidnappings. Here, the state may find itself even more threatened and frustrated, since the diffusion and anonymity of such a "class action" will make it difficult to find targets against whom to retaliate.

At some outer extreme, the state might feel driven to legislate against such transfers of wealth, again parallel to laws against the more straightforward payment of ordinary blackmail, and again quite difficult to enforce unless and until the hostage-taking menace becomes more serious. Yet even if such tactics and payments cannot be outlawed, the result for the terrorist movement involved is not nearly as powerful as when the cash is transferred directly into its hands. If the poorer people of California welcomed the goods distributed as a result of Patty Hearst's plight, they surely were astute enough, given the common knowledge of the possibilities of crime and extortion, not to attach very much broad political and sociological significance to the coerced transfer. They did not pledge their services and allegiances to the SLA. The SLA surely would have extracted a greater punch from having collected the cash itself; its subsequent undertaking of several bank robberies clearly illustrates that it would have liked to acquire more direct control over monetary resources.

Unavoidable Risk Sharing among Victims

What amounts to a marginal concession by one goverment could of course be a central push to surrender or defeat for another. States look after themselves; the U.S. might wash its hands of a regime in Vietnam while France or Austria might feel no commitment to Israel. A policy of beggar-your-neighbor, or of making concessions without concern for a weaker member of the system, will hardly be aesthetically attractive, but it shows up in politics often enough. It can be condemned as immoral, but is not prima facie irrational. If freedom is no longer thought to be indivisible, resistance to terrorist attack may not be all of one piece either.

Yet what does the weakest or most friendless state in the system then do to keep itself from going under? We have noted that Israel is more firm than other states in rejecting concessions for hostage situations. It is simultaneously no surprise that some of the fears concerning the open-ended concessions we have discussed here are articulated more often by Israelis, with particular reference to the attacks launched by the PLO. It might be easy to document that Zionist terrorists once were engaged in similar activities. Yet, that is well back into the past. Today it is easy to document that French and other governments are making concessions to Arab terrorist groups that Israel would not make itself, concessions that might well be seen as establishing a threat to Israel's continued existence.

What can a country like Israel do to avoid bearing an unfair share of the burden of terrorism? It can remonstrate with the governments of West European countries as to the shallowness of their morality where law and order are concerned. If realpolitik governs international behavior as much as many of us fear, however, this will only have some marginal effect. Much more promising are the developments that naturally force the other governments of the world simply to share the burdens of terrorism and thus to allocate additional resources to resisting and combating it, whether they want to or not.

Perhaps the Palestinian terrorists at the Rome airport will desire to inflict damage only on airplanes bound for Tel Aviv. But his example may embolden someone else to inflict similar destruction on planes bound for Belgrade, or for Milan. Although generalized morality might not spare Israel from suffering by itself, generalized vulnerability may yet find allies for Israel—reluctant allies, but allies nonetheless. The Paris and Zurich airports may have been forced to become armed camps because of the Palestinians, but they will probably be compelled to remain so in the future because of potential terrorist activity.

In this connection, it may be very important for Israelis and others confronted by terrorist attacks to remember that they have a natural ally in the police forces of the world. All such forces are upset and embarrassed by the incidence of terrorism. In terms of simple bureaucratic politics, an acceptance of terrorism is a menace to their careers. If the Israeli government feels tempted to resort to extralegal means of retaliation, perhaps with terrorist strikes of its own in the cities of Europe and America, it loses itself a powerful source of support, for it then begins to pose the same menace to police respectability that the PLO poses. Even if European governments bend over backwards at the cabinet level to avoid seeming too pro-Israel, the officials who run their police forces will for the moment have to be funtionally pro-Israel, in the very nature of being antiterrorist.

Intergovernmental Accord

Terrorism, like guerrilla war in general, requires a sanctuary, or a secure rear area to which the insurgents can flee when superior forces are pursuing them. A clear avenue of solution might therefore be to try to get every country on earth to join in opposing such tactics, on the premise that all of law and order is threatened at once when terrorism is not rebuffed and convincingly punished.

In some sense we might be quite impressed with the degree of international consensus that has been achieved here. The Chinese, who fifteen years ago might have passed for the most radical regime on the globe, made it clear very early that they would not be hospitable to skyjackers bringing captured aircraft to Chinese airports, sometimes forcing the skyjacker to apologize to the passengers involved and then giving him a tour of hard labor in the countryside.

Showing great fear of what terrorist tactics might achieve in the context of the ethnic and political dissent within its own area of control, the Soviet regime has similarly shown a general disapproval of such tactics, but with some occasional slips. One might venture the guess that the KGB is able to escape central control about as much as our own CIA is, thus remaining free to dabble from time to time with some of the less predictable and acceptable political factions of the world. Any secret intelligence service worth its name is likely to invite every new political force to dinner on occasion, just on the possibility that there may be a payoff of information or influence over the longer run. The reports that Soviet money found its way to the Baader-Meinhof Gang and that Italian terrorists have spent time in Czechoslovakia probably prove no more of a departure than this from the general Soviet aversion to terrorism.

The Castro regime, after long tolerating the skyjacking of airliners by American dissidents coming to Cuba (perhaps understandably in terms of the original precedents for this technique), then changed its stance dramatically, possibly because the international image of such tolerance of terrorist tactics was becoming very negative. Similarly, Algeria went through a phase of serving as a haven for such terrorists and then became less supportive in light of world attitudes.

However, the impact of only one or two holdouts illustrates an important technological point here, namely that the increased range of transport aircraft has left the terrorist free to exploit sanctuary possiblilities at very long distance. It may consequently take "only one rotten apple to spoil the bunch," to upset future efforts to stamp out terrorism by international agreement.

Governments and citizens in the West are also periodically embarrassed to discover that people with whom we very much sympathize can use the same skyjacking tactic to try to escape from the Soviet Union or other Marxist-governed regimes. (Again, we must remember the original Cuban linkage to this tactic.) What are we to do when a young Russian or Czech seizes control of an airliner to make his escape to Munich or Stockholm? Can we be content with a simple response of returning him to the tender mercies of the Soviet or Czech police?

For one apparent solution, we have developed the formula of "extradite or imprison." Rather than sending these fugitives from communism back to a Communist-governed country, we might show our displeasure with the means used for their escape by sentencing them to some reasonable term in a prison in West Germany or Sweden. While this solution might strike many as reasonable, some important flaws remain in it, stemming from the elementary differences between the societies on the two sides of the Iron Curtain.

First, would a Russian really be deterred by the prospect of serving time in the Swedish prison system, the model for the world in terms of humane treatment and of serious effort to rehabilitate, rather than simply to punish? If word about this got back to the Soviet Union, serious problems could arise: life in a Stockholm prison might well look nicer to the Soviets than life in the USSR in general. Yet we surely cannot ask the Swedes, as a matter of their international duty to law and order, to reintroduce an element of sadism into their penal system.

Second, the very reasons for skyjacking from the Soviet side will make some of us asymmetrically and inconsistently sympathetic to the tactic when used by refugees from communism. A dissident in West Germany or the U.S. or Japan does not need to threaten the passengers of an airliner to reach China or the USSR or Algeria or anywhere else, for he or she is altogether free to travel. It is mostly in the Communist countries that the right to show disapproval by emigrating is routinely denied.

Some Conclusions

Thus, in all of its ramifications, the problem of terrorist challenge and state response is probably too often portrayed as a once-and-for-all moral contest. "Either a state proves it has moral backbone, or it fails"—so the logic would go. The argument here has been quite different. States and societies do what they want to do, which often enough will displease social commentators or neighboring states, but which at the same time may hardly spell ultimate doom or ultimate surrender in all subsequent contests of resolve. If Chancellor Kreisky's closing of the camp for Jewish emigrants from the USSR signaled a willingness to give in to terrorism, we do not yet know that this willingness will extend to the very heart of law and order and civilization in Austria in general. Most probably it will not. Some surrenders to threat are total, as was the failure of Czechoslovakia to resist the Russian invasion in 1968; others are less than total, as fences are mended and new firebreaks are cut.

We should return then to our basic question at the start. "Why be so appalled at terrorism?" Perhaps the reason to be appalled is indeed not that society and law are in danger. We roll with the punch of terrorist attacks, and society carries on. If assassination threatens our presidents, we make do by setting forth the succession to the office more carefully and explicitly. Some good men are scared away from seeking the office, but other good candidates remain. If prisoners must occasionally be released because of an unusual sensitivity in a hostage situation, we toughen up to avoid having to release prisoners the next time. Perhaps the real cause for worry is much more analogous to the auto accidents to which comparison was made. It is simply a major nuisance to have to dodge bombs or to have to fear kidnapping.

It is true that the physical destruction incurred on the highways of Israel or the U.S. remains far greater than that caused by terrorists of any denomination. For perfectly rational explanations, however, the fear surrounding terrorist possibilities has to be greater than that of auto accidents. We are not confronted by calculating, antagonistic human beings who want to have accidents, but our adversaries in terrorist cases indeed mean to do us harm.

Terrorism is thus a major nuisance rather than a minor one. As with other nuisances, the purpose of social policy will be to see that it is contained. If the costs of tolerating the terrorist possibility become too high, other costs will be paid to reduce the risk. It may never be reduced to zero, but a reduction to zero is not possible with any of the other nuisances either.

CONTRIBUTORS

Yonah Alexander, Director, Institute for the Studies of International Terrorism, State University of New York

Moshe Amon, Religious Studies, University of British Columbia

Hans Baerwald, Political Science, University of California at Los Angeles

Gerald Bender, Political Science, University of California at Los Angeles

Nemai Sadhan Bose, History, University of Southern California and Jadavpur University, India

Rona Fields, Psychology, American University

Lawrence Z. Freedman, M.D., Institute of Social and Behavorial Pathology, University of Chicago

Robert Friedheim, Associate Director, Institute for Marine and Coastal Studies, University of Southern California

Robert Gerstein, Political Science, University of California at Los Angeles

Edward Glick, Political Science, Temple University

A. J. Gregor, Political Science, University of California at Berkeley

Stephen Grimminger, LEAA, Department of Justice

Contributors

Thomas Hachey, History, Marquette University

Frederick Hacker, M.D., Psychiatry and Law, University of Southern California

Schlomo Hasson, Urban Planning, Hebrew University, Jerusalem, Fulbright Fellow

Christopher Hatcher, Psychiatry, University of California at San Francisco

Edward Heyman, Political Science, University of North Carolina

Marilyn Jones, LEAA, Department of Justice

Richard Keiser, U.S. Secret Service

Jeanne Knutson, The Wright Institute

Roman Kolkowicz, Director, Center for International and Strategic Affairs, University of California at Los Angeles

Andrzej Korbonski, Chairman, Political Science, University of California at Los Angeles

Nathan Leites, Rand Corporation

Howard Levant

Marvin E. Liebstone, Science Applications, Inc.

A. R. Louch, Chairman, Philosophy, Claremont Graduate School

V. K. Malhotra, Director, Center for Intercultural Studies, University of Southern California

Robert Morrissey, Dean, Graduate Studies, State University of New York at Oneonta

Contributors

James Nathan, Political Science, Naval War College

Bruce Perlman, Philosophy, Claremont Graduate School

Stefen Possony, Hoover Institution

Ambassador Anthony Quainton, Director, Office for Combating Terrorism, State Department

George Quester, Political Science, Cornell University

Frank M. Rackley, Consultant

David Rapoport, Political Science, University of California at Los Angeles

Richard Sisson, Political Science, University of California at Los Angeles

Zeev Sternhell, Political Science, Hebrew University, Jerusalem

Leonard Weinberg, Political Science, University of Nevada at Reno

Leszek Weres, Political Science, Polish Academy of Science, Fulbright Fellow

Louis West, M.D., Chairman, Psychiatry, University of California at Los Angeles

C. E. Zoppo, Political Science, University of California at Los Angeles